THE WERKBUND

STUDIES IN THE HISTORY AND IDEOLOGY OF THE DEUTSCHER WERKBUND 1907-1933
EDITED BY LUCIUS BURCKHARDT
TRANSLATED BY PEARL SANDERS

THE
DESIGN
COUNCIL

First published in the United Kingdom in 1980 by
The Design Council
28 Haymarket
London SW1Y 4SU

First published in Italy in 1977 by
Gruppo Editoriale Electa, Venezia
under the imprint
Edizioni La Biennale di Venezia

Printed in Italy

Translation © 1980 Barron's Educational Series, Inc. and the Design Council

The Werkbund.
  1. Deutscher Werkbund — History
  I. Burckhardt, Lucius
  II. Design Council
  745'.06'243   TS73

ISBN 0 85072 108 3

Contents

FOREWORD
Vittorio Gregotti

Over 700,000 visitors attended the 1976 Venice Biennale.. This figure represents about three times as many visitors as the greatest number to have attended the previous 36 Biennali. Whether this was due to a more general interest in art, to increased mobility and financial resources, or to the new programs presented by the Biennale, I cannot say.

There can be no doubt, however, that the large growth of interest in the Biennale was to a great extent due to the fact that it now covered a wider field of activity than before and questioned the traditional supremacy accorded to painting and sculpture as privileged creative activities. From the point of view of the theme of the 1976 Biennale, it is a fact that design, seen as a discipline governing the production of manufactured goods, provided an excellent sample for a study of the physical environment.

Our present overproduction of goods must therefore be viewed as a significant facet of contemporary culture, of the disequilibrium brought about by the expansionist ideology of western science and technology, affecting the relationship between nature and artifact, the ever-present contradiction between scarcity of resources and overproduction, wastage and poverty, exploitation and survival.

The exhibition of design centered on one of the most important periods in the history of the emergence of design as a discipline: the history of the Werkbund associations, which were at the heart of German industrial expansion from 1907 onward.

This totally new kind of exhibition made it possible for the first time to compare original designs with their execution; it was able to represent also the ideological contradictions and differences existing among the various positions that were already present at the time the Werkbund was first established, and that continue until this day to occupy the center of the controversy surrounding the functions and perspectives of industrial design.

1. *Poster for the exhibition of the Deutscher Werkbund, Cologne, 1914.*

INTRODUCTION
Lucius Burckhardt

"Essentially at the basis of the Werkbund one always finds the dispute concerning prototypes,"[*] recently remarked a well-wishing commentator on the Werkbund. We were discussing the very real difficulty of reducing the essential features of the movement to a single common denominator that could encompass its various stages of development: in the years before the First World War, during the interwar years, and immediately after the Second War. One of its few constant tendencies has been to retain a tense interrelationship between artist and designer, between an individual object and a mass-produced article, between the principle that a design must be distinguished from its execution, and the surmounting of this dichotomy. The last point is particularly relevant again today, though in a different form; for the first time in the history of the Werkbund, it does not relate to a return to traditional craftsmanship but marks the emancipation of the consumer and his release from the grip of the producer and architect. An emancipation of this type, achieved by means of the remodeling of houses, the recycling of abandoned buildings, and spontaneous construction, could possibly appear hostile and extraneous to many of the members of the Werkbund, as did the word *functionalism* in the thirties or *prototype* in the period before the First War; but, in our threatened world today, the future itself is represented by those who put individual work on the same plane as industrial production, or even before it.

The series of essays presented in the present volume is the result of a selection made to coincide with the exhibition of the Werkbund, held first in Munich, then at the 1976 Venice Biennale, and finally in other European cities.

The first two essays recall the birth of the Werkbund out of the ruins of the dying Jugendstil movement and analyze the ambivalent attitudes of its founders, who partly returned to the ideas of the old pioneers of the Arts and Crafts movement and partly rejected them, in their search for a universal standard to be applied to the practice of art and design that would always have its basis in social values. Other contributions illustrate the changes and tensions that arose within a movement addressed to social and artistic values at one and the same time. But we were particularly interested in an area that is frequently neglected just because its external manifestations are so short-lived: I refer to garden and landscape architecture. In fact, this

[*]This is an allusion to the dispute between Muthesius and van de Velde at Cologne in July 1914 during the Werkbund.

was a central interest of the early members of the Werkbund, as shown by the first document to be published by the Swiss Werkbund, a leaflet, dated 1914, entirely devoted to garden design. The defense of landscape has again become the focus of interest of the new Werkbund, whose most notable achievement is to have been the first since the war to have drawn attention to the *Grosse Landeszerstörung*, or the indiscriminate destruction of the countryside — Finally, other essays concern, on the one hand, the ambivalent attitude of the Werkbund toward the avant-garde and, on the other, the reaction that began in the late twenties and early thirties. In this connection we encounter a theme that awakens strong feelings and causes serious psychological inhibitions in those countries afflicted with fascism. Yet whereas in Germany an exaggerated stress is often placed on the radical change of direction that 1933 brought to art and architecture as well as other spheres — so that it is difficult to understand how it was that in such a short space of time the Führer could have found so many artists and architects who were completely unknown before then — in Italy an inverse process took place, where equal emphasis is placed on a continuity of development that is just as apparent.

I believe that the error behind both of these interpretations is to be found in the historical method adopted: proceeding by means of synchronic pictures, instead of following the various movements diachronically through their different periods.

There are gaps in this volume at points where reference may be made to recent studies of the history of the modern movement. Among these, mention must be made first of the Munich catalog entitled *Zwischen Kunst und Industrie,** containing a very valuable collection of source material. But at the same time we must refer to the many excellent studies on specific themes published during the last few years: the catalogs to the Darmstadt exhibition of the work of the Jugendstil, the work by Barbara Mundt on the birth of the Arts and Crafts school, Jacques Gubler's fine study of modern Swiss architecture, and finally the book by Hüter on the Bauhaus. Writers have recently begun to take a greater interest in national socialism, and in the present collection this tendency is exemplified by the contribution of Joachim Petsch.

*Die Neue Sammlung, Munich 1975.

We are aware, however, that broad areas have been either neglected or treated in insufficient depth; there is still a need for new detailed research. We are thinking, for example, of research into the reception given by members of the Werkbund to the great international currents, into such fashions as Art Deco, now again at the forefront of interest, and into the very tense relationship that grew up inside the modern movement between those who supported a type of architecture that was essentially purified, though still "expressive," and those who represented a radical and social functionalism.

Finally we must mention another gap, perhaps the most serious we have allowed ourselves in this volume: we have brought the history of the Deutscher Werkbund to an end in 1933. Its rebirth following the end of the war, the changes and discussion that have taken place within the movement, and the problems that face it today are all matters that have not been touched upon. In this connection we have permitted ourselves some short observations. In the years immediately following the Second World War, once the spiritual and material havoc brought about by the Third Reich had been removed, the members of the Deutscher Werkbund wished to take up their work again at the point where its development had been abruptly interrupted in 1933 — that is to say, by "modern architecture" and, in the sphere of design, by what was termed "good style." It was on this terrain that the work of the founders of the Ulm Hochschule für Gestaltung, related in many ways to the Werkbund, was established. It was at the School of Ulm that significant advances in the theory of design were made between 1956 and the early sixties. But by the early sixties the Werkbund already presented a new image. Its publications and congresses became concerned with themes where less stress was laid upon objects than upon processes; the focal point of interest was represented no longer by created objects but by the decisive moment of production — both in the planning stage and in the stage of toolmaking — or again by a consideration of the physical and social side effects of decisions pertaining to design. In the Federal Republic the Werkbund were the first to draw attention to problems that we now term ecological and that were referred to in a somewhat antiquated terminology as the "indiscriminate destruction of the countryside," as previously mentioned.

Among the best-known and most lasting contributions of the Werkbund are the Siedlungen, built during the interwar years. It was expected by a number of the Werkbund members, and by others too, that after the war a similar building effort would be undertaken by the association. At that time it would have been by no means impossible from an economic point of view to build a Siedlung, but the very dimensions of the critique that had to be directed against architecture, town planning, and the Siedlungen themselves during the sixties nullified any attempt at forming a creative basis that could be translated into practice. The Swiss Werkbund took a great step in that direction when for a certain time it was engaged in planning for a great Siedlung to be built in the immediate vicinity of Zurich. Yet here, too, the Werkbund was forced to acknowledge the fact that it was inadequate to collaborate with the industrialization of the building sector; in spite of this, the design, which was eventually executed but not signed by the Werkbund, resulted in a Siedlung no less open to criticism than any other residential districts erected during the years of the economic miracle. If today within the circle of the Deutscher Werkbund there again emerges from time to time the idea of constructing a new Siedlung, then it must be pointed out that this idea now takes a quite different form: it views the Siedlung as a means of self-defense, the restoration of a district to be saved (preserved), and takes account of the wishes of the residents instead of producing a finished model prepared by an oligarchy of architects.

In conclusion, it is surprising to see how great an interest the Werkbund takes in its own past. In this it is of course following a general tendency: the exhibition held in the autumn of 1976 at Darmstadt on the work of the Jugendstil had 500,000 visitors — a greater number than to any other art exhibition held in the German Federal Republic. This sudden interest in the recent past on the part of such a wide public indicates at the same time both progressive, liberal tendencies and reactionary, repressive tendencies. It is our hope, however, that the Werkbund's rediscovery of itself and its past experiences should be viewed not in a nostalgic vein but as an attempt to overcome the mistakes and errors of the past so as to prevent a repetition of them in the future.

BETWEEN ART AND INDUSTRY
THE DEUTSCHER WERKBUND
Julius Posener

The history of the Werkbund is the main road along which the new architecture advanced. This road, however, was not straight; it changed direction several times. Even so, it is the *via regia* of the new architecture. Groups within the Werkbund opposed each other: in the twenties the Bauhaus and the Breslau Academy moved in different directions. Yet Gropius and Mies on the one side and Scharoun and Rading on the other continued being members of the Werkbund. The Werkbund, in fact, always included men of different, even opposed, tendencies. In the early years, men as different in their outlook as van de Velde, Muthesius and Schultze-Naumburg were active members. At that time already the Werkbund was labeled "an association of the most intimate enemies." And we need not be surprised that this remains true even today.

The equilibrium maintained within the Werkbund has at all times been a precarious one, and on several occasions, the Werkbund was on the point of breaking up. If, in the summer of 1914, war had not broken out, the Werkbund would hardly have survived the great controversy of Cologne in July 1914. In 1917, two members published essays outlining the Werkbund aims which were diametrically opposed to each other: in his lecture called *Craftsmanship and Mass Production,* Muthesius stood for mass production and the shaping of machine-made products and industrial design, while Adolf Behne strongly criticized industrial design and all, more or less, that the Werkbund had until then advocated. Yet Behne did not leave the Werkbund. From the beginning, members of the Werkbund misunderstood each other, fought each other, maligned each other; but they remained members.

One may well ask what kept people of so different, even so opposing opinions together. Strictly speaking, the Werkbund had no doctrine, at least, no well-defined doctrine. Nevertheless, its members all had one thing in common: They all stood for quality. But "quality" for some of them—Heinrich Tessenow, for instance—meant the excellence of craftsmanship; for others, like van de Velde, it meant the height of artistic perfection. He said so in July 1914. Others, again, applied this word "quality" to social life. One may say that Bruno Taut's emotional socialism of the years following the war was of this kind. Certain members thought that the Werkbund ought to promote a particularly German quality of work: Winfried Wendland and Christian Loercher held this view. At present, certain members of the Werkbund say that the quality of the Werkbund consists in the high standard of its members' work, whereas others feel that it is up to the Werkbund to envisage the problems inherent in social renewal. As one can see, therefore, the meaning of this word "quality" is by no means clearly defined.

All members of the Werkbund, however, share one common concern: they understand that in industrial society *every* kind of quality is being threatened. In 1907, this threat was referred to as a danger to culture; today, we speak of a threat to the quality of life itself. Perhaps it is this common awareness of danger that has saved the Werkbund from breaking up and still holds it together. For no professional association—such as an association of architects or artists—would be able to face up to this danger. Groups of this kind are too specialized, and they are bound together by specific interests. As a free association of artists—mostly, but by no means exclusively, architects—craftsmen, industrialists, men of letters, publishers, businessmen, teachers, the Werkbund occupies a position of its own; it is less specialized and more independent. For this reason it has been able to resist, so far, every attempt to pull it apart—although it often had hard trials to face——and I am fairly certain, that in future also it will resist attempts of this kind.

When it was founded in 1907, the Werkbund still retained much of the spirit of the English Arts-and-Crafts Movement: the protest against commercialism expressed by William Morris and his followers such as Robert Ashbee or, as Morris stated in unmistakably clear terms, against capitalism which forces people to use objects of inferior quality and, even worse, to produce things that are shoddy and often useless. In 1908, Ashbee asked for "quality in the product and in those who produce it." The Werkbund shared this faith: but from the first, the Werkbund was more than merely a German version of Arts and Crafts. It had realized that the only way to overcome the evils inherent in industrial production was by cooperating with industry instead of returning to handicraft as Morris and his pupils wished to do. Muthesius called them ironically "Sozialkunstgewerbler" (social artist-craftsmen). They wished to change our whole way of life completely to practice what in German is called "Lebensreform." It is true that the Werkbund also was not free from tendencies pointing in this direction: but no one among its members would have wished to retire to some small provincial town with a group of artisans and to live the life of craftsmen and gardeners, as Robert Ashbee did, as late as 1908, in Chipping Camden. In his speech, given on the occasion of the founding of the Werkbund, Fritz Schumacher declared that industrial production was the form of production that had to be accepted from then onward and that the task of the Werkbund would be "to overcome the alienation that had arisen between

2. Peter Behrens, lettering for AEG, 1908.

those who invent and those who carry out and to bridge the gap."

It may be doubted, if Schumacher has grasped the essence of the problem when he spoke of an alienation between those who invent and those who carry out. Ever since medieval times this alienation has existed, at least in the field of architecture, and Schumacher might have done better had he referred to an alienation between those who invent things and those who shape them. Be that as it may, Schumacher urged the Werkbund to concern itself with the problem of industrial design. This is something new, and by this the Werkbund distinguishes itself from Arts and Crafts. It is interesting to remember, in this context, that in 1915, in the middle of the war against Germany, the English architect Richard Lethaby tried to form a "Design Association" modeled on the Deutscher Werkbund. That one should work in a manner appropriate to the materials being used, to the task in hand, and to the function, these aims the Arts-and-Crafts people had already proclaimed. The new thing, really, was this: that the Werkbund intended to work with industry not against it. This, also, explains the quick success of the new association.

As a matter of fact, within industry itself certain advanced groups were not adverse to cooperating with the artist. Certain critics have gone so far as to maintain that in the final analysis the Werkbund was merely an association formed by industry itself for the furtherance of its own interests. This is not so; but it is true that certain branches of industry were, in fact, interested in the existence of the Werkbund. That this interest existed even among industrialists who were not themselves attached to the Werkbund is shown by the example of the commission given to Peter Behrens by the AEG in 1907. Behrens was to design everything pertaining to the AEG, from its publicity to its factories and the living quarters of its workers: trademarks, posters, shops, arc lamps, electric teapots, and other appliances. Behrens fulfilled a role without precedent—and indeed without successors—demonstrating how strong an interest certain progressive industrialists took at that time in the problem of *form*. There were several reasons behind this interest. One of them was that these industrialists wished to impress their workers by providing a pleasant and spacious factory for them to work in. The workers should realize how much their employers cared about them by providing them with such comfortable places to work. The

3. Hermann Muthesius, Michels und Cie silk factory at Nowawes near Potsdam, before 1913.

wish was to draw strength away from the social democratic party, the party of subversion, as it was then called, as implied by Walter Rathenau, the son and successor of the founder of the AEG, in the words with which he prefaced his book *Von kommenden Dingen*: "to hit doctrinary socialism right in the heart!" The worker was to be proud of his fine factory and of the firm he was working for. The young Gropius expressed a similar thought when he spoke of the "feeling for beauty present even in the workman without culture." This same beauty and grandeur, this "monumentality"—to quote Gropius again, referring to Behrens' turbine factory—was at the same time to express the standing of the firm and, as Behrens himself stated, would act as an advertisement for it. Finally, it was hoped that the solid and beautiful product of design that would come from German factories would lead to the success of German industry on the international market. The man who can be called the ideologist of the Deutscher Werkbund, Friedrich Naumann, never tired of repeating that German industry could not compete at an international level with mass products but only with articles that were "special"; that is, quality goods. And, as Muthesius pointed out, it was just as important that these goods should have a particular shape, a German shape, which would be recognized as such in other countries.

Arguments of this kind were heard also in the Werkbund itself, for two reasons. The first is that the men of the Werkbund actually believed in them. Many of them were both good Germans and socially progressive men. They saw a connection between the prosperity of industry and the well-being of its workers; and they thought the hour had come for Germany to find its "place in the sun." For many among them, in fact, there existed a clear connection between "a place in the sun" for Germany and the well-being of the German worker. There were those, too, who believed in a German mission to the world. It was true, as Muthesius pointed out, that a new form was arising which was international, because everywhere in the world objects of daily use became increasingly similar. But, he added, the blueprint for this new international style would be created in Germany. One reason for this was that the members of the Werkbund believed in the economic function of art. Another reason was that art wished to commend itself to industry, to put itself at the service of industry because, as Schumacher said in his speech on the occasion of the founding of the Werkbund, art was not a luxury, but an economic force; in fact, Schumacher went so far as to call economic efficiency the most important factor in the life of the nation ("die wichtigste der Kräfte").

This was the situation in the years before 1914, and

it was to this particular environment that the Werkbund owed its surprisingly rapid and resounding success. At that time already the Werkbund was working in the field of industrial design: Behrens designed arc lamps, Neumann cars, Gropius traction engines and sleeping compartments, Grenander coaches for underground trains. In the pages of the yearbooks of the Werkbund there appeared not only buildings, furniture, lamps, etc., but also locomotives of the Maffeiwerke (Munich), electric railways, transatlantic liners, Rumpler's airplane "The Dove," concrete bridges and steel suspension bridges. One could find in these pages reproductions of the latest posters; they also contained, however, objects of applied art in a conventional style and also paintings and sculpture following the latest fashion, which, today, appear very old fashioned. Alongside American silos, presented by Gropius in a fundamental article on the architecture of engineering, there appear the illustrated fairy tales by Erler, all sorts of putti and little animals, wrought iron candlesticks, and stained glass. These yearbooks show just how heterogeneous the Werkbund was: the Werkbund and the art favored by the middle classes in those years.

The Cologne exhibition held in 1914, however, and the great debate organized by the Werkbund in connection with it began to reveal the first cracks within the structure of the movement. The discussion mainly centered around the opposing tendencies of standardization versus free art; in other words, between the arc lamps of Behrens and the paintings of Erler. And in the exhibition area outside, the already conventional buildings in a style mockingly called neo-Biedermeier were seen side by side with the creations of van de Velde, Bruno Taut and Walter Gropius.

The war and the catastrophe of 1918 suddenly clipped the wings of German industry's forward advance. Both sides within the Werkbund were in agreement concerning their interpretation of the war: they saw it as a product of industry. Where they differed was in their evaluation of industry. Muthesius, writing during the war, saw in it a power for good, while Tessenow in his book, *Handwerk und Kleinstadt*, written at the culminating point of the butchery of the last year of the war, stated that the road to this particular hell had begun long before the war and that the development of industry was the beginning of it. At that time the poet Stefan George wrote: "To him [the poet-prophet] what means the killing of hundreds of thousands compared with the killing of life itself?" Tessenow, of course, did not express himself in the apocalyptic tones of the poet, yet his thoughts moved in the same direction. For such men as Tessenow and his friends in the Werkbund, therefore, the loss of Ger-

4. Silos for the USA, before 1913 (illustration for the article on civil engineering by Gropius, Werkbund yearbook, 1913).

5. Locomotive of the Maffeiwerke, Munich, before 1914.

6. Ernst Neumann, limousine, before 1914.

7. Walter Gropius, train sleeping compartment, 1914.

8. Fritz Erler, mural painting, 1911.
9. Bruno Taut, house of glass at the exhibition of the Deutscher Werkbund in Cologne, July 1914.

10. Marcel Breuer, dining room in the house built for Moholy-Nagy, Dessau, 1926.

man industrial supremacy signified almost a redemption. The Werkbund now turned its back on industry. Gropius decided to bring the arts back to craftsmanship and with this end in view set up in Weimar a "Bauhaus" the very name of which recalls the "building hut" of the middle ages. Poelzig reminded the Werkbund, in 1919, that it owed its existence to a spiritual impulse and not to any economic reasons. He also was of the opinion that since every technical progress changes the shape of these objects—machines, for instance—was meaningless. In the catalog of the exhibition, *Zwischen Kunst und Industrie—der Deutsche Werkbund* (Die Neue Sammlung, Munich, 1975, page 170), the text of his discussion with Walter Riezler on this subject appears: Poelzig said that redundancy deprived the shape of technical objects of any significance; Riezler opposed this opinion. In marked contrast to the ideas formulated when the movement was young, Poelzig also rejected the notion that art could have anything to do with good taste. The hour of the "Return to Art" (Adolf Behne) had come. Inside the Werkbund, people no longer spoke about functional form, the aesthetics of the machine and industrial design but about the quality of the work of the artisan and the artist; in other words, of any kind of work that is patiently developed and imparts to its object a definite shape. In fact, the Werkbund had returned to its point of departure: Morris and Arts and Crafts. Even the socialism of Morris lived again in the "social thought" of Bruno Taut. The only difference, one might say, lay in the change of atmosphere: Taut and his followers were expressionists, whereas Morris had been a neo-Gothic.

The ideas of the Werkbund have changed more than once in the course of its history of twice twenty-five years; and every time the change was so profound that it is difficult to find a common denominator. Is it to be found in the concept of quality? I do not think so, because this concept, ambiguous from the beginning, was also subject to change. I am inclined to see the common denominator rather in the Werkbund's attitude to culture, in that constructive criticism of the culture of the day for which the Germans have coined the word "Kulturkritik." We will find it active also in the phase of the Werkbund's history following the years immediately after the war.

By the end of inflation at the latest it had become clear that German industry had not, in fact, suffered any significant loss of power. During the years of prosperity between 1924 and 1930, the Weimar Republic had in reality been the continuation of the Empire although the means it employed were different. There had been a change, of course: the feudal monarchy no longer existed, and its demise signalled an undoubted advantage for the Werkbund. Friedrich Naumann already had been of the opinion that monopolistic capitalism and the working class both stood on the side of progress, while on the opposite shore stood the power of the Junker landed proprietor class. Now feudalism had gone. Apart from that the socio-economic structure of the Empire had remained unchanged, because what had happened in 1918 was not, in the deepest sense, a revolution. The Werkbund could now renew the link with industry, which the war and the post-war years had merely interrupted. Adolf Behne, whose influence during the expressionist years of the Werkbund can be compared with Naumann's position before the war, now wrote a book entitled *Der Moderne Zweckbau* and found the following formula to facilitate for the artists of the Werkbund the transition from expressionism to the new aesthetic canon of the "Neue Sachlichkeit" ("New Objectivity"): "Sachlichkeit means imagination dealing with precise facts." Walter Gropius abandoned the medievalist artisan program of the 1919 Weimar Bauhaus, and his program for the renewed Bauhaus at Dessau (1926) was based on the principle of mass production. "The vital needs of the majority of people," he wrote, "are essentially identical. A home and domestic utensils are important things for everybody, and their shape can be determined by reason rather than by artistic imagination. The machine which creates prototypes is an effective means . . . to procure for everyone diverse mass-produced articles that are cheaper and better than those made by hand. We need not fear any suppression of the individual from standardization." This is the same opinion as that expressed by Muthesius in Cologne in 1914 and again in more decisive terms in the lecture he had given in 1917 entitled *Craftsmanship and Mass Production*. The Bauhaus with its workshops for artisans was now transformed into a research laboratory where models were perfected for industrial production.

"A home and domestic utensils are important things for everyone," Gropius had declared, and therefore mass production had to be applied to them. Prototypes for homes had to be developed and an adequate formula for their architecture had to be found. This gave rise to the architecture which, in Germany, was labeled the "Neue Sachlichkeit" and later the "international style," and which we, today, term the "architecture of functionalism." The Werkbund participated very energetically in the new movement, both in the Bauhaus and outside. At the Weissenhof in Stuttgart a Werkbund–Siedlung was created (1927) which represented to everyone—admirers as well as detractors — the quintessence of the new architecture. For the Weissenhof, the Werkbund had made use of the collaboration of foreign architects: the Dutch architects, Oud and Stam, and the French-Swiss, Le Corbusier. The second exhibition of domestic building, held in Breslau in 1929, was less famous, partly owing to the obvious fact that it came second (but perhaps also because it was the work exclusively of architects who were active in Breslau: Scharoun, Rading, Lauterbach, Effenberger and others). The third Werkbund–Siedlung dates from 1934 and was built in Vienna by the Austrian Werkbund. (At that time some Werkbünde had already been set up in neighboring countries.) The new accommodation planned for these Siedlungen was furnished with a new kind of furniture: chairs made of steel by Mies and Breuer, wooden furniture by Schneck and the Rasch brothers. The furniture, lamps and kitchen utensils created at that time by the Bauhaus had the same characteristics: they were light and strikingly simple. The aesthetics of the machine had returned and only now produced satisfactory results. Within the Bauhaus itself, some members were beginning to take an interest in experimental photography and the new art of the film (Moholy-Nagy). Industrial art began to encompass a broad spectrum of activities that had been unknown until then. I have no intention to define the architecture which arose at the same time in other countries as merely an emanation of the Werkbund. Referring to Dutch architecture, this would certainly not be true, nor would it do justice to the architecture of the Russian constructivists. Yet architects like Mies, Gropius and Le Corbusier had emerged from the studio of Peter Behrens; and the very fact that Le Corbusier, Oud and Stam took an active part in the building of the Weissenhof-Siedlung shows how close they were to the Werkbund. The Werkbund, in fact, was the heart of the new movement in both architecture and the applied arts; and many of the ideas then being put into practice had already been conceived within the Werkbund prior to 1914.

Looking back from a certain distance, we gain the impression that this was the form of architecture that imposed itself on Germany. It is true that its achievement has been considerable: one need think only of the great residential districts of Berlin (Taut and Wagner), Frankfurt (Ernst May) and Celle (Otto Häsler). But in spite of this, it remained one current alongside other currents; and because it

11. *Egon Eiermann and Sep Ruf, German pavilion for the Brussels World Exhibition, 1958.*

was the most advanced and progressive of these currents, it was also the one that encountered the bitterest opposition. It was labeled cold, inhuman and intellectual; it was described as a style best suited to a hospital, but in particular it was accused of betraying the German spirit. In opposition to the organization of modern architects known as the "Ring," the "Block" was established, and such men as Blunck and Gessner worked within it; that is to say, men whose artistic development had been arrested about the year 1912 yet who, at one time or another, had also belonged to the Werkbund: for obviously there has been a place within the Werkbund also for those who held firm to tradition. As we have seen, the Werkbund has always adopted a fairly catholic outlook. After the advent of Hitler's national socialism, an attempt was made to save the organization from being dissolved by bringing its policy in line with the type of architecture acceptable to the party. We must not forget that the counterdemonstration to the Weissenhof staged by Paul Schmitthenner, the Kochenhof built on a neighboring hill and ostensibly called "Deutsches Holz für Hausbau und Wohnung" (German timber for building and furniture), was itself erected under the auspices of the Werkbund. Buildings and furniture of the then popular type of a somewhat romantic craftsmanship appeared even in *Form*. But the Werkbund could not be saved; and in 1934, it was dissolved. How serious the argument was that took place in 1933 is shown by the correspondence between Winfried Wendland and Walter Riezler recorded in the catalog to the exhibition previously mentioned.

The period separating the first from the second Werkbund lasted until 1947. In that year the Werkbund was refounded mainly through the efforts of Hans Schwippert. The Werkbund came before the public again for the first time by taking part in the German pavilion of the Brussels World Exhibition of 1958 (architects Egon Eiermann and Sep Ruf). The building itself, the garden designed by Walter Rossow and the objects displayed in the interior were good examples of the Werkbund's way of doing things. In fact, one might say that the years of Nazism had passed, like an incubus, leaving no trace. The impression made by the pavilion was very favorable.

Very soon, however, it was realized by members of the Werkbund that good industrial form could at best represent one part of the Werkbund's activities, and that this part increasingly lost significance. As I said before, the common denominator of the Werkbund, in spite of the many changes it passed through, was its protest against the threat that is latent in the age of mass production; in 1907, people within the Werkbund (and not only they) spoke of the threat to culture; now, about 1960, they began to speak of a much deeper threat: an attack upon the quality of life and on the basic resources of life itself. In 1959, the Werkbund organized a conference on the theme "Die grosse Landzerstörung" (the great destruction of the countryside). The program of this conference (October 1959) began with these words:

> For fifty years the Werkbund has been concerned with beauty, taste, form and dignity, in short with 'ennobling man's work'; it has taken an interest in objects for daily use and, at the same time, it has tried to ennoble the people who use them. This activity had a deep and valid justification. The Werkbund is not going to abandon its historic aims, it will remain active in these domains, active and vigilant.
>
> But in these fifty years [the same document continues] the world has been changing profoundly from decade to decade. What once was obvious is obvious no longer: pure air, limpid water, unsullied nature. It begins to look as though our occupation with the aesthetics of everyday life appears ridiculous, futile, subordinate, if not downright superfluous.

In these few lines the whole program of activity of the Werkbund after 1960 is condensed. It considerably enlarged its sphere of interest, no longer wishing to be thought of as the "Werkbund of teacups" (*Tassenwerkbund*). Actually, there is no lack of evidence to show that at all times the movement had concerned itself with much wider issues than the form of dishes and cups, tables and chairs. Bruno Taut always related his ideas to their social context; in 1929, Adolf Rading posed the question of the right to possess land; even the founders of the Werkbund, Behrens, Muthesius and the young Gropius dealt with problems such as social progress or the culture of the community at large. The Werkbund has never been merely the *Tassenwerkbund*, and 1959 did by no means represent a break with Werkbund traditions (as the program expressly states). If anything, there occurred a broadening of the sphere of interest and a displacement of its focus.

However, this displacement of the focus of interest and broadening of its sphere of activity has modified the Werkbund's situation. At the time of its most resounding successes, before the first world war and in the late twenties, the Werkbund was able to cooperate closely with certain industrial groups for the very good reason that their interests converged. In simple terms: at that time, German industry needed the Werkbund. Its founders did not delude themselves about this clear factual interest. Today, one may say that this common interest still exists, but it has been substantially weakened. It is true that

the Werkbund promoted the *Rat für Formgebung* (Design Council), which undoubtedly proved to be a fertile source of advice to certain branches of industry. But industry began to move away from the Werkbund and formed a group known as *Gestaltkreis der Deutschen Industrie* (German Industrial Circle for Design). Such a group could not have come into being without the Werkbund; but it did not help the Werkbund at all. Faced with the problems of the destruction of landscape and of what we today refer to as ecological pollution, the Werkbund was forced to adopt a critical attitude toward industry. It never had been accommodating; it never had been a group of yes-men. Even in 1907 it had strongly rejected the trend visible in German industry to produce shoddy things. But at that time and in the 1920s, a common interest existed, and the Werkbund was relatively accommodating in its relations with industry. After 1959, however, it became decidedly "troublesome." This does not mean that the Deutscher Werkbund is working against industry; this would be romanticism, a return to William Morris. Yet when the Werkbund fights against the pollution of the atmosphere and of rivers and expresses opposition to the danger inherent in the irrational exploitation of land which threatens entire regions ("The future of the Alpine Region," Bavarian Werkbund, 1971; "A borderline case: the Rhine," Baden-Württemberg Werkbund in collaboration with the Swiss Werkbund), it is promoting a point of view that may well coincide with the interests of local government — the Government of Bavaria actually took a concrete interest in these activities of the Werkbund. Industry, however, takes no such immediate interest in it; in fact, it feels under attack and hampered by the criticism implied. We know that by maintaining the ecological balance industry would, in actual fact, promote its own interests. But this means taking a long-term view; in the immediate present, the industrialist feels threatened and defends himself against the demand that he should install costly purification plants and filter systems. In the same way, the builder of new residential developments affecting the density of a certain region feels threatened by criticism made in public. In these domains — and others — the Werkbund aims at improved economic planning and opposes the unlimited freedom of individual planners and producers. In the final analysis, the Werkbund does oppose the unlimited freedom existing in the economic system called *Freie Marktwirtschaft* (free market economy). Whether it wishes or not, the Werkbund is critically interfering with the aims of the Marktwirtschaft, whenever it tackles problems of this nature. Its action, therefore becomes political. *Whether it wishes or not:* for some years now, a

lively argument has been in progress between those members of the Werkbund who believe that sound reasoning will persuade exponents of the free market economy such as industrialists, building promoters and others that, in the long run, the Werkbund has their own interests at heart and those who feel that this hope is unrealistic. In this connection, however, I must state that this group, also, is working unsparingly in order to promote every kind of reform that promises some success. In this sense, we are "working" on the authorities responsible for regional planning and, as the case of the Alpine Region shows, not without a modicum of success. Again, our contribution to the discussion on the conservation and development of the artistic heritage in town and country has achieved a certain success, albeit limited, and the same may be said of our activity in the vast field of education.

It is, therefore, not really important that some of us consider free market economy as hopelessly inadequate for the task of mastering the crisis in which the world finds itself today, whereas others still think that an appeal to reason and goodwill will be sufficient to bring about substantial changes. We are all agreed that substantial changes are necessary.

The road the Werkbund must travel today is steeper and more uneven than at any other time in its history. This history itself is often held against us: there are those who leave our exhibition with the remark: "Dear old Werkbund! It has a great future behind it." At its first meeting, in 1908, Theodor Fischer, at that time president, gave the Werkbund a life span of eight years: eight years, he said, would be sufficient to accomplish the task the Werkbund had set itself. In reality, not even then was its work confined within the narrow terms implied by Fischer. In 1914, Muthesius proposed a new field of activity: that of preparing prototypes; and he called his lecture *Die Werkbundarbeit der Zukunft* (The Werkbund's Task Tomorrow). He showed great foresight then: the program contained in his lecture was taken up by the Bauhaus ten years later. This indeed is the salient fact that emerges from the short panorama of Werkbund history I have tried to trace here: that the tasks the Werkbund has set itself have expanded all the time and that it never depended on its own will that they expanded. At present, indeed, it looks as though the little Werkbund may get lost in a sea of work. That, I am sure, would be a pity. For a group such as the Werkbund whose action is not motivated by any personal or group interest, a free association of individuals belonging to various professions and united only by common concerns and aims, represents an element not easily replaced in social and, indeed, in political life.

mit unsren Kräften und werden dann grössere und höhere Bedürfnisse haben, und werden auch diese stark und schön befriedigen. Wir gehen einer — Unserer Kultur entgegen. ≋ ≋ Darum werden wir einen neuen Stil haben, einen eignen Stil in allem, was wir schaffen. Der Stil einer Zeit bedeutet nicht besondere Formen in irgend einer besonderen Kunst; jede Form ist nur eines der vielen Symbole des inneren Lebens, jede Kunst hat nur teil am Stil. Der Stil aber ist das Symbol des Gesamtempfindens, der ganzen Lebensauffassung einer Zeit, und zeigt sich nur im Universum aller Künste. Die Harmonie der ganzen Kunst ist das schöne Sinnbild eines starken Volkes. ≋ In unserm rechten Stolz auf unsre

12. *Peter Behrens, page taken from* Feste des Lebens und der Kunst, *Eugen Diederichs, Leipzig, 1900.*

WERKBUND AND JUGENDSTIL
Julius Posener

"The Werkbund is responsible for the death of the Jugendstil," I was once told by an architect who was old enough to have witnessed the Darmstadt exhibition of 1901. The texts and photos the Deutscher Werkbund has assembled on the occasion of the seventy-fifth anniversary of the exhibition on the Mathildenhöhe may illustrate the attitude of the Werkbund toward the Jugendstil. It is obvious, of course, that the Werkbund could not, at the time of the Mathildenhöhe exhibition, voice any opinion: it was founded only six years later. But the founding of the Werkbund has not been the beginning of a new road; it was by no means unexpected. When, in 1907, the Werkbund materialized, its foundation confirmed ideas which had been pursued before the exhibition in Darmstadt opened. As a confirmation I invite you to read the following text written by Julius Lessing in 1893:

> To create a utensil according to its functional purpose implies, in some cases, a loss of artistic form: in most cases, however, it will lead to new and pleasant forms which reflect the spirit of our times, the machine age.

This is already the language of the Werkbund. And in 1901, the year of Darmstadt, Alexander Koch envisaged an organization very similar to the Werkbund. He called it a *Zentrale des Kunstgewerbes* (Center of Applied Art) and wrote: "In it influential artists should combine with representatives of industry, the crafts and literature." He foresaw in 1901 the form the Werkbund was to assume.

And Peter Behrens, the man whose work more than that of any other artist then living was to embody, from 1907 on, the principles of the Werkbund, had been one of those artists who had built houses on the Mathildenhöhe. In 1902 Hermann Muthesius, who is often referred to as the spiritual father of the Werkbund, gave a critical evaluation of the Jugendstil, of which more will be said later. We may say, therefore, that at the time, when the exhibition on the Mathildenhöhe was held, the programmatic lines of the Werkbund had already been laid down and that those who were to become the leading figures in the Werkbund had already taken up their positions in relation to the Jugendstil, each in his own way.

Each in his own way: At Darmstadt, Peter Behrens supported the Jugendstil, as is confirmed by his writings. The document which expresses most succinctly the convictions he held at that time is without doubt the small volume *Feste des Lebens und der Kunst* (Eugen Diederichs, Leipzig, 1900), the ornamental layout of which was created by Behrens himself. In this book Behrens wrote:

> We have understood our time, our new strength, our new needs. We can set these forces in motion and satisfy our needs. We can do more, we can use our strength on a higher plane, and we shall then have greater and more spiritual needs. These too we shall satisfy and always in a way which will be strong and beautiful. We are advancing toward a new culture — our own.

In this book, Behrens speaks of the plan for a theater and festival palace. He says:

> At the edge of a small wood, on top of a hill this festive building shall arise. Resplendent in its colors as if to say: my walls have no need of the light of the sun. Its columns are wreathed in garlands, and four long white banners will flutter at the top of four masts. Up there, in the gallery, tuba players will stand, their tunics flashing, and sound their prolonged calls far into the countryside and the woods. Slowly, the great portal opens wide, and we enter the high room. Here, all colors are deeper, to induce a calm atmosphere. If below, in our usual environment, we have provided forms that have a constant reference to everyday life following the logic of our thoughts and our sense of what is useful, here, on top of the hill, we are lifted up to a higher purpose, a goal only transmuted into reality, our spiritual needs and our need for metaphysics . . . . We are consecrated and prepared for the great art of ideology! [The German term is *Weltanschauung*.] And now the great drama of life unfolds: we ourselves are the actors in the wonderful spectacle of our severe joy!

This is Behrens speaking, the man of the AEG arc lamps, the first of industrial designers! One could imagine oneself listening to Fidus or to one of the poets of the circle round Stefan George. Let us hear more! The manifesto also contains words such as these: "We have forgotten the inadequacies of life . . . . we have forgotten, that many things were ugly through our own fault."

You see: Life, here, is being lifted onto a higher plane through art, and art is seen as completely separated from everyday life: "If below, in our usual environment, we have provided forms that have a constant reference to everyday life . . . [to] our sense of what is useful . . . ." Still, even below, we *did* "provide forms." Apparently, Behrens, at that time, recognized an inferior and a superior art. However, the time was not far distant (1909) when

13. *Peter Behrens, AEG turbine factory in Berlin, Hüttenstrasse, 1909.*

14. *Peter Behrens, electric teapots designed for the AEG, 1909.*

15. *Peter Behrens, arc lamp for the AEG, before 1912.*

16. *Peter Behrens, Pfaff sewing machine, 1910.*

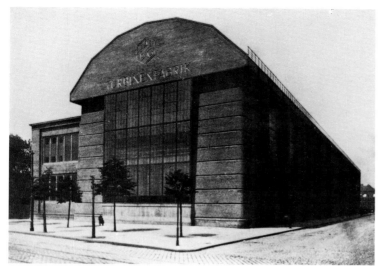

Behrens was to reconcile the two arts in the turbine factory or, to put it more precisely, when he was to subject to superior art working life even in its hardest form: the factory as a temple or, to quote the definition of the time, "a cathedral of labor." When Peter Behrens had created his famous arc lamps, an incorruptible critic, Heinrich Pudor, declared that those lamps were not as functional as was generally supposed. He called them pure art. Had Behrens, he said, really based his design on function, he would have arrived at forms that would have been very different. Yet Pudor himself was a man of the movement whose character we might indicate by referring to Fidus. He was a man who advocated — and lived! — *Lebensreform* (by which we mean a complete change of everyday life). He had himself formed one of those small, esoteric circles, which were emerging everywhere at that moment; he was a nudist; he was also a fanatical supporter of everything German, going so far as to change his name to the German form Heinz Scham.

Now the ornamental layout Behrens created for his book was pure Jugendstil. *One* side of the Jugendstil, we begin to realize was just this love of the esoteric and the clique, the sublimation of life through art, the introduction of a chosen, consecrated circle into the ritual of a higher life. There is, however, another aspect of the Jugendstil — or so it seems. Let us consider this other aspect. In 1895, van de Velde, who was one of the past masters of the Jugendstil stated: "Life is utilitarian, and those who dislike this are themselves good for nothing." And: "Industry has subjected the arts, which until now moved in the most different directions, to demands and to laws common to them all and in doing so has given them a common aesthetics." And:

> Industry has brought steel construction and, indeed, mechanical engineering to the realm of art. It has simply elevated the engineer to the level of the artist and enriched art with all those activities we may call — and proudly — art applied to industry. Very soon, people will speak of the arts of industry and construction. And in this defintion architecture will be included.

One more quotation: "The perfectly useful object, created according to the principles of rational and consequent construction, satisfies the prime condition of beauty, the kind of beauty we cannot do without." There van de Velde states the thesis of functionalism. Yet in the same essay, he says: "If the many manifestations of (contemporary) painting and sculpture that purport to the ornamental are not

17. Peter Behrens, lamp for main bedroom, before 1912.

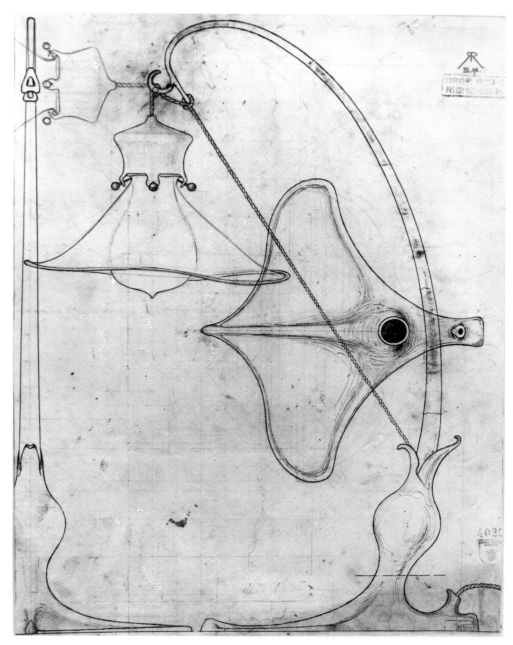

18. *Richard Riemerschmid, table lamp.*

purely and simply illusions — and how could they be? — a unified art is under way, soon we shall have to recognize it, and we shall label it 'the arts of industry, construction and ornament'." But this last proposition is the decisive one; for as far as van de Velde's own practice is concerned — and that of the Jugendstil — ornament is the aim and functionalism no more than a declaration of purpose. In the essay entitled *Ein Kapitel über den Entwurf und Bau moderner Möbel* (a chapter dealing with the design and execution of modern furniture) van de Velde desperately tried to show that a wardrobe designed with purely ornamental intention is in reality designed to suit the function of a wardrobe. His argument sounds circulatory; but the thing just would not work; and even less could it be mass-produced: it is, in fact, a piece of furniture only a good craftsman could make. However, van de Velde declares, referring to this wardrobe, that he would "in furniture, as a matter of principle, leave out any detail that could not be produced by large-scale industry." This, he said, was his way of designing furniture, and he added, that he was proud of it: "My ideal would be the reproduction of my creations on thousands of copies, certainly under very tight control." Very tight control, indeed, would be necessary in every case. And, please, take note of the expression "my creations"!

This turning toward industry and the statement that industry *has given* (he could at least have said: "will give") an aesthetic basis to all the arts cannot, therefore, be taken altogether seriously. It is a tribute he paid to the principles of functionalism, principles which at that time were by no means new: Let me remind you of the quotation from Julius Lessing of 1893 at the beginning of this study. What van de Velde really wanted, what he desired passionately, was the new style, the new ornament. He believed that this ornament *was* the style of industry, and he thought, that the creative artist was capable of creating this style; industry itself apparently could not do it. In 1914 van de Velde pronounced ten theses destined to guide the future work of the Werkbund. In one of them he states: "For twenty years now some of us try to define the forms and the ornaments which completely express the spirit of the epoch." In these theses, van de Velde also mentions "the gifts of individual manual skill," which the Werkbund ought to promote and "the joy and faith in the beauty of an execution as differentiated as possible." Industry had now been forgotten and

19

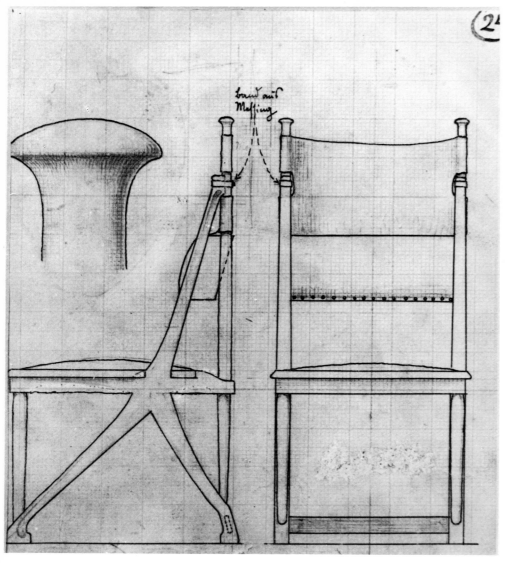

19. *Richard Riemerschmid, chair.*

craftsmanship been restored to its former rights. That van de Velde could forget industry in 1914 shows that even in 1895 it did not occupy the center of his thoughts. I do not mean to say, of course, that van de Velde did not mean what he said then: everything van de Velde has ever said was said out of deep conviction. In his case, however, the Marxist term of "false consciousness" (*falsches Bewusstsein*) is applicable. Neither the actual conditions of industrial production nor the needs of the masses were properly understood. Under the veil of functionalism, van de Velde's ideal — and his work — is no less esoteric than the thoughts to which Peter Behrens gave expression in his booklet *Feste des Lebens und der Kunst*. Both men were anxious to use the medium of beauty to overcome what they referred to as "commercialism." (In this they followed in the wake of William Morris.) This being their aim, it was inevitable that, in the beginning at any rate, only "the happy few" were in a position to enjoy this new beauty (in spite of van de Velde's call for a reproduction of "my creations" in thousands of copies).

Can it be said, then, that the move toward simplicity which occurred immediately after the Darmstadt exhibition responded to a more correct evaluation of the conditions posed by industry and by society? It is only to a limited extent that we can answer this question in the affirmative. It is true that in the years following Darmstadt designers worked on furniture for the working class. One of them was Peter Behrens; Karl Schmidt of Hellerau must certainly be mentioned; and there were others. It is equally true, that this furniture, unlike van de Velde's wardrobe, was of a standard type: *Dresdener Maschinenmöbel* (Dresden machine-made furniture), as Muthesius called the furniture made at Hellerau. But the Hellerau factory was called *Deutsche Werkstätten für Handwerkskunst* (German workshops for artisan art), which means that in their intention they were studios where artistic craft work was to be produced. The name belied the actual practice which was to produce furniture mainly made by machines. It is also true, that some architects designed houses for manual workers, Heinrich Tessenow and Bruno Taut in particular. The two tendencies, therefore — the improvement of living conditions for the working class and designing for mass production — began to play a role in the work of artists belonging to the Werkbund; but it was what we may call a sideline. Even when Muthesius at the Cologne meeting of the Werkbund in July 1914 proposed that the Werkbund should tackle the prob-

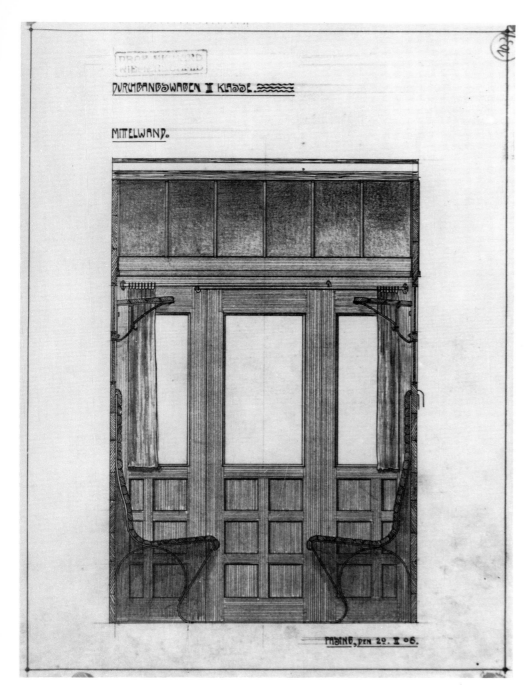

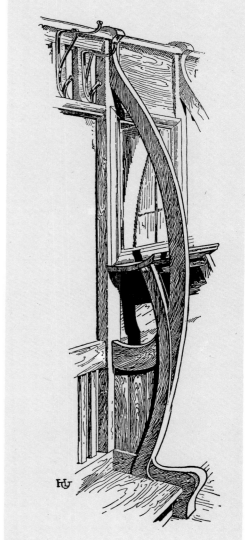

20. Richard Riemerschmid, second-class compartment, section.
21. Henry van de Velde, coat hangers, 1897.

lem of standardization, he thought it appropriate to justify this proposal with a reference to the need of German economy to export quality goods. Neither in his ten theses nor in his lecture at Cologne workers' housing is this mentioned. (And yet he called this lecture "Die Werkbundarbeit der Zukunft.")

Those who stood for simplicity (after the orgy of ornament of the Jugendstil) wished essentially to create a bourgeois culture, and they were aware that a twentieth-century bourgeois culture could not come into being outside of industrial production. This is the essential difference between the Werkbund and the English Arts-and-Crafts movement on which, however, the Werkbund was based. In their way, the Arts-and-Crafts people — that is William Morris and his followers — had been coherent. They wished to bring about socialism, and they thought the only way to achieve this was by opposing industry. This, certainly, was a case of "false consciousness"; yet in itself their doctrine was sound. The Werkbund, which came on to the scene fifty years later, could not then remain apart from industry, while industry itself had taken, in the meantime, the step which led from competitive to monopolistic capitalism. The Werkbund welcomed this development, because Werkbund people were patriots deeply convinced that in a strong and prosperous Germany the middle class was responsible for social welfare. Friedrich Naumann declared that large-scale production was already socialized; he even called it "socialistic." Now, he said, it had also to become democratic. A sense of responsibility, destined to grow in proportion to the importance of the enterprise, would bring about this process of democratization, since this was also in the best interests of the entrepreneur himself. The workers themselves would make their contribution in this direction, because large-scale industry promoted large-scale trade unions. This, then, was the formula put forward by the most progressive members of the Werkbund: let us create a bourgeois culture for the industrial age, and let us see to it that by a continuous process of "elevating" the working classes these, too, can participate in ever-increasing measure in this new bourgeois culture. This — more or less — was the view of the man who has been described as the spiritual father of the Werkbund, Hermann Muthesius.

One can easily see that in this concept there was no longer any place for the creation of a new style through the efforts of the artist. This is why Muthesius, as early as 1902 (the year after

22. *Henry van de Velde, mahogany stool.*
23. *Henry van de Velde, bedroom chair.*
24. *Henry van de Velde, dining room chair.*
25. *Henry van de Velde, chair.*

27. Bruno Taut, terraced housing in the Falkenberg Siedlung, ca. 1912.

26. Charles Rennie Mackintosh, door with leaves,
ca. 1900.

23

Darmstadt), rejected the Jugendstil. He gave the essay, in which the Jugendstil is being discussed, the significant title "Stilarchitektur un Baukunst" ("The Architecture of Style and the Art of Building"). In this essay, he also very clearly defined the role of the machine in the production of standardized artistic products. "Architecture", he wrote, "like every other work of art must seek its own essence in the content to which its shape must be appropriate. Its form, in fact, only serves to reflect its inner being. The detail, architectural style at present plays only a minimal, an imperceptible, part, if it plays any part at all." This was a clearly stated rejection of the "artists of ornamentation." Elsewhere, Muthesius is even more explicit and makes a direct attack on the Jugendstil. He declares that "the idea to create a new style, a style of the present age, alongside the historic styles is aimed solely at the surface, is, in fact, superficial . . . . Among such attempts, there must be numbered the latest productions, which look for the essence of a new style . . . by replacing the former straight window frames with curved ones . . . . This kind of modern style reverts to formalism, and I should think we had enough of formalism by now."

However, Muthesius tried to be fair even to a way of doing things he rejected. He showed some understanding of the aims pursued by the masters of the Jugendstil: "It is true that here, too, expressive capacity is the aim. What is being expressed are certain facts of construction related by empathy to the human body: A chair assumes a kind of crouching position with sprawled-out legs; a table-leg an elastic line like the human foot which is also supporting weight; the parts are interlaced and hold each other tight; a metal attachment claws itself into the wood and projects like an arm; a brass doorhandle by its own line alludes to the movement to be performed with it." Yet after this benevolent concession (introduced anyhow with the words "it is true that") Muthesius goes on to say that in a period when commercialism reigns supreme, nothing can sur-

vive of these expressive values except the formal concept of the "sinuous line" and recalls that what is known as Jugendstil is nothing but the absurd and meaningless application on a large scale of this formal concept. Even so, Muthesius was deeply aware of those creations of the Jugendstil which were in themselves vigorous; In England, he came under the spell of Mackintosh, although he did not include any of his works among the testimonials of the Jugendstil. But he did not even accept Mackintosh altogether without criticism: he pointed to the danger of esotericism in his work. He said among other things that modern man, especially in his working attire, would clash with those aesthetic surroundings.

Assuming that Muthesius' ideas express the most mature point of view inside the Werkbund — and I think they do — we may say that the Werkbund rejected the Jugendstil. The Werkbund was not "responsible for its death," because the Jugendstil movement would very soon have reached its limits even without the Werkbund; but the Werkbund has clearly formulated the reasons why the Jugendstil was irreconcilable with the machine age and, at the same time, with bourgeois culture, why, in short, it had cut off itself from reality and would end up in a blind alley. In this respect, opinion in the Werkbund, about 1907, was united; we need not even exclude the masters of the Jugendstil themselves, men like Riemerschmid and van de Velde. The fact that in spite of this the Werkbund artists were not always able to distinguish between essence and decoration is shown by certain light fittings designed by Peter Behrens at about the same time that he designed the AEG arc lamps. *Kunstgewerbe* (let us here translate it with decorative art) remained a constant danger to the Werkbund; and when in 1914 Muthesius spoke in favor of standardization, wishing to persuade the Werkbund to accept it as the "work of the Werkbund for the future" — this being the title of his lecture — and urged the movement toward industrial design, the protagonists of free art

within the Werkbund very strongly rejected his proposals.

And is this controversy not again relevant to us today? Today, also, progress is moving in the direction of industry. But it is clear that in order to eliminate its harmful effects, one has got to keep industry under control. It remains to be seen if the Werkbund philosophy of reconciliation is still valid, if it is enough to "speak to the conscience" of industry, to appeal to it, as it were, in the cause of its own best interest. Maybe our idea of what is best for industry does not quite coincide with the industrialists' own views. Be that as it may, the flight to art, so attractive again to many of our contemporaries not excluding Werkbund members, remains, say what you like, a flight: it means running away from those problems. I find it appropriate here to recall the words of Muthesius to the effect that the form of every object can serve only to reflect its essence. I am afraid, however, that today this relationship of form and content is being disturbed by — posited Muthesius — standardization. Muthesius' ideas concerning the type and standardization were, of course, quite different from those current today. He was "preaching" at a time, when it still seem possible to convince industrialists, that good design — *especially* good design — would increase profit. In fact, something good *has* been achieved in this way: no one will deny that cameras, for instance, nearly always are attractive to look at, that they have achieved — to use Muthesius' term — essential form. In the building sector, however, where good design adds nothing to profit, the situation appears in quite a different light. In the years preceding the first world war, this problem had not yet emerged, since, with the exception of civil engineering, building operations continued to be carried out by craftsmen. We shall have to endeavor to design the elements of industrialized building in a way worthy of the traditions and the intentions of the Werkbund — provided, of course, that the building industry is prepared to cooperate.

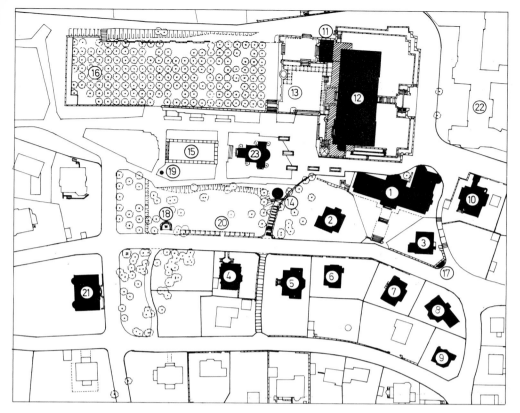

In 1892 the 23-year-old Ernst Ludwig von Hessen
und bei Rhein was made Grand Duke of Hessen.
His mother, the Grand Duchess Alice, who died
prematurely in 1878, was the favorite daughter of
Queen Victoria, and the Queen personally took
charge of her grandson's upbringing. Ludwig paid
many visits to the English court and Queen Victoria
visited Darmstadt frequently, even after the death
of her daughter.[1]

The young Ernst Ludwig received a typically
English education, reflected in all his behavior.
Count Harry Kessler, his companion at studies in
Leipzig University, described him in these terms:
"The hereditary grand duke, as grandson of Queen
Victoria, had much in him that was English. He did
not find beer houses entertaining but loved sports,
danced wonderfully, wore evening clothes ele-
gantly, had a happy, lively temperament, even
fiery, but with style. . . . Of all German princes he
was the most naturally a European and man of the
world."[2]

While he was in England Ernst Ludwig must have
come into contact with the work and ideas, and
perhaps also the exponents, of the Arts and Crafts
movement, although neither in his correspondence
with Queen Victoria nor in his memoirs is there
anything to confirm this supposition.[3] In any case,
his patronage of the arts began when he entrusted
the furnishing of two drawing rooms used by his
wife Victoria Melita in the new palace in Darmstadt
to one of the best exponents of the English
movement: Mackay Hugh Baillie Scott.[4] Baillie
Scott and the even more important Charles Robert
Ashbee stayed in Darmstadt repeatedly between
1897 and 1898, and it is certain that in those
months they frequently discussed ideas with the
Grand Duke.

The founding of the artists' colony on the Mathildenhöhe was determined by two events that took
place in England a little earlier: (1) in 1888 the Guild
and School of Handicraft was founded by Ashbee,
with the aim of achieving the unity of all the arts
and, inspired also by ideals of communal living, in
1902 it moved to Chipping Campden, where the
small community was to be transformed into an

28. Ground plan of the Mathildenhöhe, Darmstadt
(state at the time of the Second War): (1) Ernst-
Ludwig-Haus, Olbrich, 1901 (2) Christiansen
House, Olbrich, 1901 (3) Olbrich House, Olbrich,
1901 (4) Behrens House, Behrens, 1901 (5) Glük-
kert House I, Olbrich, 1901 (6) Glückert House II,
Olbrich, 1901 (7) Habich House, Olbrich, 1901 (8)
Keller House, Olbrich, 1901 (9) Deiters House, Ol-
brich, 1901 (10) House in the style of Upper Hessen,
Olbrich, 1908 (11) Wedding Tower, Olbrich, 1908
(12) Exhibition pavilions, Olbrich 1908 (13) Pergola,
Olbrich, 1908 (14) Schwanentempel, Albin Müller,
1914 (15) Fountain, Albin Müller, 1914 (16)
Sculptural decoration for the Platanenhain,
Hoetger, 1914 (17) Wall fountain, Habich, 1901 (18)
Monument to Schwab, Habich, 1901 (19) Pond,
Albin Müller, 1914 (20) Pergola, Albin Müller, 1914
(21) Messel House (22) Group of renting houses,
Albin Müller, 1914 (23) Russian Chapel, Benois,
1899.
29. Darmstadt, Mathildenhöhe, aerial view, c.
1939.

ideal commune whose means of support were those of "primitive production";[5] and (2) in 1890 William Morris published his Utopian novel, *News from Nowhere*.[6] It must be remembered that in the second half of the nineteenth century artists' colonies sprang up in many parts of Germany; these were free associations of painters, for the most part, who chose to live in rural surroundings so as to devote themselves to painting in the open air, after the example of the Barbizon school, or simply to escape from large cities.[7] But the Darmstadt "Künstlerkolonie" shared little of this phenomenon. It goes without saying that these new English ideas reached Vienna also, more or less at the same time. Here, in 1900, Joseph Maria Olbrich had already published his discourse containing a utopian vision of the city constructed on "a large open field": "We shall snow you what we are capable of; in the entire complex, everything down to the smallest detail will be guided by the same spirit: streets, gardens, tall buildings and cottages, tables and chairs, lamp standards and spoons, every article is the expression of the same sentiment. But at the center, like a temple in a sacred wood, stands the house of work, which should be an artists' studio and workshop for artisans at the same time, where the artist can always have beside him the restful and regular artisan work, and the artisan can have liberating and unifying art, until the stage is reached when both will coexist in the same person."[8]

Not only the idea for an artists' colony at Darmstadt, but its actual implementation was exclusively due to the Grand Duke Ernst Ludwig. As we have seen, his inspiration had come from England, while the architect Olbrich, who was of his own age and like-minded, proved to be an ideal collaborator. But in this connection we should not overlook the not insignificant influence of the publisher Alexander Koch, whose journal *Deutsche Kunst und Dekoration* first appeared in Darmstadt in 1897 and played a decisive role in the birth of the Jugendstil.

In contrast to all other colonies, the one at Darmstadt came into being not as a result of free discussion among a group of artists but because a group of artists was summoned to Darmstadt by the Grand Duke to live and work there; each artist received an annual salary, although modest.[9]

The project for the construction of the colony was first conceived in 1898. In the same year and in the year after, seven artists in all were summoned to Darmstadt: Joseph Maria Olbrich (architect), Peter Behrens (painter and artist-craftsman), Han Christiansen (painter), Patriz Huber (architect-decorator and artist-craftsman), Ludwig Habich (sculptor), Rudolf Bosselt (sculptor in metal), and Paul Bürck (painter-decorator). At first all that was envisaged was a building to house the studios, but by the autumn of 1899 plans were made for an exhibition entitled "A Document of German Art," which was to include homes for the artists, complete with internal furnishings. For this colony Ernst Ludwig made available the Mathildenhöhe, a hill arranged as a park, situated at the east end of the city in relation to the castle, where there were already a water reservoir, the Russian chapel constructed in 1897–99 by the architect Benois, and some villas.[10] The cost of the plot and the construction of the houses was to be borne by the artists themselves.[11]

A first plan for the colony was prepared toward the end of 1889 by Olbrich, the only architect in the artists' colony.[12] This plan was based on a system of perpendicular axes, with the studio building placed in front of the water reservoir and five villas in an axial relationship to the building; the plan also envisaged an open-air theater to the east of the reservoir. In the winter of 1899–1900 variants of this plan were produced, taking account of the slope of the terrain and placing the studio in a more northwesterly direction; this entailed a relative displacement of the axis of the houses, which now no longer formed a villa at their lower end but instead ended in a temporary structure where exhibitions could be held.[13] For the first time the design now provided for a viewing tower at the northeast of the reservoir.

On March 24, 1900, when the foundation stone of the building containing the artists' studios had been laid — known as the Ernst-Ludwig-Haus — the final choice fell on the second plan, and this plan, with the variants it comprised, was executed in 1901 for the exhibition buildings. Olbrich assumed responsibility for the design of all the buildings, with the exception of Peter Behrens' house, whereas the other artists undertook the furnishing and interior decoration. A festival held on the occasion of laying the foundation stone of the Ernst-Ludwig-Haus reveals the same artistic intention as found in Olbrich's description of a "temple in a sacred wood."

> May it be a temple, murmuring with prayers,
> and trembling with the mysterious breath
> of the beauty we are seeking
> with intense devout supplications.[14]

The sacramental nature of the colony is clearly apparent. The artists are priests officiating at the service of beauty. The artists' colony as it was officially presented to the public in 1901 fulfilled an idea that was held dear at the time: the idea of the total work of art — in other words, the unity of art and life, artist and artisan, house and decor. From this to the total aestheticization of life was a step taken by Peter Behrens, as he showed very clearly in these words, addressed to Ernst Ludwig in 1901: "In this way do we wish to view our art and live in the spirit of our time; whatever activity we engage in must, in the spirit of our time, inspire beauty, and everything that forms part of our life must acquire beauty. In this way beauty again becomes for us the quintessence of the greatest force, and to its service a new cult is born. To this cult we wish to erect a house, a dwelling in which the whole of art may be solemnly unfolded for the consecration of our life."[15]

Such ideas were not alien to Ernst Ludwig; yet in the organization of the Künstlerkolonie he was just as worried about commercial matters. He hoped to increase production, improve quality and secure a greater number of commissions for the crafts of Hessen; the artists summoned by him to Darmstadt had to work toward these goals, to be models and to have a direct output at the same time.

The significance of the Darmstadt artists' colony lies in the opposing forces of these two demands, between pure aesthetics and economic calculation. Ernst Ludwig pursued a single aim, which was clearly defined: that of reconciling the new aesthetic vision of life and the economy of Hessen. It is in the combination of these two demands that the importance of the Künstlerkolonie lies; this is the reason for the enormous impact made by the 1901 exhibition throughout the whole of Germany. On

30. Joseph Maria Olbrich, Ernst-Ludwig-Haus. **On the left,** *Christiansen House;* **on the right,** *Olbrich House (photo, 1901), Darmstadt.*

31. Theatrical spectacle, before the Ernst-Ludwig-Haus, May 15, 1901, directed by Peter Behrens, Darmstadt.

32. Joseph Maria Olbrich, Ernst-Ludwig-Haus, section, Berlin, Kunstbibliothek.

33. Ludwig Bosselt, medallion reproduced on the cover of the commemorative volume of the 1901 exhibition, showing the model of the Ernst-Ludwig-Haus.

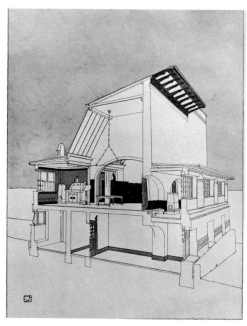

the other hand, the artists' houses, which actually were constructed on the Mathildenhöhe, with their furnishings, made much less impression.

The Ernst-Ludwig-Haus constituted the center of the colony, in both form and content: situated above the artists' houses, to which it was connected by a stairway,[16] it created the sacramental effect desired by Olbrich, enhanced by the great portal with wide-curving archway and two enormous statues (by the sculptor Habich) at the sides, one portraying "strength" (male), the other "beauty" (female), and by the compact windowless facade of the upper stories, with two truncated towers at the corners. These features illustrate the extent to which the structure was conceived in a monumental dimension. As shown by his designs, Olbrich's intention was to confer great monumentality to the structure, and this intention is clearly present from the first.[17] The pure cubic shape of the building he designed for the Vienna Secession (1897–98) has been reinterpreted here and given a theatrical quality.[18] The studios of the first seven artists summoned to Darmstadt were housed in the interior. Above the doorway were placed in large letters the words: "Let the artist show his world that which has never been nor will ever be" (Hermann Bahr) — a significant contrast to the practical expectations of Ernst Ludwig. The pseudo-religious intention expressed in the architecture of this building appears even more clearly in the commemorative medal coined by Rudolf Bosselt for the 1901 exhibition: it depicts a standing woman surrounded by the aureole of the saints and holding a little model of the Ernst-Ludwig-Haus as if she had been its founder; at her right are two censers.[19] This medal was embossed on the cover of the commemorative volume of the 1901 exhibition.

When the building was officially opened on May 15, 1901, Peter Behrens put on a spectacle, which was performed in front of the Ernst-Ludwig-Haus and summed up the aims of the Mathildenhöhe colony:

It is the symbol of the new life.
Under this sign will be unveiled
the new era for youthful spirits.
The hour has come!
Not in vain did we wait,
the sign shines forth, the hour has come![20]

The ceremony itself was conceived as "the first great festival held in the spirit of modern aesthetics."[21]

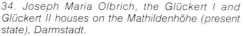

34. Joseph Maria Olbrich, the Glückert I and Glückert II houses on the Mathildenhöhe (present state), Darmstadt.

35. Joseph Maria Olbrich, vestibule with staircase in the Glückert I House, 1901, Darmstadt.

36. Joseph Maria Olbrich, vestibule of the Glückert I house (restored 1908), Darmstadt.

In an extraordinarily short space of time Olbrich designed a further six houses in addition to his own (commissioned partly by some of the wealthy citizens of Darmstadt), as well as all the temporary constructions for the 1901 exhibition. Architecturally, these houses are not of equal value; the most successful from the viewpoint of formal clarity are, without any doubt, the Habich and Glückert I houses. Although certainly not important for their architecture, they are important for their harmony between interior and exterior, and for the planning of every feature down to the smallest item of household equipment. Considering that the houses have had various owners during the course of time, as well as having suffered war damage, it is to be expected that the various original nuclei should have been dispersed and can now be seen only in photographs.[22] Only the hall of the Glückert I house, now reconstructed, can provide an exact idea of the original state. In the temporary exhibition buildings Olbrich was less successful. Only the painting pavilion can be considered a perfectly successful work, whereas the clubhouse and the main entrance to the exhibition are of an almost ridiculous bareness.[23]

Olbrich's architectural work met with harsh criticism. After the exhibition it had to be admitted, even in Darmstadt, that "the architectural part of the exhibition was considered by most people to be a failure, a failure to be explained by the fact that the solution to such a difficult task was entrusted to a single artist."[24]

The contribution of Peter Behrens, whose first work as an architect was in the construction of his own house, is the most coherent testimony to a homogeneous design for house and furnishing realized by a single artist and includes also a garden and outer enclosure. As early as 1901 the special artistic position and the prophetic significance of Behrens' house was recognized: "It is not composed of forms but is a single form from base to roof." Seen against the works of Olbrich — whose value has to remain problematical — this house showed that "on the battlefield of the Mathildenhöhe, Peter Behrens has chalked up a victory for our young architecture."[25]

The 1901 exhibition attracted the attention of a vast public, but unfortunately, owing to their cost, the furnishings put on show remained inaccessible to the middle class for whom they had been intended.

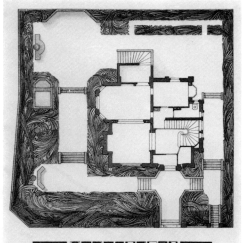

37. Joseph Maria Olbrich, entrance to the 1901 exhibition, Darmstadt.
38. Peter Behrens, Behrens House, plan of house and garden, Darmstadt.

39. Peter Behrens, Behrens House (present state), Darmstadt.

The object of Ernst Ludwig, which was to create "an elegant bourgeois art" that "would enable even the less wealthy to adorn their homes in a simple yet tasteful way,"[26] was therefore not achieved in 1901 at Darmstadt. The exhibition was criticized for offering a "poor man's style for the rich,"[27] and this signaled a change of direction toward traditionalism and also crystalized the elitist structure of the Darmstadt enterprise.

An important idea, which was foreseen in the initial phase but never executed, was the setting up of an academy where "creative artists . . . would be able to meet the most respected representatives of industry, crafts and literature."[28] This idea for a coexistence of artists, craftsmen and industrialists, broadened to include representatives of the world of letters, was a surprising anticipation of what was perhaps the basic idea of the Deutscher Werkbund, which viewed its own activity to be "in the united action of art-industry-commerce."

At Darmstadt, Ernst Ludwig was the first person to have thought openly of a cooperation of this type. In contrast to the Arts and Crafts movement, at Darmstadt the enemy was not seen as industrial production itself, but the desire was to define the role of crafts in relation to mechanized work:[29] "Craft work cannot by any means compete with mechanically produced articles by setting itself to produce only low-quality standardized goods, because by doing so it invites both economic and spiritual ruin. Furthermore, one cannot make the wheels of our industry turn back in favor of crafts. . . . Craft work must be guided, by means of a suitable artistic education and artistic models, to create individual works in which intelligence, taste, personal ideas and, possibly, the popular spirit can find expression. The machine cannot attain this result."[30]

Arts and crafts are seen in that symbiosis to which tended William Morris, the Arts and Crafts movement, and also, because they modeled themselves on this experience, the artists of the Mathildenhöhe. The boundaries of industrial production have been set, but it is not yet apparent how artistic models or good artisan designs can be put to use in mechanized production for the purpose of raising the aesthetic level and the quality of the so-called "vile merchandise." This essential step forward was undertaken only by the Deutscher

40. Peter Behrens, Behrens House, library, 1901, Darmstadt.
41. Joseph Maria Olbrich, end section of the Wedding Tower, 1908, Darmstadt.

Werkbund. However, the achievement of Darmstadt, which differentiated it from the English models, whereby it was recognized that art, industry and commerce must come together at a certain level, for economic if no other reasons, remains a fundamental postulate of the Deutscher Werkbund.

Through their participation in international exhibitions, the Darmstadt artists became widely known.[31] At the World Exhibition in Paris in 1900 Olbrich already put on show a "Darmstadt room," and in the International Exhibition of Modern Decorative Art, held in Turin in 1902, the international jury awarded him first prize for the three rooms he exhibited. But an even greater success awaited Olbrich in 1904 at the World Exhibition in St. Louis with his "summer residence of a friend of the arts." The later exhibitions of the Künstlerkolonie held in Darmstadt (in 1904, 1908 and 1914), although less spectacular than the 1901 exhibition, illustrated the beginning of concrete cooperation among artists, artisans and industry. The displays were made more flexible and convenient. For the 1908 Hessen exhibition a workers' village was built; its purpose was to show that "in the construction of small houses and their furnishings it was possible, without too great an expense, to take account of artistic sensibility."[32] Olbrich was commissioned by the Opel Company to design a worker's house of this type, complete with interior furnishing.[33]

Parallel with these exhibitions, the activity of the colony continued on the Mathildenhöhe, along with the building work there. The most important constructions of this period were the exhibition pavilions erected by Olbrich in 1907–8 beyond the reservoir and the "wedding tower" built to commemorate the marriage of Ernst Ludwig to Princess Eleonora of Solms (in 1905) but modeled on the initial plan, which provided for a viewing tower. The history of its design is documented by numerous sketches,[34] confirming its triple function: to be at one and the same time a commemorative monument, an emblem of the city and a viewing tower.[35] During those years Olbrich moved farther and farther away from the influence of the Jugendstil, as his own view of architecture developed in the direction of neoclassicism, as seen clearly in the exhibition pavilions on the Mathildenhöhe and even more so in the Feinhals Villa built in 1908 in

42. Joseph Maria Olbrich, pavilions of the exhibition on the Mathildenhöhe, 1908 (after restoration 1975-76), Darmstadt.

43. J. L. M. Lauweriks, perspective drawing of the residential complex in Hagen.

Cologne-Marienburg.[36] In 1908 he designed a wider entrance with staircase for the Glückert I house, which he had built and furnished in 1901. A comparison of the two arrangements reveals how Olbrich's work now approached traditional forms. Work on the Mathildenhöhe was completed in 1914. The final touches were put to the complex when a fountain was placed in front of the "Russian chapel," and a temple, known as the temple of the swans, was constructed by Albin Müller — summoned to Darmstadt in 1906 — and finally sculptural decorations were added by Bernhard Hoetger.

But the 1901 exhibition had been a complete financial failure. Serious tensions began to surface among the artists, with the result that some of them left the colony in 1902; it was then thought necessary to deny rumors that the association was on the point of breaking up.[37] After the first wave of enthusiasm, an invitation to the Mathildenhöhe no longer offered an exciting prospect. Nothing could now stop the artistic decline of the colony, and it became more and more difficult to obtain artists of the stature of Olbrich or Behrens.[38] The Darmstadt Künstlerkolonie became provincialized. Peter Behrens left Darmstadt in 1903, but Olbrich remained until his death in 1908: he was then the last survivor of the original group of artists. The outbreak of the First War provided a sort of timely euthanasia for the enterprise that had arisen with such high hopes fifteen years before.

During the Second War the interiors of the houses were completely destroyed, but today even their exterior appearance has radically changed, because the restoration work was too far-reaching. The house of the painter Christiansen has literally disappeared. In an attempt to define the historical position of the Künstlerkolonie, it may be stated that its ideological postulates are far in advance of the actual work produced by its members. In the inspiration behind the setting up of the community it must be recognized that it became a very significant forerunner of the Werkbund, although the hoped-for recovery of craft work was in effect very limited.[39] The glass and ceramics workshops founded by Ernst Ludwig had a short life, as did also "the studios for the study of applied arts" (1907–11), created under the auspices of private enterprise. Therefore, the "new Athens" that Hermann Bahr believed he could see in Darmstadt in 1900[40] was not realized. However, the Darmstadt colony was a stage along the road leading to the twentieth century: in 1901 it was still on the main road but later took a byway which came to a dead end.

The "model" represented by the Darmstadt Mathildenhöhe had a successor (until today practically overlooked by critics) at Hagen, an industrial city in Westphalia, where similar ideas were put into practice, though more coherently. Here, in the heart of the Ruhr,[41] Karl Ernst Osthaus, an important collector, art patron and promoter of culture, acquired in 1906 a large area of land on the outskirts of the city, "on which to give immediate effect to the aspirations of the modern movement of the garden city and art. In a comprehensive plan resolved at artistic level, large and small villas will arise. The builders will have to be bound to the common undertaking of entrusting the designs only to the greatest architects of our time. Only by following this path never trodden until now has it seemed possible . . . to create a comprehensive artistic image that could be really harmonious."[42] In an article explaining the idea of the Siedlung, published in the 1912 yearbook of the Deutscher Werkbund, Osthaus stated:

The problem of the city with an artistic appearance of its own has been coming closer to a satisfactory solution only in the past few years. There has been a single exception: Darmstadt. Here the wise artistic policy of a prince indicated the direction to be followed. The Mathildenhöhe, with its character of a permanent exhibition, was not an error when one considers the circumstances in which it was executed. However, one cannot again dwell on this approach. The next step must be taken in the direction of a culture of the city and the house without any second aim.[43]

However, Osthaus himself also intended to construct his settlement in such a way that it could be used as an exhibition. Indeed, the design for the Folkwang-Museum can be seen as an indication of his wish to create a central nucleus and at the same time to set up "a kind of open-air museum of modern architecture, painting and sculpture."[44] The conception of Osthaus lacked the pseudo-religiosity of the Darmstadt Künstlerkolonie. From the concept of a garden city adopted by Ebenezer Howard[45] as a means of furthering socialism, Osthaus took the formal aspect, for the purpose of stopping the spread of large towns by constructing satellite new towns.[46] In the intention of Osthaus, the Hohenhagen Siedlung was a unitary project, but, later, various architects were called in to collaborate in the planning stage, with the logical consequence that the final plan suffered from the heterogeneous ideas of the individual artists who took part in it. However, in 1906 such figures as Henry van de Velde, Peter Behrens and the then unknown J. L. M. Lauweriks were engaged on the project:[47] in this connection it should be mentioned that it is only recently that the central importance of the contribution of Lauweriks to the "frontal fillet" at Hagen has been recognized.[48] The houses built by Lauweriks were less costly but also much less monotonous than those by Olbrich at Darmstadt. They were occupied almost exclusively by artists, so that, by a fortunate coincidence, an artists' colony came into being,[49] which Osthaus had not originally envisaged.

For Osthaus, Hagen represented "an attempt to transfer to the problem of town planning the ideas that were already alive in the Werkbund."[50] "The Hagen impulse" — modeled on Darmstadt — made reality through the direct participation of van de Velde, Behrens and Lauweriks, and with the influence it had over Oud, Berlage, Le Corbusier and Gropius, occupies a central position in the history of architecture and design, a position that in future even the art historian will not be able to ignore.

1. For a biography of Grand Duchess Alice and Ernst Ludwig, see Gerard Noel, *Princess Alice: Queen Victoria's Forgotten Daughter* (London, 1974); Max Wauer, *Grossherzog Ernst Ludwig und das Schicksal seines Hauses* (Darmstadt, 1938); Golo Mann, "Der letzte grossherzog," in the catalog *Ein Dokument deutscher Kunst 1901–1976*, vol. 1 (Darmstadt, 1976), pp. 29–34; M. Knodt, *Die Regenten von Hessen-Darmstadt* (Darmstadt, 1976), p. 127 ff.

2. H. Graf Kessler, *Gesichter und Zeiten: Erinnerungen* (1935), (Berlin, 1962), p. 219.

3. Both correspondence and memoirs are unpublished. My thanks are due to HRH Princess Margaret von Hessen und bei Rhein for allowing me to see the documents.

4. Cf. H. W. Kruft, "Die Arts-and-Crafts-Bewegung und der deutsche Jugendstil," in G. Bott, ed., *Zwischen Morris und Bauhaus: Eine Kunst begründet auf Einfachheit*, (Hanau, 1977), pp. 25–39).

5. N. Pevsner, "William Morris, C. R. Ashbee und das zwanzigste Jahrhundert," *Deutsche Vierteljahrsschrift für Literaturwissenschaft und Geistesgeschichte*, no. 14 (1936), pp. 536–62

6. Published first in the socialist journal *The Commonwealth*. W. Liebknecht published the German translation in the social-

democratic journal *Die Neue Zeit* (1892–3). It was reprinted in 1974 in G. Selle, ed., *William Morris, Kunde von Nirgendwo* (Cologne, 1974).

7. Cf. G. Wietek, ed., *Deutsche Künstlerkolonien und Künstlerorte*, (Munich, 1976).

8. H. Bahr, *Bildung* (Berlin and Leipzig, 1900), p. 46. It is not clear whether the speech is to be dated before or after Olbrich was summoned to Darmstadt or if, in fact, it was ever given.

9. Cf. A. Wolde, "Der ökonomische Hintergrund der Künstlerkolonie," in the catalog *Ein Dokument deutscher Kunst 1901-1976*, vol. 5 (Darmstadt, 1976), p. 49.

10. For the history of the Mathildenhöhe, cf. A. Koch, ed., *Grossherzog Ernst Ludwig und die Ausstellung der Künstlerkolonie in Darmstadt 1901* (Darmstadt, 1901); the first years of the journal *Deutsche Kunst und Dekoration* (1897 ff.); Ludwig Prinz von Hessen und bei Rhein, *Die Darmstädter Künstlerkolonie und ihr Gründer Grossherzog Ernst Ludwig* (Darmstadt, 1950); J. Roether and H. G. Sperlich, *Die Darmstädter Mathildenhöhe* (Darmstadt, 1960); H.-C. Hoffmann, "Joseph M. Olbrichs architektonisches Werk für die Ausstellung 'Ein Dokument deutscher Kunst' auf der Mathildenhöhe 1901," in *Kunst in Hessenund Mittelrhein 7* (1967), pp. 7–25; G. Bott, "Ziele und Geschichte der Ausstellung der Darmstädter Künstlerkolonie 1901–1914," in *Acted du XXII Congrès International d'Histoire de l'Art 1969*, vol. 2 (Budapest, 1972), pp. 319–28 (reprinted in *Jugendstil: Kataloge des Hessischen Landesmuseums*, no. 1 [Darmstadt, 1973], pp. 13–18; G. Bott, "Darmstadt und die Mathildenhöhe," in Wietek, op. cit., pp. 154–61; catalog *Ein Dokument deutscher Kunst 1901–*, vol. 5 (Darmstadt, 1976), where are published the two essays by A. Wolde, "Daten zur Geschichte der Darmstädter Künstlerkolonie," p. 41 ff., and "Der ökonomische Hintergrund der Künstlerkolonie," p. 49 ff.

11. Wolde, op. cit., p. 49.

12. K. H. Schreyl, "Joseph Maria Olbrich. Die Zeichnungen in der Kunstbibliothek Berlin," in *Kritischer Katalog* (Berlin, 1972), p. 69, no. 10306 (fig. on p. 71).

13. Ibid, p. 69, no. 10306 (fig. on p. 70).

14. G. Fuchs, "Zur Weihe des Grundsteins," in Koch, *Grossherzog Ernst Ludwig*, p. 48.

15. P. Behrens, *Ein Dokument deutscher Kunst: Festschrift* (Munich, 1901), p. 10 ff.

16. The axis that once led between the Glückert II and the Habich houses on the south side of the Alexandraweg and practically subordinated the whole Siedlung to the Ernst-Ludwig-Haus is today enclosed by gardens.

17. Schreyl, op. cit., p. 58 ff.

18. In the work of Otto Wagner we find a series of sketches done in 1900 for a "gallery of modern art" in Vienna. Although these sketches present undeniable affinities of style with the work of Olbrich, they cannot have served as a model for him (H. Geretsegger and M. Peintner, *Otto Wagner* [Salzburg, 1964], p. 186 ff., figs. 208–10). After being officially summoned to Darmstadt in July 1899, Olbrich returned to Vienna in the same month and stayed there until September; there he may have begun work on his first designs for the Ernst-Ludwig-Haus. It is very likely that he showed these designs to his master, Otto Wagner, in whose studio he had been working since 1894. Wagner's designs for the "gallery of modern art" are clearly based on some of Olbrich's ideas, and it seems that Olbrich did not mind this. Wagner did not deliver his plans until May 12, 1900. The laying of the foundation stone of the Ernst-Ludwig-Haus had already taken place on March 24, 1900 (cf. Hoffmann, "Joseph M. Olbrichs," p. 11).

19. Illustration in Koch, op. cit., p. 286.

20. G. Fuchs, "Das Zeichen," in Koch, op. cit., p. 66.

21. Koch, op. cit., p. 56.

22. The best reproductions are to be seen in Koch, op. cit.

23. Illustrations in Koch, op. cit., p. 80 ff.; graphics of the Wasmuth Verlag, *Architektur von Olbrich*, 3 vols. (Berlin, 1901–14).

24. Koch, op. cit., p. 10.

25. F. Commichau, "Die Aussen-Architektur," in Koch, op. cit., p. 98.

26. Koch, op. cit., p. 10.

27. Ibid., p. 11.

28. Ibid., p. 12.

29. Kruft, op. cit.

30. Koch, op. cit., p. 25.

31. Cf. in this connection G. Bott, op. cit., in note 10 of this article, and the catalog to the exhibition "Ein Dokument Deutscher Kunst 1901–1976," Darmstadt 1976, vol. 5, page 67.

32. Catalog of the 1908 exhibition, p. 82.

33. The 1908 exhibition confirms that in Darmstadt the ideas of the Werkbund had met with a direct response, not only because large-scale industry took an interest in the experiment, but also because one of the principles basic to the new association had now become generally accepted, namely, that "even at factory level it was possible to produce practical, beautiful and convenient articles provided that in their planning and in the first phase of their design the right people were involved" (Ludwig von Hessen und bei Rhein, *Die Darmstädter Künstlerkolonie*, p. 42).

34. Cf. the catalog "Joseph Maria Olbrich" (Darmstadt, 1967), p. 276 ff.; Schreyl, op. cit., p. 75 ff.

35. I consider as misleading the suggestion of H.-G. Sperlich (*Versuch über Joseph Maria Olbrich* [Darmstadt, 1965], p. 17 ff.) that the first designs indicate a relationship with the idea of a triumphal arch.

36. Giulia Veronesi, *Joseph Maria Olbrich* (Milan, 1948), p. 162 ff.

37. Cf. the catalog *Ein Dokument deutscher Kunst 1901–1976*, vol. 5 (Darmstadt, 1976), p. 42 ff.

38. Cf. the account of the artists present at the Mathildenhöhe in vol. 4 of the catalog *Ein Dokument deutscher Kunst 1901–1976* (Darmstadt, 1976).

39. A. Koch (*Darmstadt: Eine Stätte moderner Kunstbestrebungen* [Darmstadt, 1905], p. VI) shows especially the surprising development of the furniture industry. But it must be remembered that the publishing initiative of Darmstadt, the Ernst-Ludwig-Presse, founded in 1907 and conducted under the patronage of the Insel-Verlag of Leipzig, although significant from the artistic point of view, succeeded only to a very limited extent in increasing the typographic industry of Hessen. Cf. also "Die Ernst Ludwig Presse zu Darmstadt" edited by the Martin-Behaim-Gesellschaft (Darmstadt, 1972); E. Zimmermann, "Die Buchkunst der Darmstädter Künstlerkolonie," in the catalog *Ein Dokument deutscher Kunst 1901–1976*, vol. 5 (Darmstadt, 1976).

40. Bahr, op. cit. (dedication to Ernst Ludwig).

41. Cf. H. Hesse-Frielinghaus and others, *Karl Ernst Osthaus: Leben und Werk* (Recklinghausen, 1971).

42. Karl Ernst Osthaus in the *Westfälisches Tageblatt* of October 8, 1906; quoted by Hesse-Frielinghaus, op. cit., p. 388.

43. Karl Ernst Osthaus, "Die Gartenvorstadt an der Donnerkuhle," in *Jahrbuch des Deutschen Werkbundes* (1912), p. 94.

44. Ibid., p. 96.

45. *Ebenezer Howard, Garden Cities of Tomorrow* (1902), ed. F. J. Osburn (Cambridge, Mass., 1970).

46. P. Stressig and J. Buekschmitt, in Hesse-Frielinghaus, op. cit., p. 369.

47. P. Stressig, in Hesse-Frielinghaus, op. cit., p. 385 ff.

48. N. Tummers, "Der Hagener Impuls: Das Werk von J. L. M. Lauweriks und sein Einfluss auf Architektur und Formgebung um 1910," *Hagener Beiträge zur Geschichte und Landeskunde*, Grosse Reihe, no. 15, (Hagen, 1972).

49. P. Stressig, in Hesse-Frielinghaus, op. cit., p. 430.

50. Osthaus, op. cit., p. 93.

BERLIN AT THE TURN OF THE CENTURY: A HISTORICAL AND ARCHITECTURAL ANALYSIS
(Not new facts, but an attempt to throw light on relationships)

Goerd Peschken with Tilmann Heinish

Berlin at the turn of the century: I was still in time to see it, when I began to study architecture in the city in 1953. But the Berlin of the years of the national unity still existed at that time: there were still to be seen facades smothered under a superabundance of decoration, superfluous pediments heavily ornamented, with iron pennons protruding strangely into the sky — a sky that could still be seen through the gaping windows made where the thin cavities in the inner walls, now unplastered, let in the light. The large stores and office blocks, put up in the early years of the century, had not been entirely burnt out, but were only dilapidated: now lacking their wooden structure, they had retained only their concrete ceilings. The large windows were boarded up or walled in, but here and there a small aperture served as an emergency window. Seen against the light, the iron trusses appeared to bulge out into the void, while the decorative sculptures on cornices and pillars had peeled off at several places, as a result of fire, or were riddled with bullet holes or splinters. The stages of the architectural history of the period with which we are here concerned could therefore be seen only against the background of the vast expanse of the ruins of what had once been the city. The city: brought to completion, as I recall, at the eve of the First War, it stretched from the Alexanderplatz to the Potsdamer Strasse, was interrupted at the west, then regrouped in scattered nuclei near the Wittenbergerplatz. Although by 1945 all its buildings were reduced to bare skeletons, they would still have been standing today if in the absurd battle for prestige between East and West they had not been sacrificed to the new, a "new" that is disliked today even by those responsible for creating it.

The city with its large emporia stood behind the old medieval city, forming a horseshoe ring: Haackescher Markt, Wallstrasse, Spittelmarkt, Hausvogteiplatz; then it spread out to the tangle of outlying districts established by the absolute monarchy: after the Friedrichstadt, the city of Friedrich, then along the Leipziger Strasse up to the Potsdamer Platz. Even before the twentieth century, completely filled-in ceilings were not known: the *Preussische Kappe,* or Prussian lintel, had already been in existence for some time, made of bricks with iron supports. But the oldest of the emporium buildings still contained rooms on the upper stories; it was only below, though on two floors, that they had iron beams and solid ceilings, with the result that, in the fire of Berlin, the beams crashed down and burst through the ceilings. The classic type of five-story emporium building, intended

44. Berlin, Leipziger Platz with view of the Leipziger Strasse. On the left, the Wertheim store with the 1926 extension.

45. Alfred Messel, Wertheim store in Leipziger Platz, 1896 and 1904 (front building).

46. Alfred Messel, Wertheim store in Leipziger Strasse, detail of second courtyard, 1904.

originally to be rented to individual stores, was first introduced into Berlin in 1885–90. The large firms had been progressively developing their trade in the direction of the large emporium and multiple store but did not adopt this type of construction until around 1895. From that moment there began the vertiginous triumphal march of the emporium store, which reached its climax in the building on the Leipziger Platz built by Messel for the Wertheim store. Messel, who participated personally in the development of the Berlin emporium-store, had in 1896–97 provided a radical suggestion for the oldest side of the Wertheim store on the Leipziger Strasse: nothing but pilasters and glass. The famous building of 1904 on the Leipziger Platz, situated in a favored position almost like a city gate communicating with the inner city, was by no means a modest structure, yet possessed an undoubted elegance of its own, so much so that it created an indelible impression on the memory of whoever could still see it. Whenever I asked people to describe the interior of this great emporium, I was given descriptions confirming that its effect was very similar to that of a Gothic cathedral: an impression of vastness, of care expended on every minute detail, an atmosphere of solemn intensity and remoteness from everyday concerns.

In 1896 Otto March stated in his book *Berlin und seine Bauten* that the influence of English and American architecture could be noted in the large stores — the influence, that is, of countries far in advance of us in trade. During the following years the German economy caught up surprisingly quickly, so that by the beginning of the new century the monopolization of retail trade not only had its own system of sale but also a special type of building where its store could be established, and in this process March played a not insignificant part. In the building development of Berlin following 1900 the symptomatic and characteristic feature has been the new importance given to delicacy and good taste. And it was this new orientation that accounts for the incredible success that came to the delicate and sensitive artist Messel. In Berlin (as in the whole of Germany) this new tendency was much more apparent than in neighboring countries, partly because it formed a contrast to the particularly ugly works produced by the previous generation. I believe that the German refined liberals who were irretrievably smashed by Bismarck, after the resounding success of his power politics pursued between 1866 and 1871, simply drowned in the current of new wealth that flooded through Berlin at the start of its expansion. In my opinion, not even nostalgia for the past can cancel the impression of coarse vulgarity created by the Berlin of the eighties — a Berlin that has today almost totally disappeared, apart from a few traces in the suburbs — where we find a coldness and complete lack of thought in the use of historical tradition. Messel's building on the Leipziger Platz expressed a clear historical intention just as much

47, 48. Alfred Messel, Wertheim store in Leipziger Strasse, details of the main building, 1904.

as these other buildings. The exterior was modeled on the style of the Jugendstil, presenting a cleverly judged mixture of late-Gothic and later styles, like the mansard roof in a Baroque style, which from the aesthetic viewpoint produced the effect of the English country house; in the interior there were unmistakable neoclassical elements, already in a Jugendstil sense, but with every form spiritualized (to use a term then in vogue). Obviously, we find here that refinement of taste typical of the second generation, accompanied by a manifest intention to glorify the monopolization of retail trade. The Wertheim store has in a sense ennobled the commercial center, just because it formed an entrance to it or gave it the tonic note.

In the calmer, less chaotic center of the city, that is, the administrative center on Unter den Linden, the most important architectural event of the years between 1905 and 1910 was without any doubt the construction of the new national library. In the studio of the court architect Ernst von Ihne, designs were made for an elegant, exquisite neo-Baroque facade. But a walk round the outside of the building — which occupies an entire block — reveals clearly, in the side streets, features that were characteristic of Berlin neoclassicism, while a glance at the open courtyards built of white-glazed bricks shows an amazing Jugendstil neoclassicism full of Viennese allusions. This happened because the young artists who worked in Ihne's studio felt themselves entitled to opt for the new tendencies, even though they did not declare themselves; indeed, neoclassicism was then the style at which, so to speak, the development of Berlin architecture had come to a halt. Farther to the south, a block on the Behrenstrasse showed — and still does show, if only partially — the genesis of Berlin neoclassicism: the great banks, which started to build their offices in the eighties and continued until the years of the First War, were the first to adopt neoclassicism, that is, even before the State itself. We can see this development, especially, in the new wings of the Discontogesellschaft at the corner of Unter den Linden with the Charlottenstrasse and Behrenstrasse. Two of the banks on the Behrenstrasse were built by Messel: the Berliner Handelsgesellschaft and the Nationalbank. The biographers of Messel have described the part he played in the formulation of the Berlin neoclassical style but have also put forth the hypothesis (Karl Scheffler and Walter Behrendt, 1911!) that the contribution by Peter Behrens was far greater than that of Messel himself. This clear, critical evaluation is itself a reflection of an irreplaceable moment in the framework of Berlin architecture of the time.

Peter Behrens formulated the Berlin (German) neoclassical style in this precise sense: he made it into an artistic current of international dimensions and even perhaps a movement of the avant-garde. The role fulfilled by Messel in the distribution sector was fulfilled by Behrens in the production sector. In the autumn of 1907 (almost simultaneously with the

founding of the Deutscher Werkbund) Behrens was made artistic adviser to the Allgemeine Elektricitäts-Gesellschaft — the AEG, as it is known — and he designed their entire industrial production, including the buildings themselves. After the textile industry and the extractive industry (mining), the sector of light engine construction was then enjoying a great success and promoting the third phase of the industrial revolution, and the AEG group had a dominant function in this process comparable to that of Ford in the USA. This new stage of industrialization led to the definitive supremacy of holdings, monopolies and large banking concerns and at the same time enabled Germany to share with the USA, side by side with England, world economic supremacy. I have deliberately anticipated this comment, since I believe Behrens's work for the AEG should be accorded great importance, if for no other reason than that it presents a historical document, or for this reason especially, even apart from a consideration of the artistic quality, which was, however, at the level of its historical moment.

For the purposes of our argument, of greater interest than the late works of Behrens is undoubtedly the first famous turbine factory built at Moabit in 1909. Behrens's factory of turbine engines is recalled today in many histories of modern architecture, where it is rightly considered to be a fundamental document, but, unfortunately, it must be said that it is in most cases related to the Neue Sachlichkeit, that is, functionalism. However, the "Turbinenhalle" is not at all "objective" — if anything, it is neoclassical and extremely expressive. Seen from outside, the visible side presents a succession of colossal laminated iron beams, on which, apart from an entablature also made of iron, there rests the heavy roof, which curves rather like a basin and which, seen from the front, creates the effect of an enormous cement block like the tombstones of prehistoric burial monuments. This impression is enhanced by the monumental blocks at the corners, squared off and sloping slightly inward, and by the glass panels on the sides, also sloping inward, which emphasize the way the supports broaden out toward the top. The whole complex is highly effective but far removed from the system of the "new objectivity"; the factory — a hangar for the assembly of parts — contains a gigantic crane, whose basic element is the gantry, not visible, situated about three-quarters up the height of the windows (in the evenings, when the lights are on inside the building, the dark shadow of this gantry can be seen). In contrast to these extremely heavy parts — the gantry and pilasters — the roof consists of an extremely light concave shape; it is not at all a monolithic block. The pilasters are half-frames, with three connecting hinges. The monumental corner blocks consist of slender cement panels. A type of architecture, like that of Behrens, conceals the gantry, but it certainly cannot be described

49. W. Martens, Disconto-Gesellschaft Bank on the Charlottenstrasse, 1902.

50. Peter Behrens, turbine factory AEG, Berlin-Moabit, Huttenstrasse, 1909.

51. Peter Behrens, AEG workshops in Brunnenstrasse, small engine factory, Voltastrasse side, 1910-11.

as objective in the sense in which this term was proposed by the new formal canon of the Neue Sachlichkeit. But Behrens applied this same method two years later in the factory on the Brunnenstrasse in Berlin-Wedding. Expression and illusion are two different things: Behrens certainly did not intend to deceive the public by his architecture. It is perfectly obvious to anyone that the glass window in the tympanum and the steel framing could not possibly suffice to support the weight of the tympanum itself, even when the base is thought of as a plinth; indeed, it has been given a sharply defined and very elegant line. To an attentive observer it is apparent, moreover, that joins of the heavy corner blocks are flanges of iron profiles, green-tinted, as are all the other iron parts as well. The skylight with its fillet of glazed segments can be seen at a certain distance and provides unequivocal evidence of the fact that the stone used for the covering is merely a stylistic device, not yet an "object" present with all its weight.

It may be that the means of expression employed by Behrens were themselves responsible for misleading people who saw in the turbine factory a coherent application of the new method proposed by the Neue Sachlichkeit — the enormous glass surfaces, the use of concrete in the tympanum and plinth, and especially the laminated iron. These materials were new at the time, and Behrens incorporated them in his building to produce an aesthetic effect. In this connection I find singularly unsuccessful the corner panels of cement, arched and slightly bulging and provided with a kind of concave line; on the other hand, the large cast-iron hinges at knee-level of the passerby are most beautiful. In his use of such devices here, Behrens seems to have gone far beyond any other European architect and deserves a place alongside the great Americans.

The change in architectural style that came about at that time in industrial building in particular is truly amazing. The school of Schinkel adapted to their own highly individual style the English model of factory with red brick buttresses and lintel. This type of lintel became so widely employed through their efforts that in Central Europe it was known as the Preussische Kappe. The factories were built of dark red brick and had large windows shaped like segmental arches, framed by a cast-iron profile, with buttresses and small pediments. Some critics described this style as an impoverished architecture (the term used then was Bedürfnisbau, or utility building); personally I would opt for the term old objectivity. Unfortunately, the inner supports hardly ever condition the structure of the exterior parts; to compensate for this incongruity, there are platforms of railway stations, with columns and cast-iron structure, and the roof has beams of bitumated wood. This type of building was influenced in the main by the requirements of utility and characterized by the use of cast-

iron, bricks and wood. It was already considered outmoded, even by Messel's generation. The Berlin city council had, in fact, appointed Ludwig Hoffmann to be the chief architect of the city, with two precise aims in view: to eliminate from schools, hospitals and commercial buildings the style of architecture that was suffocating them and to raise the artistic level of communal buildings by removing the criterion of the satisfaction of basic needs alone. Hoffmann's method resulted in an architecture that showed greater attention to tradition than did the architecture that preceded his. Behrens, too, proceeded in a similar direction in the industrial building sector; here — on a monumental scale, as can be seen — he replaced brick walls and windows in the shape of segmented arches by vast surfaces of glass between iron supports. The materials he used and the particular solutions he chose for the turbine factory tell us a great deal about the content Behrens wished to express. In this sense the I-sections are particularly revealing. In the old industrial building of the so-called cast-iron age the buttresses, as always, simplified in form, were essentially reminiscences of antique candelabra-type columns: the "old objectivity" was a stylized architecture yet was still highly traditional or even classical. Cast iron and brick were used merely as a means of creating a form legitimized by historical tradition. In the factories of the "old objectivity," characterized by the poverty of their decoration, among other things, there were produced, for example, those cupboards overladen with superfluous ornamentation, those velvet drapes, those porcelain ornaments and those door decorations that today crowd the shelves of our secondhand shops.

The I-sections of the turbine factory no longer contain any vestige of the classical column but follow the method of the new laminating technique. They no longer obey the rules of style that dictated the forms of the objects in daily use manufactured at that time and conferred legitimacy upon them: these were now new forms, which, just because of Behrens's reworking of the neoclassical style, acquired the dignity of the antique. This same characteristic is peculiar to all the other works designed by Behrens, especially his famous arc lamps. These lamps do not presume to be made of a particularly precious material, nor does their design indicate a clear desire to return to the antique. Nevertheless, it is these works by Behrens that must be considered forms of highly qualified applied art, or even pure art par excellence. The design of these lamps and of the turbine factory was not therefore intended to offend the traditional taste of the purchasers but sought to acquire for the industrial mass product — and at the same time for the mass-production of large-scale industry — the prestige that until then had been granted only to the work of art, to bourgeois ideals and to free art.

Fritz Hoeber, Behrens' biographer, explained in 1913 without too many preambles that the AEG, which by then had grown into an industry of international importance, was no longer so much concerned to advertise itself, as to impart a high degree of quality to technical precision, as always, by ensuring that its form, too, was beautiful; this was actually a theological argument. Hoeber also formulated what might be termed the functionalist ideology at its early stage — "functional beauty," "beauty in precision" — and he eventually compared factories with cathedrals.

A clearly progressive symptom was the modification to the collective consciousness brought about by the art of the new objectivity; society became aware that it was in process of change into an industrial society, living because of industry and dependent upon industry. On the other hand, the historical forms it repudiated should indicate, beyond themselves, a humanitas of which the economic and technological progress should be servant. I do not deny that this hope has for some time now been seen as completely noncredible, and the historicist pomposity behind it has been unmasked in all its falsity: I am speaking exclusively of the new element represented in the I-section. In spite of its admired and admirable honesty, this new element indicated merely itself. In that case, could it be taken as a criterion? If, therefore, this new form did not relate to anything beyond itself to those who made it and to those for whom it was made, then it could not but rule and terrorize us by what has happened in the meantime. Yet the alternative conscience or affirmative constriction was posed but not decided in this first work of Behrens, the turbine factory.

Now that we can see things more clearly, we can distinguish in the design of Behrens various aspects of the social and industrial consciousness. The aspect already discussed relates to the consciousness of the consumers, the users, to whom it was explained that mass industrial products had to be adjudged good and beautiful like the best product that had in the past been made by craft methods. This is the aspect of the new objectivity, an aspect of great importance and world impact in the years when monopolies began to take control.

A second aspect is a phenomenon that was more or less limited to Germany. The self-awareness of industry, expressed in the powerful image of the turbine factory, was certainly nurtured by the very achievements of industry: the colossal turbines that were assembled here and the chains of production of the other departments. But whose was this awareness? To whom was it addressed? First and foremost it was the awareness of the masters of the AEG and their managers, the large class of the bourgeois entrepreneurs who, thanks to modern methods of organization worked out by themselves, had made the German economy competitive on a world scale. In view of the political situation of the time, the principal addressee of this demonstration of self-knowledge was without question the German-Prussian state, still monarchic in its structure and strongly supported by the Junkers, the great landowning class. The times were ripe for the new oligarchy made up of the captains of industry, the presidents of large holdings and monopolies, and great banking concerns to make their voices heard in the state also; in other words, to play a part reflecting the standing of their effective role in the economic life of the country. This policy not only had its own official monument in Behrens's first work, but was very soon to celebrate its triumph in what was perhaps the most spectacular facade ever designed by Behrens, that of the Kleinmotorenfabrik of the AEG, built in 1910–11 on the Brunnenstrasse. This factory for the production of light engines served as a model for the embassy of the German Reich in St. Petersburg; by this act the role of the monopolies as cultural guides received its official baptism. Soon afterward, during the First War, government functions were formally granted to the great German industrialists; a member of the Rathenau family, which owned the AEG, was made responsible for the war economy.

In observing and describing these significant works of architecture, I have been surprised at the amazing similarities in the system of facade adopted in the Wertheim store and in the light-engine factory and the turbine factory (both by Behrens): colossal pilasters, a ceiling or gantry set back from the facade, and a broken roof in the manner of a mansard roof, which with the entablature forms an authentic plastic unity. By their proud and important solution these two architects have found the appropriate form through which to express the great period of the German bourgeois high society. I think it was right that the great captains of industry took the power of the state. If they had not, then there would not be such a convincing form of building that could represent their own power. I shall examine this question in further detail later on.

I have not yet concluded my consideration of the interpretation of the neoclassical version imposed by Behrens on the form just described. The colossal neoclassical pilasters are an imperial motif, obviously not limited to confirming the German Reich's claim to prestige, but instead crystallizing the imperialistic intentions of Germany toward the world — Le Corbusier saw this intention in the turbine factory of Behrens. But the fact that an industrial country with a certain supremacy to be defended on the international plane should try to acquire also a certain political prestige and to visualize its own influence reaching into every sector where its exports and imports extended seems to me just as understandable. However, when one tries to see the catastrophe Germany was soon to represent for its neighbors and for itself and in the evaluation of the role played by the

52. Peter Behrens, design for the German embassy in St. Petersburg, principal facade, 1911.

bourgeoisie in architecture — a subject I wish to treat in my contribution — then the usual pointing out of the connections between Berlin neoclassicism, and that of Behrens in particular, and the classicism of national socialism is not so much mistaken, as lacking subtlety.

In the few years separating the founding of the Werkbund and the outbreak of the First War the bourgeoisie was faced with a period of ascendence, climax, and great crisis, which was very accurately reflected in architectural history. This crisis can be detected from a careful reading of Behrens's industrial buildings, and, perhaps even more so, of the administrative offices of the AEG designed by him. However, I would rather focus my analysis on the type of middle-class housing being developed at that time, partly because at the same time we can illustrate another essential phase in the architecture of Berlin at the turn of our century. At the beginning of the century the middle-class home was modeled on the country house. To understand the significance of this choice, it is necessary to take a large step backward and look at the privileged type of house built for the nineteenth-century middle class, about which unfortunately there are so far no clear ideas or concepts. The most common characteristic form, if only from a numerical viewpoint, was the well-known Berlin house built for renting, whose architectural appearance certainly failed to reveal its unmistakable destiny and economic position. In appearance it continued to be a bourgeois house, as it had developed out of the medieval bourgeois house through the efforts of patriarchal Prussian absolutism, but with the addition of many other rooms (a development that in most cases had already occurred in the eighteenth century, when the absolutist administration was anxious to promote the expansion of manufactured goods). On the street side and usually on the ground floor this bourgeois house contained shops, while the small patriarch, the proprietor, lived on the first floor, the "noble" floor; the reception rooms looked onto the street (apart from the dining room, the "Berlin room," which overlooked the courtyard), while the rooms where the family actually lived (bedrooms, nursery, kitchen, sewing room or wardrobe) overlooked the courtyard. On the same side there were obviously also the servants' quarters. The tenants who were middle-class "renters" had their rooms on the street side on the upper stories, which from the end of the eighteenth century numbered two; in contrast, the working-class tenants lived in accommodations that overlooked the interior, where by tradition (a custom that has remained unchanged until today) they were considered subordinate and were placed under the paternal tutelage of the proprietor. In the courtyard at the rear were the craftsmen's workshops, and later, in the Second Reich, factories occupying several floors and let to various firms. The barrack-type lodging house, occupied by workers' families, which grew up during the Second Reich, covered a wider area

and often had several wings that were occupied and therefore several courtyards at the rear; sometimes there were no workshops. Like the bourgeois lodging houses, these buildings usually consisted of five stories.

The patriarchal type of residence with whitewashed facade was architecturally pretentious, and with its reception rooms facing the street side it served a precise purpose: to parade in front of the sovereign like a regiment of soldiers in dress uniform. The conviction held by historians that absolutism represented nothing more than an essential stage of the bourgeois era — or, more precisely, the era of liberal capitalism — is confirmed, in the sector of the history of building, by the fact that this same typology endured into the nineteenth century. The reception rooms — now called parlors — and the facades were intended to make an impression not only on the absolute monarch but on the no less critical eye of the bourgeoisie and so to confirm the reputation or credit of this type of residence, as it would be more accurate to say in defining its aims. This same type of house seems to have come into its own wherever the social process of late-absolutism was coherently fulfilled (or suffered), and indeed it is present with only slight differences, in Paris, for example. Besides, the middle-class patriarch, who also imitated the model of the court, was completely ignorant of the principle of equality between the sexes, so that he never tolerated two identical apartments ("suites") or even a central entrance. If there are examples of central entrances in the lodging houses, these were always to be found in houses having two apartments on the same floor (*Zweispänner*).

The fact that this type of middle-class housing was accepted as congruent by this class, since it was functional to it, is confirmed by an example: the middle-class villa of Berlin, which began to put up in Berlin after 1800, became emancipated from the model of the *maison de plaisance* and summer residence of the nobility and in a series of coherent modifications adopted the form of the town house: drawing rooms on the front (with a garden resolving the facade), side entrance, bedrooms up to the children's nurseries (on the upper floor), garage and stables in a separate block overlooking the courtyard, which was called the court as in the town house, but was not at all a courtyard. This type of villa had already been given its form around 1860, when the liberal middle class entered its final trial of strength with the Prussian landowner state — the constitutional conflict; after the defeat of the middle class and the victories of Bismarck, the *Landhaus*, or country house, met with a definite stalemate, until around 1890.

Around 1890, however, the villa again began to develop rapidly. It was enriched with a lobby extending to two stories in height, or, in the case of lower middle-class families, with a vestibule, which also housed the staircase and which not only fulfilled its own function, that of forming a

focal point for the traffic of the household to pass through, but also often was used as a living room. In this process the middle-class villa of Berlin — now mostly referred to as a Landhaus — finally lost the associations that still connected it to architectural structures favored by the court and the system of absolute monarchy. This may have been because the feudal origin of the model, the country house of England, had been forgotten or else because this derivation itself was deliberately exalted as proof of the independence attained by the middle class. But in my view an even more important factor was the change that took place in the actual way of life of the middle class, expressed by the new feature of the lobby. In the richest examples, where a large lobby extends to the height of two stories, the upper gallery communicates with the bedrooms. From below, for example, a visitor can see these rooms and the nurseries. This type of arrangement requires great discretion from the guest: he must be aware how far he can permit himself to know what is happening in the gallery. In addition, the children who grow up in this house must know just as well what type of communication with the guest is possible in the lobby, according to the time of day and the degree of familiarity and friendship. And at a meeting in the lobby in the evening all the guests must know how far they can go in making noise, and so on. In the "liberal" type of villa — by this term I would define the type of villa arranged according to the model of the town house, a type progressively abandoned between 1860 and 1890 — a rigid separation was maintained between the parlors and the rest of the house; for example, children who were too young to be admitted into society were never allowed to enter the "best rooms" unless accompanied by adults, and the women were never allowed to do any kind of domestic work in them (apart from embroidery). Through the middle of the house there therefore ran a line of demarcation between the private sphere and the sphere we might call public. The liberal of the old school, who was still patriarchal in his outlook, lived what might be called a schizophrenic life: outside and in the parlors he was liberal and had with his peers a relationship that was essentially one of equality, whereas among his family he maintained a most rigid hierarchy. In contrast, the country house with porch that was built at the beginning of the century corresponded to the needs of a more liberal and harmonious way of life, in other words, a less contradictory way; the rigorous patriarchal type of control exercised over women and children had now ceased, and what had until then been an obligation and surface convention was now internalized culture and civilization. The boundary between the public and private spheres was no longer situated between living rooms and reception rooms but at the threshold of each room belonging to each member of the family, since in its internal structure the family had become liberal. In the English house, the new style of behavior led to the use of a door for each room, so eliminating the sequence of parlors. The German country house did not manage to follow the English example, even in this sense: the civilizing process was not entirely completed. Yet never since that time has such a refined way of life existed in Germany. The finest house of this type I have been able to see (before it was recently transformed into a lodging house of small apartments) was the Neuhaus house in Dahlem, built by Muthesius in 1906. Immediately as one entered the porch there was a ceiling overhead; then on the left the porch was submerged into a twilight atmosphere (where the service areas and the kitchen opened out). Instinctively, one turned to the right, toward the part of the porch that was well lighted and on two floors, where a passage with seats on both sides formed a quiet corner partly protected by the balcony of the staircase landing. With an amazing delicacy the door of the study belonging to the master of the house was partly hidden by the first flight of stairs and set back so as not to be in too direct contact with the rest of the house and therefore protected from noise. Again, in the case of the door leading from this study into the parlor set aside for the mistress of the house, the same function of "distance" was fulfilled by a deep wardrobe recess that surrounded the door itself. Even the inner arrangement of the study (belonging to the master of the house), where there was a corner for working and concentration, a corner for relaxing, and a corner for private conversation, was highly significant in showing how this wealthy class knew how to make the most of their possessions. However, the internal partitioning of the wife's room did not provide so much individuality. Of course, the house was occupied by more than one couple (perhaps by grandparents or married children), and the Erker, or bow window, of one of these bedrooms overlooking the porch was the architectural expression of the direct relationship between a given couple and the rest of the house and their circle of friends and acquaintances. Posener has referred to the Muthesius porch as an extremely important space.

These houses provided for a well-planned and suitable type of accommodation also for the staff, who worked in the separate wing housing the kitchens on the ground floor and their bedrooms in the attics. In the "liberal" type of villa, in contrast, the servants usually had to work and sleep in unhealthy basements. For these shameful conditions the builder had to pay by raising the level of the basement to emerge above street level, for reasons of light. The result was poor communication between house and garden of a direct and natural kind, and both one and the other produced an unfortunate effect. Here the very idea of a villa, which was to live in the garden, was almost lost. It was not until the early years of the century that the country house, at least in its finest examples, finally stood at street level.

53. Hans Griesebach, Wilhelm von Bode villa, in Uhlandstrasse, Berlin-Charlottenburg, 1855, demolished.

54. Hans Griesebach, Wilhelm von Bode villa, in Uhlandstrasse, Berlin-Charlottenburg, plan of the ground floor.

55. Hermann Muthesius, Neuhaus country house, Berlin-Dahlem, Bernadottestrasse, 1906 (reconstructed).

56. Hermann Muthesius, Neuhaus country house, Berlin-Dahlem, Bernadottestrasse, 1906, general plan.

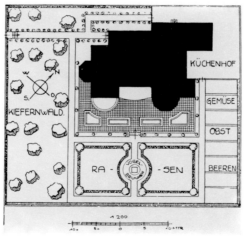

At this point it might be opportune to discuss a whole series of problems, referring to such collateral phenomena as the fashions in dress or the movements for the "reform of life," and so on. I prefer to say nothing about them apart from one single comment: the refined life-style followed by the upper middle class after 1900 was followed by a broad strata of the intelligentsia only in the past ten years. There has therefore been an interval of two generations. Then, as again now, Germany appears to have drawn near to real Western culture.

When around 1905 the works of Muthesius realized the highest expressions of this type, the country house also became a model for the town. The most elegant lodging houses in the western zone of Berlin now have on the ground floor an entrance porch paneled in wood (unlike the carriage-way type of entrance with columns as seen in the best examples, like the Kreuzberg houses built for large manufacturers) and a lift, while the entrance to the individual rooms on the upper floors is broadened to form a wide vestibule, from which the drawing rooms lead off.

The country house, therefore, was now the model for the middle-class city apartment. I think it is interesting to reflect upon this new situation. The "liberal" villa was, as I have said, arranged in a way similar to the town house, and the residential quarters of the time were, as it were, improved cities — or they were intended to be improved cities; there was still no trace of any hostility toward the city and civilization. The aesthetic effect of these villas, with their gardens enclosed behind handsome iron railings was not suburban, but pre–city — and still is, wherever the example has been retained, because with these villas the constructions follow the edges of the streets. In the case of the country house, on the other hand, it is not at all unlikely that the form it took was connected with a sense of hostility toward city life and civilization, a sentiment that was decidedly antibourgeois. Indeed, the very term country house suggests an implicit flight from the town. The unity that had now been achieved in the life of the upper middle class in their own country houses, though fine in itself, risked becoming neofeudal. The important distinction between the public and private spheres was undermined. The nobility had not known this distinction, and in the marriage bed its function was always constitutional. In this context the aesthetic relationship between the house and the plot of land is of interest. The houses built by Muthesius on the Rehwiese and his Cramer house stand at the edges of large public parks, where they enjoy a panoramic view over the gardens and appear to protrude into them almost as if they were claiming a right to something which, to use an expression dear to liberals, the builders had not

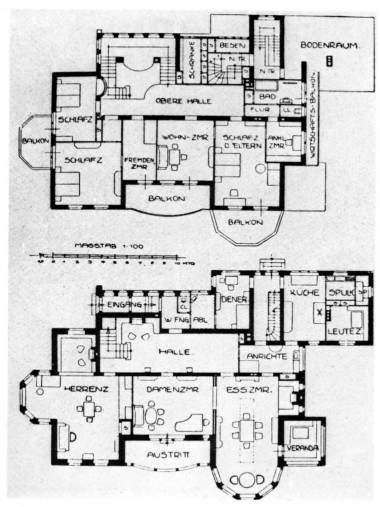

57. Hermann Muthesius, Neuhaus country house, Berlin-Dahlem, Bernadottestrasse, 1906, ground plans.

58. Hermann Muthesius, Neuhaus country house, Berlin-Dahlem, Bernadottestrasse, 1906, entrance with staircase.

Page 47

59. Peter Behrens, Theodor Wiegand villa, Berlin-Dahlem, Lennestrasse, 1911, plan of the ground floor.

60. Peter Behrens, Theodor Wiegand villa, Berlin-Dahlem, Lennestrasse, 1911, facade overlooking the street.

paid for. Here, rights that had existed since feudal times seemed to be resurfacing. But this relationship could also be inverted: for example, the Neuhaus house stands on a relatively small plot. Muthesius had made the garden into a work of architecture by constructing a terrace and relative loggia. Today, however, these features have been sacrificed in the reconstruction of the house, and it is apparent that the building is too large in relation to the land on which it stands: it is rather ugly and stumpy, like the houses in most of the residential districts of yesterday and today. Its ugliness is due to its own (unreal) pretentiousness in exerting its right as a villa to have its own area of space and to enjoy that isolation that would be indispensable to it, but that in reality it does not have. In this is reflected a consequence of a very precise factual reality: the terraced housing that is the most common form of house building in the Western tradition made a very limited impact on Berlin.

In the case of the country house, the relationship with the external world, or the public, becomes less intense. Muthesius's own house stands between the Potsdamer Chaussee and the Rehwiese, and faces the quiet woodland area. In the Neuhaus house, however, a slender strip of conifer woodland runs between the garden and the street, so that the garden no longer stretches in front of the house but is at its side. Of course, by that time the Potsdamer Chaussee no longer signified that close contact with the outside world — with the common people — that it had had in the past, when the state chancellor, Prince Hardenberg, or Prince Charles of Prussia occupied summer residences in this same avenue and had their gardens and terraces right on the edges of the street. The reason for the change was that some of the traffic had now been progressively absorbed by the railway, and, in addition, by the beginning of the century the most prominent citizens passed through the avenue in cars, already traveling fast for the time, and therefore could not be easily recognized and greeted. I do not mean to discuss here the level attained by German middle-class culture, as we have seen, but would simply like to record that the external conditions and form of the Landhaus permitted few civil alternatives. In its political and economic implications, what may be said is simple and short. The economic foundation of liberalism, as we know, is the independence of many individuals, but, as has been made clear in the first part of my essay, this hypothesis had by now become outdated. Because it was now the monopolies, holdings and large banking concerns that conditioned and determined the situation, the very basis of middle-class freedoms had been overthrown. If it was now felt essential to preserve the culture and freedom of the city, this meant that these values should represent a form of life that had been acquired and was therefore a political form; these values should be an obvious possession of the majority of the social classes. Until now this

observation concerns not only Germany: the problem is posed in all industrialized countries. What follows, on the other hand, relates specifically to German history.

Once liberalism had been shattered by Bismarck, it was unable to recover; this was due to the fact that its economic period had already reached its conclusion. The class that had now regained a bourgeois consciousness was a new class. There is no doubt that the refinement of a villa with porch is to be interpreted as a typical second-generation phenomenon, of a generation that succeeded the first newly rich *arrivistes* who had emerged in a period of national unity. This was the generation that shared in the new confidence of those who believed in monopolies and wished to have them and to use what they could provide. This class was now close to taking government power as well and to making its own voice heard in the world. However, ought this class to seek patiently to restore the weakened power of the middle class, civil awareness and sense of freedom, or ought it not rather to align itself with the well-preserved conservative and feudal military system of the Prussia of the powerful Junker landed proprietors and, in short, make a pact with the countryside? This alternative is explicitly clear in the very contradictoriness of the Landhaus itself. Society and the social strata were forced by history to face decisions before it had been ascertained that they were ready to do so.

It is well-known what the choice was. And this choice determined the destiny of the countryside as well as the destiny of the middle class itself; it was a decision that did not have to be taken under the pressure of a contingent reality, but for reasons of an internal nature. This is confirmed by the new life-style of the middle class, again manifested in the structural transformation brought to the Landhaus. By about 1910 the type of country house containing a porch, built in a generalized style that was capable of multiple solutions, had reached the end of its historical season. This led to the transformation of the Landhaus, the most radical transformation in the whole history of the German middle-class villa. From this moment the villa turned its back on the street, wishing to form a protective barrier for the defense of its garden, and again included a central entrance. The living rooms were now moved to the garden side, set back in relation to the house, while the service areas (garages and dustbins) were put in front. This plan has remained unaltered until today. For the history of architecture what this signifies is the perpetuation of the late-absolutist model of the eighteenth-century *maison de plaisance*. This happened because the eighteenth-century arrangement of the drawing rooms with their alignment *en suite* was readopted in the Landhaus. Posener described this development as reactionary and regretted that Muthesius himself was not able to avoid following this direction, which had been

known even in his time. But the real protagonist in this scene was without any doubt Behrens, and this was seen very clearly in the house he built for the burgomaster of Hagen (and future reich chancellor), Cuno, at Eppenhausen near Hagen. This house was built in 1909, and in spite of its corner position none of the bedrooms has windows overlooking the street side. The style of decoration resembles that of a fortress. Its entrance is in the center and its general plan is symmetrical; the rooms are arranged *en suite*. The porch has been reduced to a simple entrance hall that houses the staircase, and the parlor intended for the lady of the house seems to have been "imprisoned."

A greater differentiation is apparent in the famous house constructed by Behrens in 1911 at Berlin-Dahlem for the archeologist Wiegand, the son-in-law of the owner of Siemens. Built in the form of a Greek temple out of limestone blocks, the house even has a very solemn peristyle, which forms a framework to the entrance door. Apart from its other function, however, this peristyle also has an aesthetic function: through the heaviness and concision of its spatial form and its detail it has to counterbalance the effect of lightness imparted by the delicate wooden paneling of the vestibule, an authentic antique piece of Turkish rococo taken from an Ottoman palace. Nothing in this house was to seem lightweight. However, the effect of these walls is too rigid and appears even formidable and uninviting, just because the vestibule has been reinterpreted in a somewhat ambiguous way. The original intention was to make it possible for people to sit on the floor, whereas now it was a background to the moment of the exchange of greetings between the guest and the master of the house, which usually takes place on foot. We may justify certain architectural ingenuities (Behrens was a painter and graphic artist), as, for example, the rather confused and unfortunate siting of the staircase and the cramped arrangement of the service areas (the kitchen door being clearly visible just opposite the dining room); yet these examples of lack of attention to detail make Behrens's work appear quite clumsy when compared with the very sensitive work of Muthesius. The intention of the builder and architect is perfectly fulfilled in the living rooms; their form is almost stumpy, tending toward the shape of a square, and this, added to the intentionally heavy surfaces of the structure, to the doors and hinges, confers a formal rigidity on the rooms, as if to impede too spontaneous a relationship between the occupant and the room itself. Seen from the garden side, in contrast, the house is characterized by an almost solemn symmetry, with the exception of the service wings and pergolas; the central part contains colossal pillars. The whole of the garden side of the house is invisible from the exterior. The Wiegand house stands on a corner site, and on the side that overlooks the side street Behrens has added a service courtyard and then a trellis, which is walled in to its full height at its outer

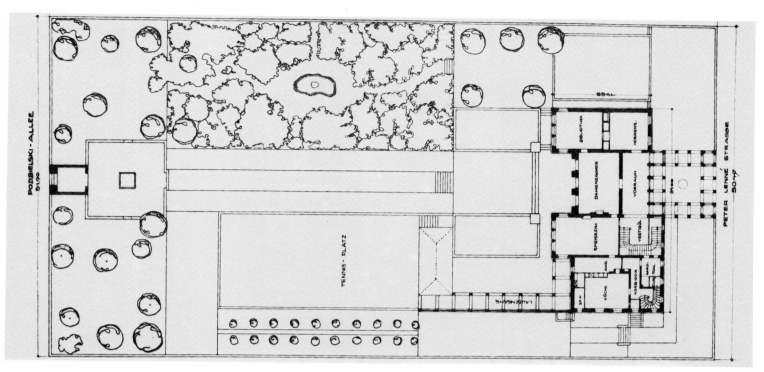

47

61. Peter Behrens, Theodor Wiegand villa, Berlin-Dahlem, Lennestrasse, 1911, design for the garden side.

side and stands apart from the main building. Although it cannot be seen from the street, the garden of the Wiegand house produces a more severe and formal effect than even the vestibule and rooms of the house, and this is due to the monumentality and symmetry of the facade. The house built for the upper middle class therefore wished to remain aloof from public life, but at the same time behind its heavy front door decisions had to be taken that concerned the whole of society. It was even said that Wiegand had wanted to have this house built so that he could offer hospitality to the emperor. Wiegand organized many archeological expeditions and, as I have been told by an archeologist, was behind German imperialism in the Near East (the Baghdad railway) and had "plundered Asia Minor for Germany."

It is surprising how well the great artistic achievements of the past — for example, those monuments of Greek imperialism, the altar of Pergamon and the gate of Miletus — adapted to the German scene. Wiegand must be accorded some of the merit if today there exists the Pergamon Museum: he labored in the twenties with determination and obstinacy to get the work started again according to Messel's original design. In reality the Pergamon Museum was never completed. Today this museum is considered the most important monument to German imperialism of the time of the Kaiser. Although it was planned only five years before the Wiegand house, it so far contained no hint of the violence that a society inflicts on itself when it decides to turn toward military power. Yet at the technical and cultural level of the builder of the Wiegand house and at the artistic level of its architect, violence itself becomes architecture. Obviously, there was no lack of lesser examples. For a study of such examples one need only cross the threshold of the offices of the Ministry of the Marine (1911) at 72 Reichpietschufer, where the shortsighted policy of the naval war machine of the dying empire had its headquarters. But to analyze this lobby would be to take things lightly. It is obvious that in other sectors influences were felt whose importance has not ceased to be apparent even today: in housing for the middle and lower categories of users — workers, clerks, civil servants; in the policy of traffic planning for the towns, public parks and even town planning. It would have been useful to have considered this matter, too, but I thought it preferable to examine the area that seems to have been of most significance. At the same time, I hope that the aspect I have considered will have helped to illustrate the historical situation that was one of the many factors the Werkbund had to face at that time.

ENTWURF FÜR EINEN TISCH
UND VIER STOCKERLN.

THE NEW LIFE-STYLE
Othmar Birkner

Since the subject I have been asked to write about is the new life-style, I should like first of all to ask a number of questions and discover if, and to what extent, the years during which the Werkbund was being founded (1907 in Germany, 1913 in Austria and Switzerland) were really distinguished by a new life-style, which groups or social strata were affected by this new way of behaving, and whether the new style was already present or was procreated directly by the Werkbund movement. Then, if there really was a new life-style, to what other contemporary or earlier style was it contrasted?

The new life-style! Was it not actually a return to the Gothic or Renaissance, or even the Jugendstil? This cannot be said, since after the first decade of the century, and while the second was drawing to an end, the Jugendstil — as is known — together with the western monarchies, entered its death throes.

When columns of smoke were still rising from the battlefields, the general situation was confused, if not close to chaos. It is therefore impossible to try to analyze it today, at a distance. But let us see what was happening in Central Europe, on neutral territory: Zurich 1918, Berne 1918. The first great Swiss exhibition of the Werkbund was held on the Limmat. In the capital of the Confederation, Germany displayed an architecture that was almost purified and an applied art without any kind of "arrogance, ostentation and false modesty."[1] The program of the Zurich Werkbund spoke of "elevation and ennobling of the culture of the home." A statement of this nature provides a sufficiently clear indication of the social circle to which it was being addressed. It was to the circle of those who already possessed a tradition of the house. And it was asked of them that they should raise and ennoble the concept of the home. What is surprising, on the other hand, is that here there was no attempt to bring about the desired change by proposing models of elegance, or examples of the most recent styles of ornamentation or applied art, and so on. In the exhibition rooms there were aligned "homes for the middle class and the workers." Then, the good middle-class citizens went to visit the pavilions to cast a glance at the simple articles of furniture designed for the homes of factory workers and even to be reminded by some mentors: "Raise the culture of your home!" Was this a challenge to the bourgeoisie? And did it all end in a scandal? Far from it. Indeed, the simple articles of furniture designed for the average middle-class citizen and the worker did not first flourish in working-class circles, to be later adopted by the higher classes of society, but, on the contrary, were first welcomed by the snobbish aristocracy. In this connection, mention should be

62. *Josef Hoffmann, furniture design for a working-class home.*

63. *Theodor Hiller, house design for a master wheelwright.*

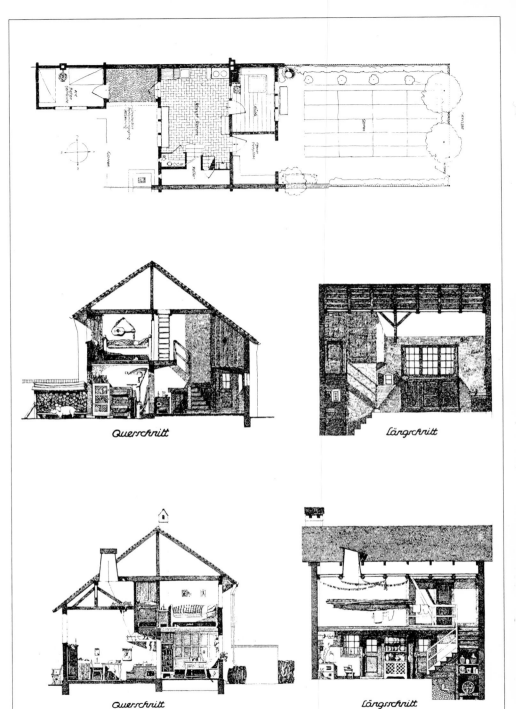

64. Heinrich Metzendorf-Bensheim, house for teachers, ca. 1914.

65. Wilhelm Kienzle, living room for a working-class home shown in the exhibition of the Swiss Werkbund, 1918.

66. Max Häfeli, design for a "one-family house for a life in conformity with nature," 1918.

made of the competition held in Vienna in 1899 for the design of inexpensive good-quality furniture for workers' homes. The result was artistically satisfying and the exhibition put forward a series of solutions that were simple from a formal viewpoint and interesting as constructions. Yet this was the furniture that aroused the interest of the wealthy citizens; the aristocracy found the furniture on display particularly delightful and perfectly suited to their country homes.[2] The movement that began in the nineteenth century in England for the production of the simple and inexpensive object of daily use was in fact welcomed and supported mainly by the wealthy classes. On the other hand, Ruskin's decision, for example, to found a "workers' museum" in Glasgow and so help to bring about the emancipation of the working class was ridiculed and dubbed a failure by Richard Muther in 1901.[3]

Therefore, the middle-class citizen who visited the Zurich exhibition in 1918 was a visitor who was perfectly prepared, as is confirmed by the examples quoted. Even to a lesser extent was this same visitor likely to be amazed by the new directions taken by gardening: countless blue cabbages, and especially the beauty of seasonal green vegetables, which at the most tolerated a few flowers of a peasant's garden among them. Of course, this development was an outcome of the war and its shortage of raw materials — potatoes were grown in the public gardens — but it led to most extreme consequences, for example, the Utopian plan of Max Häfeli, "Kleinhaus für naturgemässe Lebensweise" (small house for a life according to nature). But the World War with its extreme manifestations was only one phase of a development that had begun to be clearly delineated around 1900. If we wish to refer to a postwar period, compressed in time, we cannot fail to take account of the accurate comment by Osbert Lancaster to the effect that the postwar period began "from the point of view of art history, even before the fatal pistol shot at Sarajevo."[4] I would take issue with Lancaster, in the sense that, although it is true that signs of the crisis were already present in the period when the Werkbund was founded, their roots go back to the nineteenth century and, moreover, they cannot be judged purely from an artistic viewpoint, because they already represent "the new life-style." Indeed, while there were in Vienna around the year 1900 aristocrats who found the simple furniture designed for workmen to be "chic," in Zurich eighteen years later cabbages came to replace garden flowers. And this did not occur because there were in 1900 in Vienna only decayed aristocrats or because more hunger was suffered in Zurich than in other cities of Europe. Also, the cabbage was not even merely a symbol of the innocent pleasures of a simple life, an echo, as it were, of the eighteenth-century pastoral comedies.

67. C. F. Voysey, country house with thatched roof, ca. 1897.
68. Interior of the "little home" by C. F. Voysey, 1905.

69. Otto Ingold, kitchen-living room in a working-class home, ca. 1910.

The equally innocent concepts I have selected as the titles of the following paragraphs cast doubt on the actual innocence of these modes of behavior.

AUTUMN BRANCHES

> In our regions autumn is not prodigal in flowers. . . . But in the flower markets one may see an unusual phenomenon, which is something new: autumn branches with red, white or black berries, such as one might pick from a bush when out for a walk along our suburban lanes and then put one or two of them in a vase. . . . There is no doubt that this spontaneous gesture is an unmistakable symptom of a significant growth in the cult of flowers native to the locality. . . . It is amazing to what extent a single branch can stimulate to beauty. Sometimes it can be a real educator.[5]

These sentences by Joseph August Lux are taken from a volume bearing the very significant title *Geschmack im Alltag* (taste in daily life). Books of this kind were very common in the last years of the nineteenth century, but especially so after 1900. In fact, they were so popular that no middle-class home was without at least one such book. Some were simple manuals, but some were finely bound volumes: one might call them breviaries of modern culture, guides "to a new notion of life and good taste." Among the many apostles, reformers, pioneers, and so on, there is at least one name that is still remembered today: that of Paul Schultze-Naumburg, with his "Kulturarbeiten." No sphere of activity was exempt from the efforts of Schultze-Naumburg and his acolytes, from clothing to furniture, paintings, and even autumn branches. To be precise, by 1908 these were no longer the sophisticated branches favored by the Jugendstil, who arranged them in a delicate Gallé vase. These were common branches that could be picked from a bush growing at the side of the street, to be taken home and put into a rough handmade pottery receptacle. Their autumn coloring underlined the grace of their spontaneous beauty, which was not artificial but natural. And flower gathering was no longer the province of the aesthete, but of the chubby baby running freely over the meadows. The sophisticated iris gave way to the daisy gathered spontaneously. And the students of the Arts and Crafts schools no longer repaired, sketchbook in hand, to the greenhouses where palm trees grew, but instead went into the fields and stopped on the banks of a stream. The modest had been discovered. In December 1898 an article appeared in the journal *Innendekoration zur Ausschmückung und Einrichtung von Wohnräumen,* and after this the transformation that had taken place in England was seen not only to be in advance of the rest of Europe — with reverent respect Adolf Loos called the English "Pfadsucher" (scout boys) — but also to be the most surprising. In fact, the English had brought back from their colonies experiences that confirmed the view of "the strangeness and whims of that nature which was still at liberty in the virgin forests." And then the "artists of the English crafts movement," the followers of the "new style," showed that they were able to discover the rugged beauty of their own country and from this to draw equally rigorous consequences, as when they succumbed to the charm of the exotic — especially Japanese culture. Although this was still only the year 1898, it was no longer possible to label as followers of the Liberty style the artists who adopted a more modern trend — for example, such men as Charles Francis Voysey. In particular, Voysey himself was accused of "coarseness," although this roughness was vigorous and full of character.[6] Carl Larsson's *House in the Sun,* of 1897, was equally important, with its emphasis on the work of the "simple village carpenter." It was for the houses and interiors designed by Larsson that the autumn branches, wild flowers or other wild vegetation was best suited. At the same time the villa became transformed into a country house, the parlor into a vestibule, the park into a vegetable plot. And how did the owners of these new residences dress? In brief: linen replaced silk, and now that the mistress of the house no longer had to be tightly corseted, she came to the door wearing a fresh muslin dress and bearing a bitter and rather tart berry protruding from a thorny barberry twig.

This process would really have been innocent if it had stopped here. Soon, however, it seemed that the leaves began to drop from the branch, leaving a bare, thorny structure like the ubiquitous cactus, which then became the symbol of the Bauhaus, founded in 1919. But our mistress of the house procreated the generation that twenty years later was to be sent to the battlefields of the Second War. And she was a good mother, in fact, she was meant to be the mother of a good generation since . . . and here we come against the second problem.

DRESS

"The female conspirators, in company with their husbands, brothers, fiancés, uncles — in short, whoever was their protector — repair to the tailor's workshop. For the occasion, these men provide themselves with good revolvers. They put under the nose of the artists the model they have chosen and, threatening to kill them on the spot, force them to swear to execute them faithfully. It seems clear that this is how things must have been." In his essay "Mode und Zynismus," Friedrich Theodor Vischer had shown as early as 1879 how an area had been invaded where tolerance was out of place. In this sense even the cultural battle waged by Schultze-Naumburg started with fashion. In 1901 his booklet *Die Kultur des weiblichen Körpers als Grundlage der Frauenkleidung* (culture of

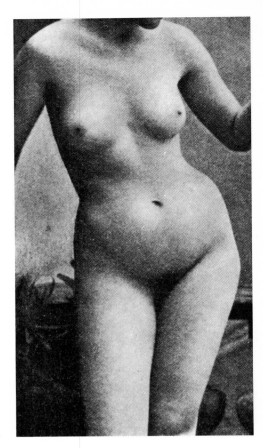

70, 71. Paul Schultze-Naumburg, Die Kultur des weiblichen Körpers, *1901.*

the feminine body as the foundation of dress) was published, and by then a series of radical transformations was already taking place, culminating in a number of reforms: to the house, the garden, school, marriage and diet. But within this fanatical process of reform, the reform of dress in particular could be seen as the key to a reform extending over every sphere of life. In all other fields one could close an eye, but not in dress, since a reform that upset the whole style of dressing in accordance with the hygienic principles laid down by Schultze-Naumberg affected not only aesthetics and ethics but — and not least of all — anatomy, too. Thanks to the process of reform that liberated women from the slavery of the corset people could rediscover the beauty of the female body, the *heiliges Gefäss* ("sacred vessel"). In the opinion of Richard Hamann and Jost Hermand, a close study of the work of Schultze-Naumburg arouses the suspicion that behind this adoration of the female there lay a deep-rooted discrimination against women as individuals. The "sacred vessel" was at best a beautiful object whose function was to welcome the male seed and transform it into a fruit.[7]

In this climate woman became the idol of the "national rebirth" and was placed on a very shaky pedestal. Fashion itself was then made a matter of nationalism, indeed possibly the most important. The dread that the corset might crush female fertility brought certain intellectual circles into an atmosphere close to panic. The corset came to be viewed as glaring evidence of the French assault upon the German "national spring," and in this moment of nationalist fervor the first "German day of the tailor" was instituted in August 1900 at Krefeld. For the occasion the director of the Kaiser Wilhelm Museum, Friedrich Deneken, called upon the best-known artists of the day. Such men as Bernhard Pankok, Richard Riemerschmid, Paul Schultze-Naumburg, Henry van de Velde — architects who joined the Werkbund in 1907, the year of its foundation — then attempted to "storm the barricades of the reigning fashion, which until that moment had appeared invulnerable";[8] they produced sketches for a "special exhibition of modern female dress."[9] The painter Alfred Mohrbutter helped to set up the exhibition at Krefeld. Among other things, Mohrbutter produced living tableaux similar to the pantomimes of the Swiss Emile Jaques-Dalcroze, which had a marked influence on the painter Ferdinand Hodler. Some of Hodler's paintings, for example, *Das Lied aus der Ferne* of 1906 or *Femme joyeuse* of 1909 and 1911, were already inspired by the new female fashion, which respected sensible hygiene and diet: clothes that hardly indicate the waistline, or not at all; flowing dresses mostly made of linen. The Krefeld exhibition was followed in 1902 by an exhibition in Berlin entitled "The New Female Fashion," which was an

72. *Emile Jacques-Dalcroze, pantomime, ca. 1900.*

73. *Ferdinand Hodler,* Femme Joyeuse, *1911.*

74. *Alfred Mohrbutter, outdoor dress, 1904.*

Toiletten aus der Frühjahrsmodekollektion der Wiener Werkstätte, entworfen von Professor Hoffmann.

75. *Josef Hoffmann, fashion designs, ca. 1910.*
76. *Franz Zelezny, sideboard panel, 1898.*
77. *Mathias Feller, dressing table in the Feller country house at Agram Jurievska Ulica, 1912.*
78. *August Endell, train sleeping compartment with washbasin, 1912.*

"expression of the consequences of the theories contained in the book by Schultze-Naumburg."[10] The reformist phenomena had now been translated into manifest reality, but, in spite of this, the new tendencies took a very long time to penetrate to the wider public. If we look through a popular fashion magazine of the time, such as the *Wiener Mode*, we cannot fail to notice that the narrow waistline, the so-called wasp waist, continued in favor, though in an attenuated form, as late as 1910. In an article dated 1911 mention was first made of the works of the Wiener Werksätte and their fashion department directed by the decorator and artist-craftsman Eduard Wimmer. Apart from Wimmer, the painter and artist-craftsman Kolo Moser and the architect Josef Hoffmann — president of the Austrian Werkbund from 1913 — were fashion designers. In Vienna, where as early as 1898 Adolf Loos had attacked the whole concept of fashion and declared that modern dress should not in the first place be "beautiful," but that the criterion of dress should be "goodness," the Werksätte brought out models that in comparison with the fashions shown in Krefeld and Berlin were quite outlandish in their color combinations and choice of materials. On the other hand, the great fashion industries, such as Drecoll and Goldschmidt, showed no hesitation in adopting the new program. They could count on a clientele composed almost exclusively of members of the nobility, who revolved around such prominent figures as the hereditary prince Ferdinand von Lobkowitz (the same Lobkowitz who was one of the most fervent protectors of the "Weiner Dalcroze-Verein").

The Bathroom

The only room in the house that was "real . . . logically resolved" was the bathroom. "A modern bathroom like this can be likened to a piece of scientific apparatus, where ingenious technology celebrates its triumphs and where the introduction of any kind of art would produce only a disruptive effect. Form created exclusively by function is in itself so expressive and awe-inspiring that it creates an aesthetic satisfaction in no way different from artistic pleasure. Here we have a really new kind of art, which has no need at all of expressive lines. . . ."[11] By reasons of hygiene the reform of life began with dress, and so it was quite logical that the reform of the house had to begin with the bathroom. From this wonderful room with its hygienic equipment a renewal of the culture of the home, the house and the city could be expected. Muthesius gave expression to thoughts at that time that instinctively call Le Corbusier to mind — the Le Corbusier, that is, of 1920, who for the program of L'Esprit Nouveau formulated the following principles: "The house is a machine for living. Baths, sunlight, hot and cold water, warmth adjustable to the desired level, the preservation of food, hygiene, beauty obtained through the medium of propor-

tions." We are by now well acquainted with Le Corbusier's reference to the "machine for living," and in addition we have had time to ask ourselves at a distance of fifty years whether we are correctly interpreting Le Corbusier and his ideas. On the other hand, the remarks by Muthesius quoted earlier, and written right at the time of the founding of the Werkbund, are much less known. And these remarks of his are surprising even to someone well acquainted with the cultural scene of the time; in a period when handwoven cloth was the ideal, his views were even more unexpected. The young Werkbund was divided between artisan and industrial production, and Muthesius himself was one of those who violently criticized the industrially produced art form. But before we write off Muthesius as a man of contradictions, I should like first to tackle a fundamental question, that is, to ask whether there does not lie concealed behind the "objectivity" of the bathroom, so violently evidenced, a fair dose of romanticism. It is the romanticism concealed behind the comparison between the "machine for living" and the transatlantic liner that immediately gives rise to an association with the sea, unknown distances, and the fascination and adventure of travel. In the same way, the remarks made by Loos contain similar overtones, if we read into the new experiment in living a romantic passion for adventure. In 1898 Loos wrote that the time had now come when "plumbing" no longer signified only the pipes installed for fountains with sparkling water "to be gazed at," but also the pipes installed for "baths, showers, water closets."[12] In the structure of this sentence the words *fountain* and *bath*, *shower* or *water closet* are close to each other optically. But to Loos or Muthesius the bathroom was much more "fantastic" than the fountain: in Vienna, when someone turned on a tap, he set in motion the workings of the forced conduits — the Alpine source had been captured and aqueducts cut over a distance of many miles. In the expression "forced conduits of a stream water" was contained as much proud romantic bombast as when Nietzsche called his Zarathustra a "book of Alpine air," so praising him in the highest possible terms. In any case, it would be an error to read into Loos's glorification of the bathroom any suggestion of approval for mass-produced hygienic equipment. Loos described the plumber as a craftsman, like the tailor, smith, or the sculptor in wood Franz Zelezny, who inlaid his furniture according to instinct rather than design, like the old masters of Medieval times — all true artists! However funny this may seem to us today, for Muthesius the bathroom without "expressive lines," that is, without the ornamentation dear to the Jugendstil, represented the point at which technology attained the full maturity of the artist-craftsman. Nor could this be otherwise at that time, in the age of art! In a lecture entitled "Wo stehen wir?" which he gave in

1911 and later published in the first yearbook of the Deutscher Werkbund in 1912, Muthesius described the years betwen 1890 and 1895 as an era of "ferment and effervescence." The Jugendstil, the "interchanged baby of modern art," had generated a temporary "confusion" but had in the end conquered the great movement of industrial art, which had "as objective the reform of all our culture of expression." The new spirit extended "from the sofa cushion to town planning."

The Roof

> And nothing . . . is more natural than the fact that, since the achievements of technology and traffic have been greeted with sincere enthusiasm, there should have resurfaced in us a nostalgia for absolute beauty; we do not want to believe that from this time onward the satisfaction produced by accuracy and extreme functionalism must replace those values that used to satisfy and raise us up in the past. One cannot therefore claim that the results obtained by the engineer are in themselves unified expressions of artistic style. Art does not come about through the practice of functionalism, but it is pure intuition; it is the satisfaction of physical ends transferred on to the spiritual plane.[13]

If we were surprised earlier at what Muthesius wrote in 1912 in the first yearbook of the Deutscher Werkbund, where he reproduced his country houses built with artisan methods, we are no less amazed and intrigued by the words of Peter Behrens on functionalism and intuition. This is even more true when we consider that Behrens formulated these ideas in connection with his plans for the Berlin AEG. This indicates that function and material did not dictate a given form of roof and did not compel the architect to adopt a given solution; this is confirmed especially by the water reservoirs of the same period. From this angle the "manifesto of Gropius's Bauhaus of 1919 seemed the reverse of progressive,"[14] and if the Bauhaus flat roof created a stir, why was this not only for technical reasons? How did Siegfried Giedion present his idea of a "liberated way of living"? His call for "light — light — air — light — opening — air — air — air — opening — opening — opening" was like the cry of a humanity that felt threatened by the danger of dying of suffocation. A no less militant attitude was shown some years later by the Deutsche Bauhütte. In its pamphlet entitled *Bausünden und Baugeldvergeudung* (building mistakes and wastage), it described such phenomena as the Weissenhof as "an offense to the German fatherland," resulting from a "mania for foreign styles." Such matters as the controversy concerning the flat roof or the roof with two gables, which was a technical question at the time of C. F. Ehrenberg and C. L. Engel, became a hundred years later one of the numerous questions that proved fatal to an entire population, if not indeed to the whole world. The same undercurrent of aggressiveness could be described in F. T. Vischer, as long ago as in the

Auf hiddensee.

Auf hiddensee.
Variante mit Dach.

79, 80. Emil Högg, two versions of a country house, with flat roof and gabled roof, 1904.

time of the polemical "educators." In the second half of the nineteenth century and until the first few decades of the twentieth, a mentality was imposed on people by this aggressiveness that not even the Bauhaus could escape: it was felt in the way of exerting pressure, of criticizing and judging — and in the end persecuting — whoever was of a different opinion. It was while this spiritual situation obtained that the Werkbund was started. The Werkbund argued in the language then in general use, it could continue to evolve and be fertile so long as it permitted a dialectical exchange to take place within itself. When in 1933–34 the Werkbund was required to present a compact and united front, it ceased to be alive.

The new life-style began during the nineteenth-century stylistic pluralism, which grew more and more coarse grained. The youthful Werkbund was active in an atmosphere of growing intolerance, and in this intolerance the roof, whether flat or gabled as the case might be, inevitably tumbled down. One final question remains: Can it be true that the era of the pioneers, reformers, educators, those who tried with all means in their power to solve the problem of human happiness, is already a chapter of history?

1. F. Hallwag, "Die deutsche Werkbund-Ausstellung in Bern," in *Innendekoration*, year XXIX (Darmstadt, May 1918).

2. "Arbeiterwohnungen," in *Das Interieur*, year I (Vienna, 1900), pp. 65–69.

3. R. Muther, *Studien und Kritiken II* (Vienna, 1901), pp. 201–10.

4. O. Lancaster, *O Du mein trautes Heim* (Vienna, 1950).

5. J. A. Lux, *Der Geschmack im Alltag* (Dresden, 1908), p. 106 ff.

6. "Englische Gewerbe-Künstler Neuesten Stiles," in *Innendekoration*, year IX (Darmstadt, December 1898).

7. R. Hamann and J. Hermand, *Stilkunst um 1900* (Berlin, 1967), p. 178.

8. "Sonderausstellung moderner Damenkostüme," in *Dekorative Kunst*, vol. 6 (1900), p. 414.

9. Cf. n. 8, vol. 7 (1901), p. 41.

10. "Die Ausstellung 'Die Neue Frauentracht' in Berlin," in *Dekorative Kunst*, vol. 11 (1903), p. 76 ff.

11. H. Muthesius, *Das Englische Haus*, vol. 3, 2d ed. (Berlin, 1911), p. 238.

12. Adolf Loos, "Ins Leere gesprochen," in *Sämtliche Schriften*, vol. 1 (Vienna, 1962), p. 72.

13. P. Behrens, "Der moderne Industriebau in ästhetischer Beziehung," in *Zeitschrift für Beton und Eisenbeton*, year III (Berne, August 1912) (with illustrations of Behrens' architectural work for the AEG).

14. G. Salle, *Jugendstil und Kunstindustrie* (Ravensburg, 1974), p. 90.

Erwin Barth	GA[1]	public park, Berlin (1926–29, 89 hectares) public park Jungfernheide, Berlin (1920–23, 160 ha)	article in *Form*
Friedrich Bauer	GA	Schillerpark, Berlin (1907–13, 25 ha)	DWB[2]
Alexander Boecking	GA		article in *Form*
Max Bromme	GA	public park Lohrberg, Frankfurt (1912–28, 14 ha) Sportpark, Frankfurt (1920–25, 40 ha) Brentanopark, Frankfurt (1928)	DWB
Josef Buerbaum	GA	public park near Solingen (1913–16) city park, Bottrop (c. 1928, 12.5 ha) public park Letmathe (c. 1928, 6.25 ha)	DWB
Fritz Encke	GA	Klettenbergpark, Cologne (1905–6, 4.5 ha) Blücherpark, Cologne (1910–13, 17 ha Vorgebirgspark, Cologne (1909–11, 13 ha) Sportpark Müngersdorf (1920–23, 24 ha) Raderthalpark, Cologne (1923–24, 27 ha) Rheinpark, Cologne (1914, 1920–28, 22 ha)	DWB
Carl Heicke	GA	Ostpark, Frankfurt (1906–8, 38 ha) Huthpark, Frankfurt (1911–13, 18.7 ha)	DWB
Herrmann König	GA	city public park Stade	DWB and article in *Form*
Max Läuger	A	city public park, Hamburg, design (1908)	DWB
Ludwig Lesser	GA	public park Frohnau near Berlin (1908)	DWB
Harry Maasz	GA	public park, Lubeck (1913, c. 45 ha)	DWB
Lebrecht Migge	GA	Wolhdorf Park public park Rüstringen (1913) public garden Hamburg-Fühlsbuttel public garden site Dobbengelände, Oldenburg public park Schönfeld near Leipzig (1913, 22, 54 ha)	DWB and article in *Form*
Ferdinand Hölscher	GA	city public park Hamburg-Harburg (1913–27, 54 ha)	DWB
Fritz Schumacher	A	city public park Hamburg (1908–9, 180 ha)	DWB
Martin Wagner	A	Jugendpark Pichelswerder, Berlin, plan (1916)	DWB

1. GA = garden architect   2. DWB = member of the Werkbund
   A = architect

PUBLIC PARKS
Inge Maass

This subject is marginal, in that it is situated outside the field of the debates and activities of the Werkbund. At the same time it represents the kernel of all planning for outdoor life before the First War and in the twenties and thirties.

During the seven years of the Werkbund yearbooks and the eight years of the journal *Die Form*, two issues were devoted to the theme of garden architecture: no. 3 of 1928 and three years later no. 4 of 1931.

In the first articles the discussion centered on the appropriate style for the gardens of villas and country houses, pergolas and garden furniture. The "sculptural-architectural" tendency was weighed against the "landscaping" tendency, which ran under the banner of the 'individual growing and developing plant' (Allinger, 1928).

Many years later, more than twenty years after the first public parks were created (Schillerpark in Berlin, Vorgebirgspark in Cologne, Ostpark in Frankfurt) and after the famous competition for Hamburg Park, an article appeared — the only one, in fact — on public parks. Alexander Boecking described "Public Green Zones in Town Planning" (*Die Form*, 1931, no. 4) and here provided the first and last survey of this important chapter of building activity, in the prewar and postwar years, by the artists and for the artists of the Werkbund.

The writer of the article was Boecking, not L. Lesser (*Volksparke heute und morgen*, 1927), nor Harry Maasz (*Der Volkspark der Zukunft*, 1913), nor Encke (*Der Volkspark*, 1911), nor even Heicke or Bromme. All these men were members of the Werkbund and designed popular public parks. Boecking possessed neither of these characteristics.

Therefore, does not this circumstance throw a singular light on the Werkbund, its members and its program? Over a period of twenty years parks were being designed and built, the political parties were engaging all their efforts to bring them into being, and thousands of people were visiting the parks each day: in the Werkbund no one reported on them or even discussed them. Did this "association of artists, professionals, industrialists and businessmen" remain obtusely limited to the family garden when the question of open spaces arose?

Two things have to be dealt with first, however: we must present for the first time, and 50 years after the fact, the work of a professional group, all members of the Werkbund, and we must discover the reason for this delay.

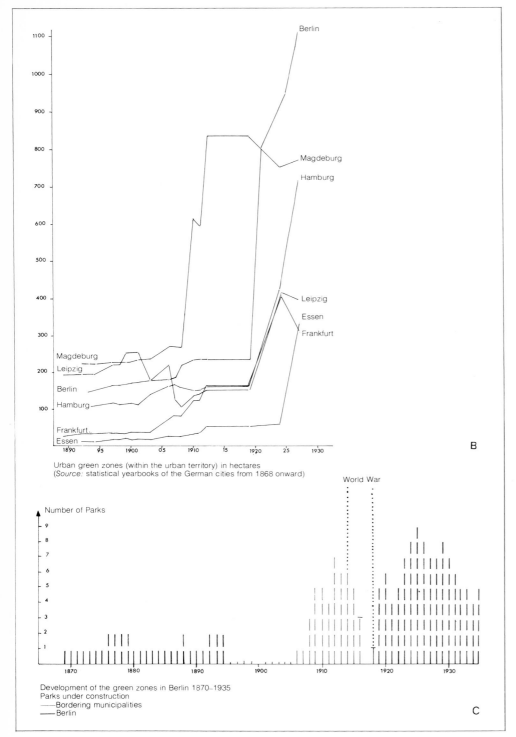

1100
1000
900
800 — Berlin
700 — Magdeburg
— Hamburg
600
500
400 — Leipzig
— Essen
300 — Frankfurt
Magdeburg
200 Leipzig
Berlin
Hamburg
100 Frankfurt
Essen

1890 95 1900 05 1910 15 1920 25 1930

B

Urban green zones (within the urban territory) in hectares
(*Source:* statistical yearbooks of the German cities from 1868 onward)

World War

Number of Parks
9
8
7
6
5
4
3
2
1

1870 1880 1890 1900 1910 1920 1930

Development of the green zones in Berlin 1870–1935
Parks under construction
——— Bordering municipalities
——— Berlin

C

The list contained in Figure A is provisional, and incomplete, taken from the catalogs of the Werkbund and from contemporary reports; this list is, however, quite impressive. Among the members of the Werkbund who mainly designed family gardens, there were many who also created great parks. We might, in fact, say that almost all the great popular parks of the time were created by the garden architects of the Werkbund.

The municipalities bought up hectare upon hectare of land, developed them and laid them out as public parks, town gardens and pleasure gardens. Both large and small towns took part in this movement. A study of the increase in green zones in some of the towns of Germany, before and after the war, reveals in all cases a considerable surge forward after 1919 (see Figure B).

To some extent these increases are due to the incorporation of suburbs. If one considers the building activity that took place over the same period, a more realistic picture of the increase in the development of green communal zones can be obtained.

One of the many examples (Figure C shows the number of parks that were constructed simultaneously in Berlin) shows clearly the timid start of a new policy for green zones in 1906–7 and the great leap forward after 1918.

It is obvious that the case of public parks represents a development of far greater dimensions than the case of the family garden.

What was the level of debate within the Werkbund in relation to this radical change in the growth of green zones? The diagrams show that before the war parks were constructed only sporadically, whereas after the war both the form and content of what had until then been the usual public parks changed abruptly.

The *urban public parks* were the parks of the middle class and were therefore constructed and arranged to meet the needs of this class. In these parks a single type of behavior was given formal expression: a walk in the park was no longer the calm stroll of the simple and modest middle class of earlier times but was now modeled on the behavior of the aristocracy as a way of showing oneself to the world. Other vital needs that had already found expression, such as places for children to play, were now relegated to dusty and gravelly corners of the park.

". . . in constructing new urban public parks, people thought first of all of 'strolls' and arrived at a new type of park that cost little but could create in the smallest possible space the same effects as the park of the stately home and that, in a pattern of tortuous paths bordered by hedges, could offer long itineraries; by planting many bushes, which limited the field of vision, it was intended to make

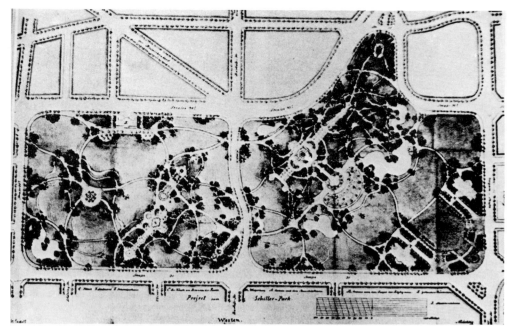

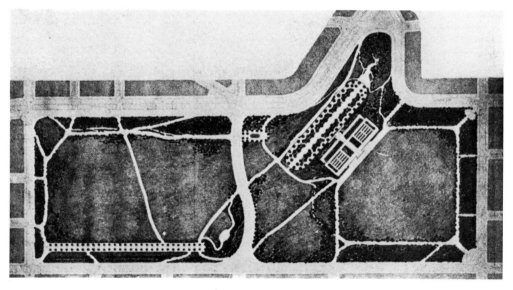

the stroller forget the limited area of land at his disposal . . ." (Hegemann, 1913).

It is possible to complete the picture provided here by Hegemann. The function of showing oneself to society, which was to be fulfilled by the middle-class park, was aided by the monuments and commemorative tablets to middle-class history; statues of the sons and heroes of the middle class were erected. In choosing the plants various educational aspects (scientific, dendrological and geo-botanical) merged with the penchant for ostentation and exoticism. Who has never seen those flower beds that, in imitation of a tapestry, finish up looking like fruit tarts composed of variegated ornamental plants, speckled red and green? The only public entertainments were concerts out-of-doors (bandstands) and sometimes boating. Camillo Schneider (garden architect and member of the Werkbund) made a famous criticism of the Tür-kenschanzpark in Vienna (Mächtig's design for the Berlin Schillerpark of 1899 can be taken as an example instead): "As soon as one enters one feels as though the park is ill, suffering from seasick-ness. An undulatory movement, entirely arbitrary, useless and irrational, runs through the garden. One ascends, descends, sees swollen hills and flattened valleys, the whole interspersed with clumps of woodland and crossed by paths whose route seems mysterious. In the end one reaches a hole, where a pond, completely lined with cement and fed by an obviously artificial stream, contorts itself spasmodically" (C. Schneider, 1904). I have paused at this judgment by Schneider, because it provides us with the first information we have concerning the specific positions taken by the Werkbund.

Schneider's criticism is clear; yet, unlike Hegemann's, it fails to point to the kernel of the matter. Schneider was concerned about the failure of the design itself. The consequence of his criticism would therefore be: rectilinear paths in place of tortuous paths, white painted wood in place of black wrought iron, palisades in place of iron railings, terraces instead of hills and undulations of the land.

Bauer's design for the Schillerpark completely fulfills all these conditions, and it was gladly welcomed. Nevertheless, this example was an exception, since the specific field of activity of the Werkbund architects remained the small plot of land: the family garden. On this little plot the new form was widely applied but without questioning its underpinnings, that is, the way of life and the bourgeois existence of the middle-class family who could afford to own this type of garden.

If we look at the new stylistic elements used here, we notice with surprise the recurrence to harmonious

81. Hermann Mächtig, design for the Berlin Schil-lerpark, 1899 (not executed).

82, 83. F. Bauer, competition design for the Berlin Schillerpark, 1907.

historical epochs, to their habitability and intimacy. There are quotations from the Medieval garden, from the Biedermeier and rustic garden with their elements: vegetable garden and ornamental bed, gazebo, fountain, seat; and even the types of flowers found in the late Middle Ages have returned, characterized by their symbolic as much as their utilitarian aspects (lily, columbine, rose, mallow, box, and so on). The numerical growth of the middle class and the increasing competitive pressure upon the classes of small tradesmen and artisans, consequent on the passage from capitalism to imperialism, constitute the background to the inner contradictions that are reflected here between the ostentatious style of life of the great feudal bourgeoisie and the type of home and garden constructed for the poorer strata of the middle class that had recently evolved, such as tradesmen, intellectuals, high civil servants, and the like. Really new dimensions were not apparent in the reform of the family garden, since it was not in the middle-class villa that the new concepts were expressed and developed, but in the working-class districts of the towns.

The stylistic reform of the family garden was therefore doomed to failure: the new form could easily be reproduced and was eventually advertised in catalogs just as any other commodity. Many of the Werkbund garden architects published these catalogs for a new clientele (for example, Buerbaum, *Neue Gärten-Aus meinem Arbeitsgebiet* [1928]; König, *Gärten von heute* [Hamburg, 1926]; or the catalogs issued by various firms specializing in landscaped gardens, such as the Ochs and Schnackenburg & Siebold of Hamburg).

Concerning the change in style, we read in a comment that appeared in the first yearbook dated 1928: "So we find in many places those cold gardens at whose sight the owner must feel his heart freeze ... a few typical trees, weeping willows, poplars or perhaps birches; they cannot so easily be mistaken ..." (Allinger, 1928).

We see how the contrast between the old and new in the family garden grew up *inside a class* and how in consequence the reform remained limited mainly to its outward appearance.

With regard to public parks the two trends moved in opposite directions. A change in form was not possible without a redefinition of function, in other words, without a debate that would involve the whole population, now seen in the role of consumer. It was no new thing for the mass of the population to use the park in common with the middle classes and so cast doubt on its class character. The contradiction between old and new, in relation to the park, was therefore a contradiction between classes: between bourgeois and pro-

84. *Franz Lebish, design for a garden, Vienna.*

85. *"Bathing prohibited," from Berlin und seine Bauten, 1906.*

letariat. From the city public park there then came into being the communal park — a completely new product.

In Germany the foundation of the Reich marked the beginning of a vast expansion of industry and a consequent rapid increase in the urban population; in Berlin the two million mark was quickly passed in 1900. The city spread into the countryside, and in the newly constructed working-class districts thousands of people were crowded together in cramped conditions. Bad living conditions, poverty and malnutrition caused a precipitous rise in the number of TB sufferers, and TB became the scourge of the century.

Sunday was a day off — the Sunday free from work was introduced in 1891 — and everyone hurried out into the open air. It had long been impossible to reach the outskirts of the city on foot, and where there was not enough money to pay the cost of transport the green areas had to serve instead. It therefore became the custom to go to the bourgeois public park. Many descriptions of the time speak of the overcrowding of these parks; the maintenance staff complained of the increase in vandalism and police reports spoke of continual transgressions.

The struggle for the use of free space was more strenuous than our Werkbund artists realized. Requests for land that could be used for play and leisure by everyone had been coming in to the authorities for some time before the garden architects sat down at their drawing boards to tackle the problem. The struggle for free space was far from peaceful, as can be seen, for example, by the prohibition against bathing in the waters of the public parks, still in force in 1907, a regulation that the police had to make people obey by imposing fines.

In a report of the Berlin city administration around 1890 we read: "Iron railings have had to be installed to protect paths and fields from damage: since the park (Friedrichhain) is very close to the city gates, it is the one most visited and therefore the one most exposed to possible vandalism."

And in 1893 when the Viktoriapark at the edge of Kreuzberg, a densely populated working class district, was opened, the council's report stated ". . . that the park . . . although its present size is barely sufficient to serve as a place of recreation for the neighboring zones, yet on Sundays and holidays it is frequented by large crowds of people."

Hegemann viewed this development in a wider perspective and drew attention to the possibility that the situation might harden if buildings continued to be erected on the free areas of space that remained.

86. *Skating rink in the Berlin Schillerpark.*

61

"What little urban public entertainments and outdoor athletic activities remained and developed in Germany under these adverse conditions would rather find refuge in areas not specifically designed for it: in streets, in backyards of gymnasia, on parade grounds, on developed land not yet built upon, in the remaining woods at the outskirts of town, or on meadows not yet developed as building real estate." (Hegemann, 1913)

Such descriptions yield three essential elements: the squalid conditions in which the mass of the population lived, the resulting competition for the use of public areas of space, and the changed attitude toward the planning of cities and green zones. If the preceding descriptions were characterized by a fear of the socialist specter, by repugnance for the working masses or even perhaps by compassion for poverty, a new attitude had now emerged. Garden architects and, more especially, council officials became more and more willing to meet the interests of the public. They began to write in glowing terms of children's games, the joys of bathing in the open air, Sunday outings, relaxation in the meadows.

A frequently quoted example was that of the Dammtor meadows in Hamburg. Boecking mentioned them in his article in *Die Form*, and Harry Maasz and Hugo Koch also gave them as an example: "The Dammtor meadows in Hamburg in the center of the city are a clear demonstration of the great desire felt by the city dweller to be able to stretch out on the grass" (Boecking, 1931).

In 1908, when he was already a city administrator, Enke reported on the attempt made to open to the public two meadows in the area of woodland that belonged to the city of Cologne: "Encouraged by this example, we have recently given permission to use a lawn area in the public garden measuring about 30 hectares. . . . It was almost a moving sight to see how great and small, rich and poor, behaved when they were no longer constrained to walk about through narrow paths and could move freely over grassy meadows. If I had not already believed that what we need is a public meadow, then on this occasion I would have been convinced of it" (Enke, 1908).

The construction of the Ostpark in Frankfurt in 1906, the Vorgebirgspark in Cologne in 1909, and the Schillerpark in Berlin in 1908 marked the first appearance of parks that were sharply differentiated from public town parks, because here the main users were the mass of the population. In these parks the battle for free zones was settled in favor of the popular masses. As we have seen, this development was not due to the efforts of a single artist but was the result of a long struggle that was

87. *Unemployed men working on the construction of the Rehberge Park, Berlin.*

88. *Sports field in the Rehberge Park, Berlin.*

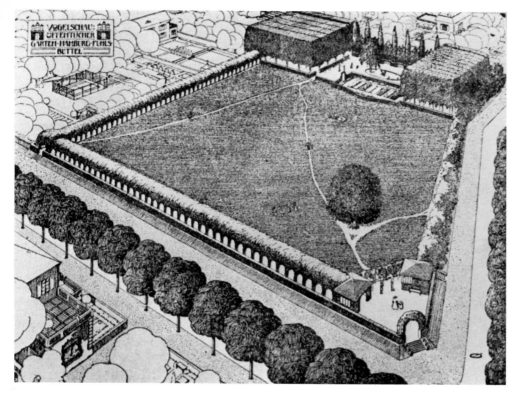

in reality centered around other sectors of social policy. Yet, its effect was to act on communal policy as well, in the matter of public green zones and, hence, on the complex of tasks dealt with by the communal authorities and on their awareness of these responsibilities.

The total achievement of the prewar years was modest: a few small and isolated concessions seemed intended only to keep the working class quiet. But after the war the situation changed, since the November revolution questioned the principle of class positions of privilege and power. In order to "save the state" further social concessions were necessary. In this situation the growth in the construction of public parks satisfied two functions: public parks met the needs of the mass of the population and were useful and rational, and by such works the social state was put to the test.

The measures taken with regard to the construction of gardens required a high intensity of labor but little outlay of materials. They therefore fulfilled a most useful function by providing work for the armies of unemployed who had formed in the large towns after the war and represented a political danger.

The creation of new jobs and appeasement was the impetus behind this enormous building activity. However, these constructions were meant to satisfy the needs of the people as well as to fulfill their function, to preserve the bourgeois state.

Public parks were therefore products of the revolution — even if it was a revolution that failed. The program for these parks and the form they took represent clear evidence of material progress: a "piece of nature, where the populace can move about as lords in their own property, at their pleasure" (Kohlrausch, 1910). Although this judgment of Kohlrausch is incorrect so far as property is concerned, it is, however, pertinent in that here for the first time areas were made available and equipment was installed that satisfied the real needs of the population.

In the center of the parks large meadows were laid out, consisting of enormous grassy expanses covering almost half the total area of the parks. They were meadows for festivals and for recreation, meadows where people could stretch out on the grass (Schillerpark) and meadows for children's games (Schillerpark). One can imagine how painful and disagreeable these meadows, where vast crowds gathered, must have seemed to the middle classes. "Mobs" it was termed in all police reports. But planners had now realized that it was essential to create these open spaces in which the mass of the people could congregate.

89. L. Migge, perspective view of the public garden in Fuhlsbüttel, Hamburg.
90. Max Bromme, public park in Lohrberg, Frankfurt, 1930.

The meadows form the basic nucleus of the public parks. Paths disappeared, except where they were created spontaneously as passageways.

Harry Maasz in his book *Das Grün in Stadt und Land* (1927) devoted a whole chapter to paths. In Migge's design these paths traverse the great central meadow.

It was accepted that public parks were open spaces, "green rooms." Plants were not to be visual or emotional stimuli but were to serve an architectonic purpose. They provided the framework for open spaces for leisure. In consequence, the significance of the botanical characteristics of the plants — their texture or structure — became secondary to the effect they would produce when massed. The concept of "mass plantings" now appeared. Local plants were given preference over exotic plants. In contrast to the well-known English or American models — often quoted — where an arcadian landscape was maintained, in which sheep could pasture, the public German parks now returned to the classical tradition. They were built on an axial and symmetrical pattern and contained the typical features of Baroque gardens — avenue, tree-lined circle, copse — where the favorite trees were lombardy, poplar, pyramidal oak, globe-shaped acacia, surrounding symmetrical ponds and fields. The other architectural features were associated with playing fields, run by the many clubs formed for various sports, and "stadiums and fields for competitive sports."

Other open spaces were the public-gardens, built on a regular axial pattern, with ornamental flowers and plants, and these gardens, especially in the early public parks, were intended to replace the family garden (which many citizens lacked).

In the older parks — for example, the city public park in Hamburg, but also the Berlin Jungfernheide — all areas of the park were often related to a central axis with laid-out grassy surface and pond. In later parks this regular arrangement was broken, and the individual constructions were distributed through the panoramic sections of the park, which was arranged around a central nucleus clearly recalling the pavilions or pleasure lodges of late-Baroque gardens (e.g. Rehberge).

When mass needs became the criterion for planning, the program went far beyond the need to run, to rest, to play, and to indulge in organized sports. Such needs had been satisfied by the middle classes for many years in their private gardens, clubs or holiday resorts but now came within reach of the mass of the population. In summer the middle-class families continued to go to the seaside so that the children could play on the beach and bathe in the sea, but now every other child could

play in the water and with sand. Quantity was converted into quality, and new forms and contents were established. If it was desired that health and enjoyment should be available to everyone, then it became necessary to create new forms and new equipment: wading pools and sandboxes, places set aside for sunbathing, open-air schools and copses with hammocks. Bourgeois morality was cast to the wind. People could undress, and an aristocratic pallor was no longer thought desirable. School journeys, cultural events, visits to botanic gardens and museums — benefits once confined to the middle classes — were now open for anyone to participate in, in the public parks, although the benefits differed in quality. Gardens were set up for schools, as were greenhouses for the propagation of seeds, open-air theaters, and fields for ball games; these were the new forms and new contents.

In his article Boecking set out a complete program:

> The public park existing today is the type of green area structured in the best possible way to serve as a park. It contains within itself all the requirements that the great mass of the people have for their free time.
> For the children: playing fields; fields for gymnastics and running; sandboxes surrounded by benches and play areas; meadows or ponds with showers; sandy areas on which to stretch out; solariums, protected from the wind, for sunbathing; drinking fountains; equipment for games and sports.
> For the sportsman: football pitches; fields for hockey, handball and volleyball; tennis courts; rifle ranges. If there is sufficient space and costs permit, there may also be a sports arena, a running track and fields for the throwing of the javelin, the discus and the shot put. If conditions permit, swimming pools, boating lakes and skating rinks must be provided, as well as a hill about 30 meters high for winter sports.
> For those in need of rest: extensive fields set apart, with deckchairs to be hired, and paths where people can stroll; many points at which seats are placed, both in the sun and in the shade, where panoramic views can be enjoyed.
> For those who come to have a good time: wide roads to walk down, concert sites, special greenhouses, open-air theaters, small zoos, merry-go-rounds, swings, fair booths.
> The following buildings: the central casino and cafe; small milk bars near the playing fields; dressing rooms; games huts; places where spectators can watch at sports pavilions; a shelter from the bad weather; and public toilets.
> [A. Boecking, "Soziale Grünanlagen im Städtebau," *Die Form*, no. 4, 1931]

The program set out by Boecking was not a utopian vision but was actually implemented in numerous parks. However, this unified beginning,

the park of the 1920s, which in its program took account of the harmonious development of physical, spiritual, musical and social capacities and needs, soon began to disintegrate. Places intended for sports activities became differentiated: sports parks came into being (in Frankfurt and Müngerdorf), school gardens were set apart, swimming pools became separated from the parks and commercialized, and the "Schrebergärten," or garden allotments, were put together in sizable colonies.

As we have seen, the garden architects belonging to the Werkbund took up various positions. The first group, represented by the majority of the members, consisted of designers of private gardens, who continued to confine their activities to the plot of land, the middle-class family garden. Their position remained almost unchanged after 1920; at that time, too, gardens were being established, although they were simpler and smaller. A parallel phenomenon existed for architects: the exhibition entitled "Sun, Air and House [!] for Everyone" was an exhibition held by the Werkbund in 1932 and addressed to the owners of summer homes!

The other group consisted of garden architects who were also members of the Werkbund but expressed their views with surprising circumspection, considering the fact that, for the most part, they were employed by the city councils and were therefore right at the center of the debate. These planners could not retain a detached attitude to the problems connected with the policy of establishing parks. Willy-nilly they showed concern for the needs and aspirations of the populace and in addition were in a position to convert them into an appropriate form: in the public park. For them what Riezler said in 1914 in his famous discussion of the ideas of the Werkbund is valid; new forms and new art can arise only if the artist can retain a close bond with the base:

> I should like to refer again to the remarks made by an earlier speaker, and an image that, in the way it has been applied, is extremely characteristic for an understanding of this circle of people. . . . He compared art to a pyramid, and it was no accident that he declared that what is important is the apex, since everything depends on the apex: "We must start from the apex." Well, ladies and gentlemen, imagine to yourself a pyramid where one starts from the top. This is simply the symbol of the conception of these persons that it is possible to create a base for art and forms by starting from an individual, standing completely detached from any kind of reality. I am convinced that things are quite different. Where there is no base, one will never be able to attain . . . a complete solution. [Riezler, 1914]

That this concern for the populace indicated what

was in essence a tepid attitude among the Werkbund garden designers is shown by certain statements. Migge, for example, wished to employ the new garden culture to make a contribution to German chauvinist foreign policy:

> In the aspirations of the nations, like any other kind of phenomenon, horticulture is an objective mirror of the social-political and spiritual structure of each period. Consequently, also, the future garden culture of the twentieth century must. . . be the authentic expression of our conditions of life.
> [So far so good, but —] we are creating a garden culture that, in detail, expresses in a characteristic way the community of a nation and that bears within itself the future, that is, the possibility of becoming the sign of a cosmopolitan whole.
> . . . Germany undoubtedly possesses the most favorable position. And I think it will be something more than a simple impulse toward self-preservation that will encourage us to take the initiative in this field of the economy so important and promising: the new gardens "made in Germany." [Migge, 1913]

In his book *Gartenkunst im Städtebau*, Hugo Koch, a member of the Werkbund, goes straight to the point: "The populace enters the scene as a spiritual force; it cooperates in the struggle for existential values, for ideal values, which were once the province of the few. Even the lowest sections of society have understood the value of rejuvenating the body and spirit."

Koch hoped that the public park, with the "pioneering work" of the "cultured strata of the population," would "in time overcome the forces of subversion" (Koch, 1921).

The reactionary aspect of the new concern for the populace and their living conditions is particularly apparent in the statements by Migge and Koch: the culture of the garden = a contribution to the success of Germany's foreign policy or a way of solving difficulties in home affairs. Harry Maasz, as well as Enke, expresses himself more prudently: "We have begun to think about the people, their needs, their right to have their own large communal garden, which until recently . . . appeared to be the exclusive prerogative of the rich. . . . The social concept of the park is the ace up our sleeve" (Maasz, 1913).

We console ourselves by noting that these tepid and reactionary quotations unwittingly reveal something more: the fact that these garden architects admitted that the impetus of their art was the populace. What they built was worth more than their theories. The public parks are a visible sign of progress — and they still exist.

91. *Shallow pools for children in the Rehberge Park, Berlin.*
92. *Lawn with deck chairs in the Rehberge Park, Berlin.*
93, 94. *Playing fields in the Rehberge Park, Berlin.*
95. *Toboggan course in Rehberge Park, Berlin.*

"EVERYONE SELF-SUFFICIENT" — THE URBAN GARDEN COLONIES OF LEBERECHT MIGGE
(From the flight to the harmonious life of the countryside to the idea of socially involved garden architecture)
Inge Meta Hülbusch

Werkbund in its history is characterized especially by its members or collaborators in the fields of the figurative arts, design, and architecture and town planning. Among these, the garden architects and landscape designers, by the very nature of their task, remained embroiled in the trammels of a feudal and bourgeois tradition, on the one hand, while, on the other, they operated within the orbit of a movement with clearly defined racist and national-socialist intentions, seeking to recover the cultural heritage of the local Fatherland. Not the town, nor modules for urban living, nor even the means of production of the industrial urban reality could be their central problem if for no other reason than that these issues took them away from their traditional bourgeois relationship with art and nature, and possibly represented a threat to them. For their breviary they therefore took the manifestos of the national youth movement. Paul Schultze-Naumburg, an architect and member of the Werkbund, which he left at the right moment, in 1927,[1] was highly thought of for having stated the ideological basis for landscape planning, relating it to the concepts of national heritage and nature. At that time landscape was not yet in fashion, or at least it was to a much lesser degree than after 1960, when the Werkbund followed the previous fetishism and abandoned the city to the call: "Landscape must become the law."[2]

But the stage was now reached when people again began to sabotage the life of the city, as they have continued to do until our own day. The landscape designer today who seeks for a garden architecture where his interest in the world of work might be pursued looks to the Werkbund for an interlocutor or dialogue, and his main purpose is to uncover that episode of the history of the discipline that can retie the broken bonds between the architect and the town planner — and thus restore the original conception — in the ambit of the construction of workers' colonies. This is of particular interest in the history of the discipline itself, because, with the mystical appearance of "landscape" viewed as an object of professional attention, the architect of the free spaces of the city again withdrew into a dream of miniature landscapes and again sought to substitute "landscape" for the city.

The garden architect Hermann Mattern joined the Werkbund in 1930, and in his work he too fell victim to the call of landscape. Also in the role of garden architect — and he was the last of the ranks of Werkbund members who before 1933 worked in their own specific professional field — there entered on the scene Leberecht Migge, who joined the Werkbund in 1912 and worked in Worpswede from 1920.

Worpswede in the Twenties

The situation Migge found when he arrived at Worpswede, and that encouraged him to stay there, presented a highly contradictory image.
Worpswede was still well known as an artists' colony, although in the opinion of many people, among them the painter Otto Modersohn, the village had declined into a residential colony. The Bremen businessman Ludwig Roselius (who joined the Werkbund later, in 1925), believing that "it was part of the duties of the Hanseatic citizens to cultivate the arts,"[3] had close links with Worpswede. Roselius was the patron of the painter Heinrich Vogeler, who in 1909 took part — as designer — in the journey to England of the Deutsche Gartenstadtgesellschaft[4] and then designed residential settlements for workers and houses with gardens. Bernhard Hoetger, who joined the Deutscher Werkbund in 1915, had been in touch with Vogeler since 1914, and both men were in contact with Karl Ernst Osthaus.
At Worpswede the various conceptions of "landscape" were concentrated, even though this fact was not generally known to the public until much later. What did the presence of such men as Roselius, Osthaus, Hoetger, Vogeler and Migge represent for Worpswede?
In the twenties Hoetger left his personal imprint on Worpswede by his constructions for Roselius and Osthaus; these were monumental sculptures — Niedersachsenstein, the Osthaus complex, the Worpswede cafe, the picture gallery — "Lietzenburgen," as Ernst Bloch called them,[5] which stifled the clear lines of Vogeler's delicate constructions. Hoetger designed the whole Weyerberg complex. "With 'vast meadows in the grey of twilight,' but also with the later Worpswede, the characteristic element of the best feature of the Secession is realized: the peculiar liberty of the sunset has existed since then, always in the countryside. Nietzsche's Pan here acquired completely Nordic features: the landscape of Zarathustra, in its first effect, was concentrated and moved into the distance, even at a 'geopolitical' level, from spring, from the morning, from Italy . . . deviating gently toward the northwest, into the autumnal triangle of Lower Saxony, England, Scandinavia. . . ."[6]
Worpswede was the plastic realization of the "sunset" put under the protection of patrons; it was a kind of "park for the preservation of nature," like the Lüneburg heathland of Alfred Toepfer.
Preparations for this "sunset" were now disturbed by the "socialist residential community," the school for work created by Heinrich Vogeler. Leberecht Migge was interested in Vogeler's experiment and participated in it. He spoke of land reform, work, and sunshine, for which land on the Weyerberg was needed for gardening, tree nurseries, and so on. He did not wish to beautify Worpswede and make it into an attraction for North Germany, but wanted to conduct an experiment in order to show that the basic conditions of life in postwar Germany could be improved. Migge did not surround his house — the "Sonnenhof" — with a "natural" garden but taught his wife and children to grow vegetables in hotbeds.
This initiative was related to his discussions with Vogeler, who reproached Migge for trivializing social problems: "He believed a revolution was not necessary if people were enabled to build through their own efforts and around their own homes the basis for their own sustenance. In this way everyone will be happy."[7]
In 1920 Migge, who had organized the Jacob Ochs flower-growing business in Hamburg, founded a school for settlers at Worpswede.[8] Who then was Leberecht Migge?
Was he, as he liked to describe himself, a garden architect who, as would appear from Vogeler's accounts, placed himself in the tradition of the "reformers"? Was he an outsider who practiced gardening "in the Chinese manner",[9] in opposition to the biologically dynamic agriculture of Rudolf Steiner? Was he a successful and snobbish garden architect, who at Worpswede was providing his family with the opportunity of conducting the household according to "Chinese methods," that is, in a calm, leisurely climate? Or was he an excellent designer of Siedlungen, who demonstrated that "country life," rather than "life in the country," was the form that necessarily had to be taken by a colony?
In Worpswede itself, where he lived with his family for eleven years, very little is known of him; his colleagues themselves, even the youngest of them, cannot assign him a place.[10] The works produced by Migge on commission had a great influence upon his colleagues and had the effect of intimidating them by more or less directly criticizing their own lack of ideas. Migge's suggestions ran

counter to the interests of the professional associations. He declared that civic and social green zones should be replaced by the "green zones of the settlements": "Common to all of them is the fact of representing not 'the soil' but 'gardens,' and in actual fact what they are creating are small gardens, ever smaller."[11] "Furthermore, apart from the fact that the city may be useful or harmful, is the reality that it exists"[12] and must therefore be made suitable for living in: this was to be done by dismantling the centralized administration, restructuring the old urban zone and reconstructing the internal economy.[13] And since the "large city is a mother of gardens,"[14] the result is that "garden cultivation = class privilege" and "garden art = cultural privilege;"[15] social gardens will therefore be established alongside (and respectively in place of) the gardens of the intellectuals: "I am actually an enemy of monopolies, even my own monopolies. The profession of gardener must not remain apart at such a significant moment in the development of a 'green Europe.' But in this connection the route passes through labor."[16]

Migge's discussions and work with architects and town planners engaged at a sociopolitical level are here apparent.

He saw the problems with perfect clarity. For him labor implied manual work, intellectual work, political work: "The ultimate reason for our failure as colonizers is in every case the question of how to pay for the land."[17] In his view, there was, for the time being, only one answer to this question: by increasing the yield of the land. This was a realistic approach but it met with resistance from politicians and colleagues engaged in the same sector.

"If it is true — as our politicians are almost unanimous in thinking — that a genuine civic sentiment can grow only out of the soil, then logically it follows that the citizens can be educated to a solid civic consciousness only on their own urban soil."[18] "Our cities [are] really the inborn supporters of economic colonization."[19]

"The socialization of urban green space is one of the most important tasks of our time, and nothing must stand in its way any longer" was how Migge expressed his hopes in 1913.[20] In this declaration he faced the problem of the availability of urban land and at the same time considered the wasteful use of this land and criticized the resident of the Siedlungen for wanting to consume without producing.[21] A "people without space" was in his view only a pretext in the discussion concerning the ownership of the land, which he later stigmatized directly and practically in the example of the aggregation of communes.

In 1925 Migge asked of the city: "One cannot plan for a cultivated or green belt around the city, nor can one leave it in the city area as a free space, but it must be deliberately programed. . . ."[22] In order to prevent the setting up of extensive settlements with a consequent shortage of land, it was necessary to start from the assumption that no more aggregations should be set up.[23]

But Migge was not very well liked by his colleagues, because he demanded quality in their work and continually criticized them. Even the greatest figures were not excluded from his criticisms: his comments on the gardening exhibition held in 1927 at Liegnitz ("Gugali"), "Yet another exhibition of gardens for the rich — when will we have a modern exhibition for the poor?"[24] would force those subjected to them, in self-defense, of moralizing.

Migge brought his bitter arguments with his colleagues to an end when he left the German association of garden architects (BDGA) in 1928. The neglect by architects of the garden and its function, and their emphasis on the formal and aesthetic aspects of the garden, provoked his comment on the gaps in collaboration within the Werkbund and led him to describe the 1927 Stuttgart exhibition in these terms:

> It is creating a great stir. Types of housing suited to the time should be proposed. All the heads of international modern architecture (with the exception of a few talents) have been invited. A new mode of constructing and living may be reduced to three formulas: *improved technique, cheaper building, appropriate gardens.* In this context I believe the so highly vaunted "new form" to be of secondary importance, but in Stuttgart this is what is put first. In Swabia a demonstration of a particular solidity and economy should have been provided. And new *gardens* annexed to the new dwellings were evidently held to be superfluous. Were they not indeed part of the work, esteemed Werkbund workers?!²⁵

How had these contradictions been arrived at? Meanwhile, at the Werkbund congress of 1911 Muthesius was still holding the view that "broad social strata like the aristocracy and the rich" were contrary to the Werkbund because they find the moralizing tendency of the movement irksome and the bourgeois profession associated with the new theory of art is suspect to them."[26] In 1913 Migge wrote in *Die Gartenkultur des 20. Jahrhunderts:* "I am somewhat prejudiced in favor of artistic practice in our present-day community of life, at least with reference to the determining influence exercised by art in this community."[27]

Of course it must not be forgotten that Migge was a gardener, a garden architect, and could clearly

distinguish between the need to safeguard nature in the garden and the need to construct a garden as an autonomous work of art. As he wrote: "No, to us who are men of today the naturalism of the garden is of no use. From whatever angle we may approach the problem, it is dwarfed before the reality of how the world goes and the new vital consciousness we have all acquired. There emerges — and this is a characteristic feature of the present formal rhetoric of the garden — a vicious circle, tracing a path without end from nature to science, from reason to art, and back again to nature."[28]

Migge was of the opinion that "everything is good and useful that becomes universally right in its value," and this led him to the development of types of gardens that he imagined, for the most part, as "gardens for the hundred thousand, small and tiny gardens for industrial towns and garden cities. This type of garden was to be the basis for the 'work rhythm' that comes from multiple and constant familiarity with all the little spiritual characteristics and all the real activities that, taken together, make up the enduring life of the garden. . . ."[29]

Migge exhorted people to take part in the struggle, "the happy and joyful struggle for the supremacy of the garden. Hurry to where we have the opportunity to transform our own country into a country of flowering gardens, where everyone, however poor, may have his share."[30] The misery brought about by the First War, which caused Heinrich Vogeler, too, to revise his opinion,[31] made Migge change his concept of the "Schrebergarten," especially when he saw the hunger the war brought in its wake. In his *Prinzip der Selbstversorgung,* or principle of self-sufficiency, he declared that the interest of land holdings consists of their yield in nature; in other words, the garden could live off its own fruits. "Every family must be self-sufficient on its own land by acquiring its own vegetable, fruit and animal produce."[32] He took as his model the orchard and vegetable garden areas of Eastern Asia, created by technology and intensive land cultivation, with the result that abundant harvests were obtained and the soil was made lastingly productive. "In these plots a building is never an end in itself, but every construction, including the home, is always a means to the end of obtaining greater yield from the soil."[33] To the "settlement that must grow according to biological laws" (see ill. 96 and n. 34), he added a variant, "the well being (see ill. 97 and n. 35). Together with Otto Haesler, Migge tried to put these ideas into effect at Celle (see ills. 98, 99 and n. 36), and with the Kiel city administration he planned a "cultivated belt" that would encircle the town and would be based on the agrarian recycling of refuse.[37] Migge always took an interest in "self-sufficiency" inside the city: small family gardens in the garden city of Hellerau, Schrebergärten in the garden city of Leipzig-Marienbrunn, the Siedlung at Duisburg-Neudorf (1929) and at Dessau-Ziebigk (1926) (see ills. 100, 101 and nn. 38, 39), and the Golzheimer Heide Siedlung (1927). Ernst May collaborated in the planning of the Praunheim settlement and the great Heddernheim Siedlung in 1927–28, and it is surprising to observe that they have features corresponding to the design shown in illustration 102 (see n. 40), produced during the war years. In Siedlungen, where it was not possible to "construct gardens," Migge tried to make garden patios that would provide the greatest possible autonomy for the householder: for example, in the wooded settlement at Duisburg-Neudorf (1929), in the wooded settlement at Zehlendorf-Schönow (1928–29), in the garden patios in Berlin-Neukölln, and so on. For every block belonging to the Deutsche Gartenstadtgesellschaft (German society for the garden city) in Berlin-Pankow, Migge provided a courtyard on which every apartment looked out, each with its own pergola (see ill. 103 and n. 41).

The "horseshoe" of the great Britz Siedlung at Berlin by Bruno Taut and Martin Wagner (1924–28) fulfills Migge's intention of connecting public and private green zones together.

The followers of Oswald Sprengler attacked the large city as responsible for the crisis of the West: the disintegration of the family, celibacy, decadent behavior, pessimistic view of the future — all culminating and being manifested in the decline of the birth rate.[42] It is only if we take into account these attacks upon "the excessive civilization of the urban environment" that we can realize the extent of the hostility encountered by Migge when, instead of recommending a "return to the countryside," he wanted to transform the large city into an autonomous entity that would not exploit the adjoining countryside.[43]

At this point it must be stated that Migge was a gardener, a technician ("Europe: a garden — this is my green Gospel")[44] — not a romantic lover of the countryside who idealized the peasant and saw in him eternal man. But his struggle for greater productivity ("Better Management," 1910) could cause him to be accused of pessimism in relation to culture, since this attitude clearly contradicted his own idea of "life on the land," which, according to Sombart, represented the environment "in which the soul can develop."[45] Frecot, Geist and Kerbs make a mistaken judgment on Migge in putting him in the same category as the advocates of land reform,[46] who believed the city to represent "the deformation of human life." For him, reforms did not represent an alternative to communism and capitalism, but he criticized the fact of being "colonizers," in the sense of "feeding off the land," which could serve as a basis for provisioning in times of crisis. His interests did not therefore coincide with the concrete effects of a generalized crisis that posed these problems for him. He engaged in building for the working class, so as to lift an intolerable weight from the shoulders of working-class families whose whole lives were spent in indigence and who saw their existence continuously threatened. According to Migge, production by the family as a means of lightening their financial burden would occur by increasing their minimal area of living space and broadening their sphere of social regeneration.

Werner Hegemann attributed the housing crisis in Berlin in the twenties to objections made by banks and speculators to any modest suggestions for improvement:[47] the "old Berlin vice — the 'cult of the street,'" as Eberstadt described it — augmented building costs, because of the heavy rates imposed on properties facing onto the street, so making it impossible for most people to own a small house and thus accelerating the rise in the value of land."[48] In London, where low houses were the norm, the price of building plots was much lower, and London was twice as large as Berlin at that time. In Stockholm it was possible to purchase small cottage-type houses on a long lease at a reasonable price, with permission to build onto them at a later stage. "Every reduction in the costs of production made by the labor force, that is to say, every lasting reduction in the price of goods essential to the life of the worker, owing to the iron laws of political economy must unfortunately lead to a general reduction in the value of the labor force and, consequently, a corresponding drop in wages,"[49] thus disappointing Migge's expectations that his idea would find general application. The transformation of the "useful garden" into a "social garden," which as a "civic garden" would be an expression of the egalitarian distribution of the wealth of society and of the possibility of making use of it, represented a useful free space, which it was very difficult to obtain. In any case, it was seen that Migge's proposed move toward the socialization of urban green zones was not capa-

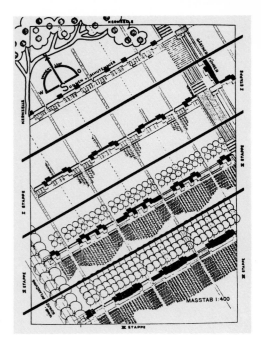

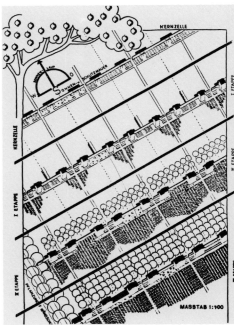

96. L. Migge, "House that grows," along the supporting wall in the "Siedlung that grows."
97. L. Migge, "House that grows," variant "optimal state" for the peripheral Siedlung.

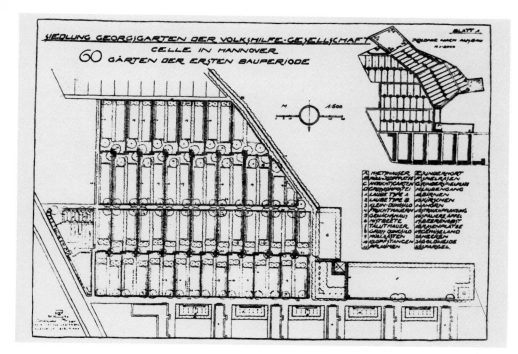

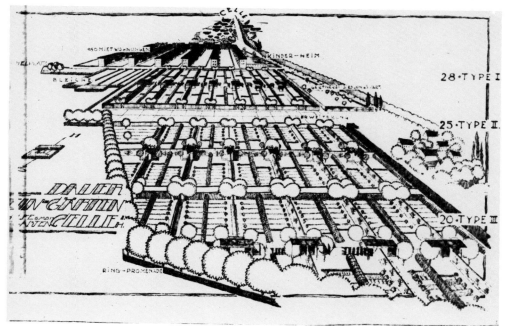

98, 99. L. Migge and Otto Haesler, Georgsgarten
Siedlung in Celle: example of "barracks" with small
gardens for intensive culture by each of the tenants.

ble of political realization, since the few examples
of areas having the double function of serving
housing needs as well as free space, with a relative
margin of tolerance in the interpretation of these
functions, had inroads made into them by building
and land speculation (e.g., the Siedlungen in the
Ruhr mining areas). This is where his proposal fits
in for the utilitarian preservation of land, which
would respect its fertility and its natural and vital
resources, which had in the meantime been taken
over by large-scale capital (the chemical industry,
building industry, atomic industry, and the like) and
brought to ruin.

There remains the question of the role Migge
assigned to women and the family, one cause of
the hostility with which his ideas were received. It is
obvious that even if people were to live in a
"Siedlung seen in its process of growth," as
conceived by Migge, this would necessitate a
model of family life different from that of the middle
class. The family would have to become once
again a center of production, as he had imagined
in his own "Sonnenhof" in Worpswede, where
Migge's wife and children each had their own
place within this self-sufficient system (as occurs
today, for example, in the case of the wives and
children of peasants who work part-time), whereas
he kept a margin of mobility for himself so that he
could give lectures and direct his studio in Berlin.
And it is in this that we see the contradiction
between Migge's concept of family production and
his own behavior, since he left his family with the
task of producing and left himself freedom. Speaking about himself in 1927, he described himself as a
"weekend Siedler," staying in the Sonnenhof only
at four-weekly intervals.

From this there followed also the conflict between
the need for a bond with the soil and with the
settlement's activity and the need to teach and
design outside of the Siedlung; at the same time
the contrast was apparent between the modest,
sober life of the artistic scene at Worpswede,
where an idyllic existence constructed its own
Lietzenburgen (fantasy castles). The contribution
of experiments and discussions made by Migge at
Worpswede came to represent for him the flight
from the city. To abandon Worpswede, which kept
him far from the daily problems of city life, signified
a return to the city from his "experimental laboratory."

Was Heinrich Vogeler then right to criticize Migge
for being nonpolitical? Where had Migge failed? In
the influence of the technocrats? His idea was
technically so perfected that it left no room for

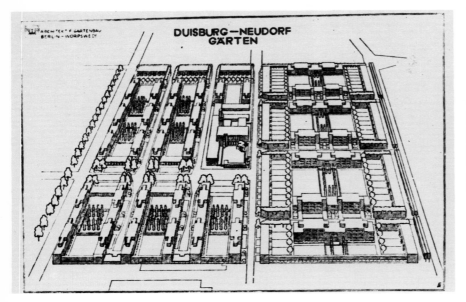

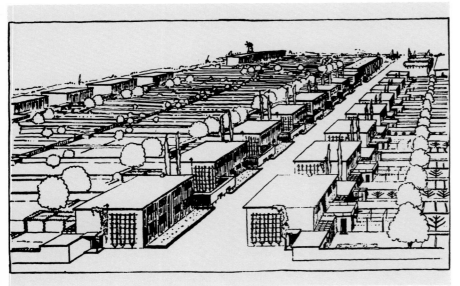

100. L. Migge, Duisburg-Neudorf, gardens.
101. L. Migge, Dessau-Ziebigk, perspective view of the working plan.

102. Design for garden with walls and trellises.
103. L. Migge, courtyard in Berlin-Pankow. A pergola for each dwelling, paths and play area.

objections; so far as I know, however, it was never publicly discussed among experts, in spite of his many publications.

In order to establish an economic "architecture of Chinese gardens" in Central Europe, where the dream[50] was of "old, shady, village lime-trees, idem meadows, mossy roofs, mold-covered tombs, and similar antiquities," and to propose these as an alternative to the large city required far more support than Migge could summon. The ideal of a classless society, which attracted the members of the Deutsche Gartenstadtgesellschaft as well, could not be attained under the conditions of the twenties by establishing and constructing Siedlungen.

It was Migge's merit to have fought to improve economic conditions within the framework of existing possibilities, whereas many members of the Werkbund were simultaneously making various attempts to smooth things over. For example, Ludwig Roselius suggested to Heinrich Vogeler: "Go on painting; give vent to your feelings in color. Leave it to men who have studied practical work to realize socialist ideas."[51] Whereas the authorities who controlled the policy of Worpswede in 1920 granted Heinrich Vogeler in Bremen the guarantee of a certain idealism, on the other hand such men as Bernhard Hoetger and Leberecht Migge passed for "pure Communist speculators."[52]

In this connection I should like to quote Werner Hegemann again:[53]

But Berlin, even after the revolution, did not think of organizing rationally its enormous housing shortage, in the same way that the Reichstag took care not to promulgate a housing law, which had been promised and was absolutely essential, and, in addition, that the Prussian Minister of Social Assistance, who has for Berlin ... greater functions of control — that is, a greater responsibility as compared with other cities — has been careful not to use his own powers to press for a considered housing policy. It seems that these necessary social provisions can be achieved only through revolution. During and soon after the revolution, land was offered to small groups of settlers within the perimeter of present-day Berlin also. Today, however, these small Berlin settlements are starved of land and people have to leave the urban area in the tens of thousands, just as they did in the years before the war, and look for the home they need outside the confines of the city — the home so longed for, which the fickle Reichstag, the lazy ministry and equally lazy Berlin deny them.

Is the "Communist speculator" then the only one

who was not lazy? Migge was well aware of his own position, as shown by a slogan of 1928:[54]

No fine culture without Knigge,
No good Siedlung without Migge.

Until now, the "guild" of landscape designers has through ignorance neglected the problems posed by Migge and also his contribution to the development of a garden architecture that corresponded to the conditions of city life.

1. For all information concerning the Deutscher Werkbund, see Zwischen Kunst und Industrie — Der Deutsche Werkbund, the catalog of the exhibition "Die Neue Sammlung" (Munich, 1975).

2. Ibid., p. 453.

3. Statement by his son, Ludwig Roselius, in the guide to the Roselius-Museum für Frühgeschichte in Worpswede, 1st ed.

4. Heinrich Vogeler illustrated the book about this journey, Aus englischen Gartenstädten (Berlin, 1910).

5. E. Bloch, "Herbst, Sumpf, Heide und Sezession," in Verfremdungen II (Frankfurt, 1965), p. 73.

6. Ibid., p. 70.

7. Cf. Heinrich Vogeler's recollections of L. Migge, quoted by J. Frecot, J. F. Geist, and D. Kerbs, Fidus (Munich, 1972), p. 39.

8. The Worpswede school for urban colonists conducted theoretical and practical courses and organized lectures. In the monthly magazine Siedlungs-Wirtschaft such topics were discussed as the growing of crops, the use of refuse, domestic economy, town planning, and the organization of the Siedlung.

9. "Chinese cultivation": using the rays of the sun in areas suited to cultivation (terraces, walls, etc.).

10. In this connection my thanks are due to Hans Hubert and Fritz Kühl, the Netzel family, Mrs. Schwarz and Mr. F. Wiggers (Worpswede) and Mrs. E. Schargorodsky (Posteholz) for the information provided by them. I am also grateful for the help of Tilman Störmer (Kassel), the grandson of Leberecht Migge.

11. L. Migge, Siedlungs-Wirtschaft, no. 1 (1929), p. 2.

12. Migge, Die Gartenkultur des 20. Jahrhunderts (Jena, 1913), p. 6.

13. Migge, Siedlungs-Wirtschaft, no. 12 (1927), p. 90.

14. Migge, Die Gartenkultur, p. 90.

15. Ibid., pp. 2–3.

16. Migge, Siedlungs-Wirtschaft, no. 4 (1928), p. 32.

17. Ibid., no. 6 (1925), p. 48.

18. Ibid., no. 1 (1925), p. 3.

19. Ibid., no. 1 (1925), p. 2.

20. Migge, Die Gartenkultur, p. 28.

21. Migge, Deutsche Binnenkolonisation (Berlin, 1926), p. 16.

22. Migge, Siedlungs-Wirtschaft, no. 3 (1925), p. 19.

23. Ibid., no. 6 (1926), p. 61.

24. Ibid., no. 7 (1927), p. 49.

25. Ibid., no. 10 (1927), p. 77.

26. Quoted in Zwischen Kunst und Industrie, op. cit., p. 61.

27. Migge, Die Gartenkultur, p. 139.

28. Ibid., p. 144.

29. Ibid., p. 150.

30. Ibid., p. 157.

31. C. D. Erlay, Worpswede — Bremen — Moskau — Der Weg des Heinrich Vogeler (Bremen, 1972).

32. L. Migge, Jedermann Selbstversorger (Jena, 1919), p. 8.

33. Migge, Die wachsende Siedlung nach biologischen Gesetzen (Stuttgart, 1932), p. 11.

34. Illustration from Die wachsende Siedlung, p. 8.

35. Illustration from Die wachsende Siedlung, p. 40.

36. Illustrations from Siedlungs-Wirtschaft, no. 6 (1926), p. 35, and no. 12 (1927), p. 96.

37. A panorama of the plans for Kiel is provided by Der Ausbau eines Grüngürtels der Stadt Kiel, written in Kiel by L. Migge in 1922 in collaboration with the city planner Dr. Hahn.

38. Illustration from Siedlungs-Wirtschaft, no. 6 (1929), p. 42.

39. Illustration from Siedlungs-Wirtschaft, no. 2 (1927), p. 10.

40. Illustration from Jedermann Selbstversorger, p. 36; cf. "Modell eines Vierer-Gartens in Heddernheim (mit Spalieren und Mauern)," Siedlungs-Wirtschaft, no. 12 (1927), p. 91.

41. Illustration from Siedlungs-Wirtschaft, no. 8 (1928), p. 59.

42. According to K. Bergmann, Agrarromantik und Grossstadtfeindschaft (Meisenheim am Glan, 1970), p. 195.

43. Some contemporaries who took a pessimistic view of the role of culture went so far as to describe sports fields as an expression of cultural decadence. Cf. Bergmann, op. cit., p. 196.

44. The last sentence in Migge, Deutsche Binnenkolonisation.

45. W. Sombart, Das Wirtschaftsleben im Zeitalter des Hochkapitalismus (Munich, 1928). Quoted here from Bergmann, op. cit., p. 198.

46. Frecot, Geist, and Kerbs, op. cit., pp. 15 and 39.

47. W. Hegemann, Das steinerne Berlin, Bauwelt-Fundamente (Braunschweig, 1976), p. 328, quotes R. Eberstadt, "The building laws represent the principal area where the 'feasibility' of town planning is expressed, which changes nothing but requires an ever greater expenditure of financial resources, legislative regulations and hence a great bureaucratic apparatus, and, while arousing new expectations, in reality succeeds only in consolidating the errors combatted elsewhere."

48. Hegemann, op. cit., p. 330. In Hellerau (Dresden), according to Barbara Hütter-Söhne (Die Rezeption der Gartenstadtidee in Deutschland [Hanover, 1976], p. 67), the streets in the residential zones were less reinforced and were therefore less "costly" for the owners of land abutting these streets.

49. F. Engels, Über die Umwelt der arbeitenden Klasse (Gütersloh, 1970), p. 185.

50. L. Migge, in Bergmann, op. cit., p. 163.

51. Erlay, op. cit., p. 42.

52. Ibid., p. 173 ff.

53. Hegemann, op. cit., p. 338.

54. L. Migge, Siedlungs-Wirtschaft, no. 5 (1928), p. 39.

DISTANT GOALS, GREAT HOPES: THE DEUTSCHER WERKBUND 1918–1924
Wolfgang Pehnt

The first annual meeting of the Werkbund after the war was held in Stuttgart September 6–9, 1919; the session was described by some critical observers with more skepticism than hope. The following tendency had emerged: the Werkbund had to find for itself an active role of its own and show itself to be the conscience of the nation; it had to oppose all the tactics of commercial policy — in other words, it could no longer fulfill the function of "diligent agent for the export of artistic craft work." Finally, instead of conforming to the demands of the importing country, it had the duty to satisfy the internal needs of its own nation: quality, in the name of honesty, decency and sincerity in its own way of feeling and thinking.[1] The debate that had taken place in 1914 concerning the ideas of Muthesius, and therefore also the Werkbund's function in industry, now became of secondary importance.

To tell the truth, the strategic positions taken up by the opposing parties had changed sides. The new composition of the presidential body — 21 members — provided a kind of guarantee to the possibility that the policy of the Werkbund could be revised in the direction of a moral idealism. With Bruno Taut, the presidency was enriched by one of the most fervent admirers of van de Velde, in the great conflict of 1914. The architect Otto Bartning and the painter César Klein were artists who — like Taut — expressed the ideals of expressionism. The group that had fought in Cologne against commercial opportunism and defended the freedom of artistic creation, even where this was not in question, was represented by Karl Ernst Osthaus, Walter Gropius and van de Velde. Finally, in Hans Poelzig the Werkbund had a president whose most notable feature was his original genius, as his sketches and designs confirm; in spite of his attempts to confer on industrial buildings and on the civil engineering constructions designed by him a *Sachlichkeit* (objectivity) of monumental dimensions, his contemporaries saw him as one of the most authentic of expressionists. Taut had already proclaimed him "dictator in artistic matters."[2]

The change in the presidency of the Werkbund was preceded by a flurry of intrigue on the sidelines. As he had been in 1914, Gropius was the "great charge of dynamite,"[3] the impassioned defender of artistic creation as the realization of individual faculties, as well as the impassioned opponent of a Werkbund policy favorable to industry. In this opposition he took up an attitude surprisingly in open conflict with his earlier statements[4] and with is own action in support of the standardization of the building sector. In correspondence with his friend Karl Ernst Osthaus, Gropius continued his struggle against "the deeply reactionary presidency of the Werkbund" and once more announced his intention of resigning if such odious men were to remain at the head of the organization. Gropius was referring to Ernst Jäckh, general secretary of the Werkbund, whom he found suspect for his numerous diplomatic and organizing activities, and Peter Bruckmann, who as a manufacturer was thought to nurture marked preference for an industrial policy. The Werkbund then seemed likely to develop into an "attack upon culture."

For his part, Poelzig was thinking of setting up a new association, an "Antiwerkbund," which would bring together the old generation of artists who were being neglected — such as Henry van de Velde or Hermann Obrist — with the new generation and expel the generation in the middle, consisting of successful men who were prepared to accept any compromise. Yet in spite of this plan Poelzig decided to accept the presidency of the Werkbund in 1919, when he came to the conclusion that it would not be easy for him to create a second time an instrument as effective as the Werkbund. "The Werkbund is unrepeatable," he wrote, "and one cannot suddenly make something else flourish in its place out of nothing."[5]

As expected by everyone, in the speech he delivered in Stuttgart, Poelzig announced that he would refuse every compromise, every opportunism and submission:[6] he wanted the Werkbund to be seen again as a spiritual rather than a commercial movement. *Again*, he emphasized, as if the essential stimulus of the Werkbund had not been the union of the two elements, for the conflict of interests between capital and production, on the one hand, and between artistic intention and social usefulness, on the other, always formed the core of its argument. But without Poelzig the Werkbund would have become either an association of entrepreneurs or an association of artists. Now he asked that the guiding principle behind all work undertaken should be the love of creation itself. One must "absolutely" refuse — he declared — to think of using work for commercial ends; at the most, such a purpose had to be "entirely secondary." Commerce and industry were synonymous with prostitution. In these terms he outlined the utopia of preindustrial production, which people thought had passed into oblivion when in 1907 the Guild of Handicraft of Charles Robert Ashbee disbanded and the Werkbund was founded. In opposition to planned consumption and stimulated demand brought about by industrial society, Poelzig indicated the durable product at both a practical and aesthetic level; in opposition to the division of labor found in large-scale industry he favored the execution of the complete process of manufacture by the artist and artisan. At this time

Poelzig and his friends held extremely vague socialist theories, consisting mainly of a naive critique of capitalism. This group, which opposed the earlier establishment of the Werkbund, showed a marked aversion to the entire party political system and believed that the community had to take the place of parties. The alienation of labor was attributed to the way processes were divided in industrialized production, to the practice of commercial immorality, rather than to the impossibility of owning the means of production and merchandise. For the Werkbund even, such ideas were sufficiently explosive material in view of its composition at the time. Indeed, financiers like Bosch asked themselves how they could consider financing the organization when it had a president whose aim was to tell industry to "do it alone."[7]

With regard to the old prewar controversy concerning the type or prototype, although Poelzig claimed the right to "free art," he assumed an attitude that differentiated only in its overtones from the positions upheld in Cologne by Peter Behrens, Richard Riemerschmied, Walter Riezler and Karl Schaefer — in other words, the factions disposed to mediate or those who sympathized outright with Muthesius. The view put forward was, in essence: mass-produced goods, and even less so, individual works, should not arrive at their definitive form through a reductive process, a process of continual eliminations, but had to arrive at their "essential form" by availing themselves of the whole spectrum of formal hypotheses. But the new president of the Werkbund rejected out of hand the unbridled fantasy and solipsist excursion — the "aviary of birds of paradise," the term applied to the Werkbund ironically in 1914. Poelzig believed that "typical forms" were indispensable to the industrial mass-produced article. On this question one can say that at least the opposing factions had drawn closer together: from all sides rose the call for discipline, the acceptance of a common artistic will (but how to attain it?), the spirit of the Bauhütte, the rejection of particularism and individual interests. The historical climate made its own contribution.

The reevaluation of the crafts was therefore seen to have a decisive role. "There is no substantial difference between the artist and the artisan," according to the Bauhaus manifesto of 1919. Poelzig went even farther and defined crafts as an "absolutely spiritual" activity. Crafts, standing apart from art only in degree and not through principle, forged a link with the mystical entity called "the people," but which from a sociological aspect remained vaguely defined. The policy of putting resources into agriculture, which was pursued in the period immediately following the First War, aimed at removing a part of the labor force by taking it out of the city and into the countryside, and for this reason seemed to add

104. Hans Poelzig, design for concert hall, Dresden, ca. 1918.

DOMSTERN

105. Bruno Taut, star-shaped dome, in "Alpine Architektur," Hagen, 1919.

grist to the mill, so to speak. Heinrich Tessenow could already see the children of his generation living as artisans in small provincial towns and constructing there an incredibly rich world.[8] But in this glorification of idealized artisan work, people lost sight of the actual world of work as it then existed in reality: repair shops or small industries with inadequate technical equipment, which were harmed rather than assisted by the efforts of the reformers.

From Adolf Behne to Heinrich Tessenow, everyone in those years evoked in the same emotional terms, and equal imprecision, the image of a community, among the various productive forces, which would draw its original strength from a mysterious dialogue with nature, for the people, with fresh and pure instinct, loved "exciting and vigorous forms" and "strong fearless colors." "To them the future artist will turn, to the instinctively serene soul of the people, which does not fear color, the splendor of gold and delight, the infantile joy in beauty," Gropius wrote in the first months after the war, but not only in the Bauhaus manifesto, since in all his articles of that period Gropius described crafts as the only possible source of renewal.[9] The Werkbund was the mouthpiece, the expression of the ideas of its adherents, when in 1920 it devoted its sixth yearbook to crafts in ancient and modern times (*Handwerkliche Kunst in alter und neuer Zeit*), published after the volumes devoted to art in industry and commerce (*Die Kunst in Industrie und Handel*, 1913) and to traffic (*Verkehr*, 1914), where the preindustrial past was reviewed. The yearbook advised the making of objects that would provide a record of the family, the city, or the state: bookbindings and tapestries, tulle embroidery and batik work, souvenir mugs of weddings and little jewel cases. Much space was allowed for dense ornamentation, taken partly from flower motifs and executed partly in the rough Expressionist style then in fashion. The level of taste was uncertain.

A characteristic feature of this situation was the actual interpretation given to this return to the past, neither a simple rediscovery nor the consequence of an interest in the world of antiquity, but rather a pragmatic significance. Before the war, Friedrich Naumann, who was convinced of Germany's potential competitiveness in the world economy, had defended "the large industrial concern" and declared there was no place for the "charm of the small workshop, the diligence of careful individual work, and the imitation of what was made in the good old times."[10] The difficulties of the final months of the war resulted in the advice being given to practice these virtues for a very simple reason: they were useful to the national economy. The Treaty of Versailles had cost Germany a considerable part of its resources of coal, iron, minerals and other raw materials, but, on the other hand, she still had, as before, a great potential labor force. In this situation the only way to get out of the serious position seemed to be to increase the export of manufactured industrial products by means of artisan processes, and this could be achieved in spite of the ever greater shortages of raw materials. In his book *Sittliche Diktatur* of 1920, issued by the Werkbund, the art critic Karl Scheffler warned that every wastage of material was a dissipation of the national wealth and that every importation of raw materials from abroad transformed Germany into a colonial nation. But the practice of crafts, which entailed a great deal of labor, proved to be in the final analysis a piece of shrewd economic policy. In the making of goods the greatest incidence of labor costs, compared with other costs of production, was judged positive.

The social and artistic ethic, whereby the worker was to be given back the joy in his labor if processes were no longer split up, was therefore in line with the socioeconomic ethic based on the careful working of material by the loving hands of the craftsman. The more courageous interpreters even managed to connect the two themes: "Whatever happens, one thing is certain: only the redefinition of work can counterbalance the loss suffered when articles are mass-produced. For perhaps the first time in the history of the German economy, the granting of new dignity to man becomes the necessary condition of existence."[11] Scheffler's argument followed the same line of thought. In fact, Scheffler drew his conclusions by throwing a bridge, perhaps rashly, between the opportune, and then necessary, "ability to renounce" and that which was desirable in the politico-economic field. At all events, the work as he defined it would be victorious, because it convinces and dominates by making use of elements that are present together in truth, in the force of action, in imagination, and in morality."[12]

But in those months when great emphasis was being laid on the crafts, only a few people of good sense were able to understand that craft work, executed individually and, therefore, costly, could in reality appeal only to the interest of amateurs. For reasons of commercial psychology, if for no other reason, the German goods produced by individual artist-craftsmen encountered great difficulties, particularly in those countries that had been the enemies of Germany. The disappointment aroused by the exhibitions held internationally, such as the traveling crafts exhibition held in the USA in 1922, helped to remove certain illusions.

In a similar way, considerations of functionalism and the new morale found themselves in agreement on the theme of color. On the one hand, color appeared as a very effective means of creating form and was an effect easily obtained; on the other hand — in conformity with the view of the proletariat of their time held by artists — it seemed the most suitable way to arrive at a popular art in the twofold sense of art close to the people and fed by the people. As Gropius said, "The people demand color," and he used color as the expressive means of those classes who were proud of their own class and no longer wished to continue to imitate the rich middle class but to replace respectable bourgeois behavior by spontaneity and vitality.[13] In Expressionist painting and (in its verbal use of color) in poetry also, color was no longer used simply to serve a descriptive function but to express an emotional value quite separate from the empirical impression. Architecture followed the same itinerary — no longer working with the color of the material, the equivalent of color as used by the painter in reference to the object, and employing in its place the entire chromatic scale for the new residential settlements and for the restoration of old buildings. But the violent, brilliant interplay of colors was intended not only to express and stimulate emotions but to be the sign of a new spiritual awareness. "Color [is] the messenger of the ultimate cosmic entities, of the intimate, very rich forces of tension between the gentlest delicacy and cruelest ferocity," in the enthusiastic words of Adolf Behne. Meanwhile, as town planning adviser (*Stadtbaurat*) of Magdeburg, Bruno Taut had spread color throughout the town; even before the war, with his Wohnkolonie, his *Tuschkasten* (box of paints), in Falkenberg near Berlin in 1913–15, he had given a color dimension to everyday life. Color became for him the symbol of the great Dionysiac banquet of life: "Yes, everything must be a feast — work, life and even death. We Europeans no longer know how to die joyfully, and we therefore clothe death in dark colors. How different things are in the East!"[14]

The Werkbund had taken an interest in the use of color for some time, and many of its members supported Taut's *Appeal for Colored Buildings* (1919). In the Cologne exhibition a pavilion built by Muthesius contained a so-called exhibition of color. Here textiles, tapestries and mosaics were displayed, and their flat design, enlivened by brilliant colors, produced the impression of familiar household objects. These objects formed the decorative basis for the propaganda of the Bayer Leverkusen and the BASF with regard to the luster of their products. In addition, at the Stuttgart congress and also in the years that followed, wide-ranging discussions were held among the Werkbund members concerning the color chart of Wilhelm Ostwald. This chart was produced as the result of an earlier initiative by the Werkbund itself and was intended to establish a system of color harmonies, but most of the artists rejected the idea, and finally the presidential body rejected it also. However, the real impulses behind this revival of color — "the sense of a frugal purity" (Bruno Taut), color as "salvation" (Walter Gropius), the "pure melody of color" as a "sound of the universe" (Adolf Behne)[15] — had very little impact on the great marketplace of ideas and pragmatism that the Werkbund had always been, however many transformations it underwent.

Most of the discussions of this period followed this pattern: whereas before 1914 the Werkbund itself had taken the initiative, this was usually no longer the case, and the Werkbund took up ideas that had been generated elsewhere. While belonging to the older generation, many of the militants in revolutionary associations — like the Novembergroup in Berlin and the Künstlerräte (artists' councils) and Aktionausschüsse (action committees) in Berlin, Darmstadt, Dresden, Karlsruhe, Cologne, Munich — were also members of the Werkbund. It is therefore difficult to measure how much was due to the Werkbund in the development process of the postwar years and, still more so, to assign its role in the debates concerning the new human society, the total work of art of religious inspiration, or the work of art that would elevate mankind instead of keeping within the bounds of pure economic calculation. Indeed many skeptical comments were to be heard in the Werkbund against the megalomania or the excessively outlandish style found in some designs, such as the works presented by Taut and Gropius at the exhibition for unknown architects held in Berlin in April 1919. Gropius said, "When the revolution broke out, the Werkbund should have put itself at its head, but it let the moment pass and now people feel very harshly toward it."[16]

What the Werkbund could, and did, undertake at that relatively late time was to act as a catalyst in relation to the groups scattered about the Reich and to mediate between the small esoteric groups, on one side, and public opinion, on the other. It achieved an artistic-political success — "its most important action," according to Gropius — when it managed to obtain a research establishment in artistic matters from the so-called Reichskunstwart, at the head of the Reich Ministry of the Interior. The new studio, directed by Edwin Redslob, who was the director of Stuttgart Museum, was responsible for presenting the image of the Reich, from postage stamps and bank notes to international exhibitions. But it cannot be denied that several of the Werkbund's activities — which were of course affected by the incipient inflation — seemed more like wearisome and wasteful exercises than the result of deep conviction. The 1920 yearbook, with its attempts to revive the artisan techniques of the past, perfectly mirrors this climate, a feature of which was the interminable discussions held concerning style and type, mechanized work or manual work — topics that were far from exhausted at the Stuttgart congress of the Werkbund but dragged on for years in the publications of the association. As Wilhelm Ostwald said in Stuttgart, at every meeting the members of the Werkbund went right back to the beginning in a completely irrational way.[17]

The cultural policy that the Werkbund pursued from the time of its foundation and intensified after 1918 was consequent and, to a certain extent, also positive and fertile, From its publications, in which the members made their ideas known on pedagogic matters, there emerged agreement on a considerable number of points. For example, Otto Bartning, Theodor Fischer and Richard Riemerschmid, writing in Werkbund publications, or Bruno Taut in a leaflet for the Arbeitsrat für Kunst, Berlin, started from the conviction that the isolation of the individual arts should end and they should be brought together into a new synthesis; if this view was accepted, then it became obvious that the various teaching institutions — the art schools, schools of arts and crafts, and the architecture faculties of the polytechnics — must be unified. Since crafts were highly considered at that time, it was natural it should be craft work that would form the common basis for all professional training within the applied arts sector. The old "rigid caste hierarchy, with the artist's haughty presumption in his attitude to the skills of the artisan and with the false ambition of craft itself — the claim to an ornamentation of genius — cuts up and separates them root, stalk and buds, and so renders the whole educational system sick and sterile, together with all the artistic life that derives from it."[18] These thoughts fitted in with the Werkbund's principles for the reform of the schools. In the spirit of this movement, in fact, the new art schools would be part of a single reformed school, in which professional training would play a central part.

The plans for the reform of the art schools in that period allowed for *Lehrwerkstätten*, or studios for apprentices; to tell the truth, this idea was not at all an innovation of the postwar years and neither was the suggestion that the students should periodically do practical work in craftsmen's studios. Riemerschmid, who was then head of the Munich School of Arts and Crafts, decided that teaching should be in the hands of artists (the Bauhaus "Formmeister") and artisan laws should be formulated by heads of studios (Werkmeister), a practice that had already produced good results in the Breslau Academy under Poelzig or in van de Velde's School of Arts and Crafts in Weimar. The profits from private and state commissions would go to the schools, and at the same time these

106, 107. Walter Gropius, Sommerfeld House, view of exterior and interior, Berlin-Lichterfelde, 1920-21.

commissions would be an enormous stimulus to the creativity of the students. At the basis of such proposals was the idea, implicit or explicit, that every human work "should manifest itself through forms and colors and in visible means express its own essence and that of its creator."[19] Yet the works of those people who had received this type of training revealed a character more expressive than practical: they were works with their own significance, rather than useful tools, and this was true of whatever place they occupied in the scale between the crafts and the higher arts. In addition, the everyday object was always viewed as a means of expression, to which the artist had to give a form. The most publicized outcome of these ideas was the Bauhaus, founded by Gropius in 1919. When in June 1920 Gropius had to defend the budget of his school before the Thuringian Landtag, he indicated a series of initiatives and similar institutions where the same principles were about to be introduced or were already being applied. This demonstration was not only a tactical move, made in a situation that was politically difficult, but also expressed how widely the ideas put forward by the Bauhaus — only one of many institutions, although probably the most active, thanks to the artists summoned by Gropius — were meeting with general acceptance.

Otto Bartning was the main influence on Gropius, in detail as well as in his general thought.[20] In the statement that accompanied the request for a "Lehrenstalt als künstlerische Beratungsstelle" (teaching institution as a place for artistic information), presented by Gropius to the Weimar ministerial authorities in 1916, Gropius again returned to the topic of the mechanization of work and the industrial production. He dropped this viewpoint in the first three years after the war but returned to it again in the process of clarification or self-criticism carried on within the Bauhaus after the autumn of 1921. In its general program, however, the Bauhaus of 1919 still expressed the utopian idea of a unification of all the centrifugal elements in a great work of architecture, while, on the other hand, it turned toward a socially inspired attitude tinged with romanticism — the same attitude that set in motion a whole flight of correligionaries in the Werkbund and the Arbeitsrat für Kunst. Bartning wrote: "the ultimate significance of every artistic activity is not the single entity; its ultimate significance is the total entity, or, as we say, the Bauwerk, the architectonic work." And Gropius, too: "The ultimate aim of the Bauhaus, however distant it might be, is the unified work of art, the great construction." Craft work, therefore, appears as a part or stage of the journey leading to this goal, in other words, the part which can be taught. But art is grace: "Only the artisan trade and science can

be taught and thus evaluated," wrote Bartning; and Gropius: "Art is born above all methods; by its nature it cannot be taught, whereas a trade can."[21] The artists who in practice guided the Werkbund soon after 1918 defended the explicit forms and models. Indeed, when, in his letters to Gropius, Poelzig considered the idea of forming an anti-Werkbund, which would bring together the artists of van de Velde's generation and those of the young generation, he declared that "the oldest and youngest (unlike the in-between generation) were turning again in spirit and style to the Gothic principle."[22] Speaking at Stuttgart, he was more prudent. He substituted "Medieval" for "Gothic" and tried to make the resemblance in style comprehensible by quoting a concrete example: the new skeletal constructions, as in the Gothic system, tended to dissolve and rearticulate the forces. At that time there were many artists who modeled themselves on the art of the Middle Ages: Poelzig and Gropius; Osthaus and Bruno Taut; Paul Scheerbart, Taut's friend who was a poet and saw in the Gothic cathedral an anticipation of his architecture incorporating expanses of glass; Peter Behrens, who, after his late (and temporary) move away from monumental classicism, in 1922 constructed in the romantic manner then in fashion a "Dombauhütte," or cathedral building, for the exhibition of industry in Munich, and used for the porch of the IG-Farben building at Höchst (1920–24) the ribbed roofing of the first Gothic period cathedrals; and, finally, the platoon of architects who were ready to follow any fashion and were still, at the end of the twenties, decorating their designs with ogival windows, portals, arches and lacework. This neo-medievalism, for which such works as *Formprobleme der Gotik* (1911) by Wilhelm Worringer and *Geist der Gotik* by Karl Scheffler had prepared the path, was obviously not determined by stylistic interests alone, because if during the Middle Ages art and crafts were one and the same thing, on the other hand, faith — as far as could be supposed later — was the connecting link between all components of the population, while the arts (and this was an argument of particular fascination to architects) had prospered under "the protective wing of a great architecture," the "ars magna."

If one excludes religious architecture and utopian projects of similar inspiration, one cannot say that the apparatus of forms based on the Gothic dominated the scene unopposed. The architectural fantasies of Poelzig, who was town planning assessor in the city of Poppelmann, and of Georg Behr were indeed lost in a form inspired by the Baroque. On the other hand, the most spectacular of the not very spectacular constructions designed by Gropius between 1918 and 1922, the Adolf Sommerfeld house in Berlin-Lichterfelde, repre-

sented an intermediary stage between the Scandinavian wooden house and the "Prärie-Blockhaus." Moreover, there were many artists, among them Bruno Taut and the young Hans Scharoun, who were fascinated by the East to at least an equal degree as by the Gothic. However, the prevailing and decisive aspect of this influence remained that of "what is mysteriously arabesque and ornament,"[23] in other words, the message of the Jugendstil, which was chronologically the closest to it of all the stylistic eras; constant reference to van de Velde and Obrist showed how these undeniable sympathies persisted. And it must be said in this connection: Although it cannot be denied that the creations of the Jugendstil were not directly addressed to the "people," but to a well-defined body of experts and intermediaries, yet they were inspired by a will to bring about reforms that aimed to redefine life in all its expressions, while availing themselves of various means and claiming their own rights.

The choice of models was not free from argument. Whatever the forms used in specific cases, the impassioned discussion that broke down the barriers between fields of activity and materials was directed against the "return to the Renaissance in the conception of bourgeois classicism" (Poelzig)[24] and attacked the parsimony shown in the Cologne exhibition by Josef Hoffmann, Hermann Muthesius, Karl Siebrecht and — at least on this occasion — Wilhelm Kreis also. Nevertheless, bearing in mind the repertory of forms in use in those years, coalitions were still possible and alliances could still be formed, which would be unthinkable around the mid-thirties, when the Neues Bauen movement was set up. Between a house designed for workers by Ernst May around 1920 and one by Paul Schmitthenner or Paul Schultze-Naumburg there was not the slightest difference: a simple cube with sloping roof; small windows in the roof often functioning as "bull's-eyes"; the window bars and framing with a pleasing appearance. Everyone could subscribe to the aims of encouraging crafts and creating a colorful image in the house and utensils: moderns and conservatives, the Dürerbund, the Heimatkunst (national art) movement and the Heimatschutzbewegung (movement for the preservation of the national heritage). The irrational vocabulary employed by all these groups did more than was necessary; that is to say, it kept hidden the discords that only in the late twenties had been revealed as irreconcilable contradictions. It was very symptomatic in this connection that in his appeal, made in the hope that works of great value would arise through the joy in manual work and that by sacrifices a new society would be created, Scheffler should address himself to the most disparate

108. Ernst May, Siedlung with leasehold property, Goldschmieden-Neukirch, ca. 1920.

109. Paul Schmitthenner, house for four family units in the garden city of Staaken near Berlin, 1914–16.

110. Ferdinand Kramer, brass ewer, execution: Emil Graf. Shown in the exhibition "Form ohne Ornament," 1924.

111. Brass ewer, execution: Staatliches Bauhaus, Weimar. Shown in the exhibition "Form ohne Ornament," 1924.

112. Dorkas Härlin, receptacle. Shown in the exhibition "Form ohne Ornament," 1924.

113. Ferdinand Kramer, stove of polished metal, execution: Emil Graf. Shown in the exhibition "Form ohne Ornament," 1924.

114. Emanuel Josef, ceramic stove, execution: Grossherzogliche Majolika-Manufaktur Karlsruhe. Shown in the exhibition "Form ohne Ornament," 1924.

groups: "Whoever stands on the right politically can see in this teaching a manifesto of a conservative tendency, while whoever is on the left can find it revolutionary. Moral actions are always both things at the same time: conservative and progressive."[25]

In the Werkbund exhibition entitled "Form ohne Ornament" a regrouping of factions of opinion was outlined.

The exhibition was set up in 1924 by the Württemberg section of the Werkbund and taken to many German cities. The theme of the exhibition made it possible for extremely diverse products to be shown side by side, since they had merely to fulfill the condition imposed by the theme, which was the rejection of all ornamentation. The most disparate objects were put on show: glass fireproof bulbs for laboratories, the austere relief engravings of Ferdinand Kramer, Bauhaus furniture influenced by De Stijl, wall lamps and hanging lamps of dubious pseudocubist taste, furnishings reflecting the lower middle class's classical leanings produced in the workshops of Swabia, a late-Expressionist majolica stove by Emanuel Joseph Margold, and several pleasingly rounded ceramic articles, some of which were of a turgid massiveness. However, the various products shown one beside the other revealed not the slightest affinity among themselves and indeed expressed their absolute incompatibility.

In the Werkbund's publication describing the results of this exhibition, attention was rightly drawn to the opposition between technical form and primitive form. At the basis of the rejection of ornamentation there were, in fact, contradictory attitudes, although these converged in the defense of a conventional historicism, which had not been superseded in any way. The designer of the "technoid" utensil saw ornamentation as an incoherent interference with the pregnant significance of form, which for him was the equivalent of a patent of objectivity, functionalism and economy. On the other hand, the artists who took primitive form as their model did not wish to have any extra ornamentation, since this appeared too "culinary" to them, and they feared it might take away the clear-cut rigor of their creations. Even respect for the properties of the material used, which was dominant in both these conceptions, started from completely different presuppositions. The defenders of the technical form acknowledged its legitimacy and subordinated themselves to it, since violence wreaked upon the material contravened the very ideal of a form that would be both logical and economical. Those who supported artisan simplicity took account of the peculiarities of the materials they used on various occasions, because they knew that only by taking account of the conditions imposed by the material could their work acquire the impression of vitality, naturalness

and organicity. But it is undeniable that this exhibition, where works diametrically opposed in both concept and execution were displayed, represented to most attentive observers the existence of two irreconcilable directions. "In the primitive form and in the pure form two different conceptions of life are opposed: on the one side intellectualism, on the other, vitality; on the one side technology, the machine, organization, on the other, the soul, the human being, the community; here, rationalism, reason and knowledge, there, sentiment, religion, mysticism; here, the will to power, there, universal love."[26]

In this new opposition, the former contrasted outlooks, which for many years had characterized the debates held within the bosom of the Werkbund, became outmoded; these debates were carried on between those who supported individualism in art and the economists, the politicians of the Realpolitik, the industrialists, who were working for the political and economic development of the country and increased exports. The new orientation of the Weimar Bauhaus was certainly the most spectacular symptom of the change that had occurred in the avant-garde. The change of direction brought about by the influence of Van Doesburg and Le Corbusier had begun as early as 1922; the seal was set upon it by the exhibition in Weimar held in August 1923, where the unity of art and technology was proclaimed. In the same period the Werkbund met in Weimar itself, so testifying to its own interest in the evolution of the Bauhaus and confirming its own active presence and sympathy with the existential crises of that institution. The progressives ranked themselves on the side of large-scale industry, since they saw in industrial production what might be termed the spirit of the time in action.

The spirit and the power. In comparison with other sectors of society, industry had stood up well to inflation. Loans that had been contracted for new investments had lost all their value, and during the period of inflation industry had found a way into the world market by dumping; the policy of dumping resulted in an allied situation in which inflation could be contained. Foreign currency that could be spent as a result of the ratification of the Dawes plan helped to consolidate the preeminent position of industry. Consequently, the role of crafts became limited: now crafts could serve to educate the public to develop their ability in sculpture and painting, while handwork — the individual article — could serve as a prototype as the designers had not become familiarized with the methods of industrialized production. But as an autonomous value, the crafts had lost their fascination to a noticeable degree. "Technology has now arrived; it is an extraordinary power; in a century it has transformed the world from its very foundations. It would be madness to imagine that the history of the

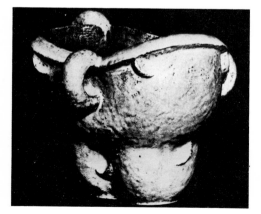

ORIGINAL BUDERUS KRAMEROFEN

world could ever annul this great achievement or that some new vision of life could supersede the work of technology."[27] In 1926 an industrialist was once again at the head of the Werkbund: the same Peter Bruckmann whose candidature had been firmly rejected in 1919.

The position that artists and critics adopted in favor of the aesthetics of the machine did not necessarily imply any political acceptance in relation to the ownership of wealth in a capitalist society but was rather a simple taking of position in favor of given conditions of production. The two stages of planning and execution had now become separated for all time. Design had to correspond to the needs of rationalized industry, and these very real demands were crystallized in the late twenties in a perfect "superstitious faith in rationalization."[28] Then the conditions posed by production were recovered in the aesthetic qualities of the products themselves, and the rational, "economic" model, in the sense that it was clearly reproducible, ennobled the compulsion that accompanied the birth of the products: "Lower costs, improved technique, improved form."[29] The precarious marriage between conservatives and progressives was dissolved in this tone; because, after the period of inflation came to an end and the phase of reconstruction was in progress, anyone who considered himself progressive could not fail to be present wherever large-scale mass production was being planned. Many of the members of the Werkbund disliked this change of direction, as can be seen from the arguments put forward by Poelzig and Walter Riezler in 1922. One cannot, of course, impute to Poelzig, one of the greatest architects of industrial building in the prewar years, a shortsighted aversion to mechanized labor. Yet he was convinced that productions that were of a purely technical character and resulted from practical needs alone had to be considered expendable without regret. In Poelzig's view, only objects created out of love and planned for eternity could claim to be thought beautiful. A significant change of positions was therefore taking place. This is confirmed by the fact that an opinion like the one held by Poelzig, which only a few years earlier would have passed for the herald of a new aesthetic vision, now came up against opposition. Riezler, for his part, was convinced that a technically "mature" and perfected form could not so easily be superseded by new modern forms developed later, because the content of its inner life, whatever it might be, cannot grow old insofar as it is form.[30] The supremacy of the artist over the engineer ceased to be acknowledged. If, therefore, the generation of artists of the first postwar years insisted on the affinities between the artist and the artisan, now in contrast the close bonds between art and technology were loosened.

For the artist this development meant that he had to redefine his own role and function in society. At the outside, the artist could even work for industry, since he thought himself to be more capable of "seeing the essence" and grasping the essential than were the engineer and designer who had always been engaged in the area of production. And he could also presume to know better than the others how to select the best solution from among many possibilities, since he had a surer instinct to guide him. But it was no longer possible to conceive of an object produced as the creation of a subjective artistic will and at the same time as a communal work born out of a fraternal collaboration. This development in the genesis of the product was a by-product of the new division of labor, where the individual contribution remained within the ambit of preestablished functions. The closest we can come to defining this type of cooperation is to think of a team: the community of manual and intellectual workers, supported by religious and cathartic sentiments, had now vanished.

Even the hoped-for synthesis now assumed a new character; no longer was it the total work of art that stood outlined against a far-off horizon — for architects, the "great construction," the new cathedral — but a kind of self-regulating system. If the tasks they undertook at that time had found a solution adapted to their essential substance, a harmonious equilibrium could have resulted. The older generation testified to this hope as much as the new. Indeed, Riemerschmid proposed "following things and materials, because (unlike men) they are incorruptible." Laszlo Moholy-Nagy, who was the new type of artist-engineer, postulated in place of total art "the total work," "in which each individual contribution would flow from biological necessity and emerge in a universal necessity."[31] In a period when functionalism had not yet lost its innocence, the faith in harmony and accord was dominant; this climate was created by the essential nature of things. Because designs created in conformity with the purposes, the material and the procedure of technology are logically linked by a current of sympathy, they are realized not as a result of an act of choice but out of necessities that are almost biological; the satisfaction of functions leads not to new conflicts but to universal harmony. In this interchange of decisions and solutions there resided the illusory nature of the newfound convictions. Their spokesmen permitted everyone to reject the old concept of style, understood as a unifying link between every act of formal creation, in the certainty that the new style would be more likely than any other style to be spontaneously engendered by the "essence": but what essence?

1. W. C. Behrend, "Zur Tagung des Deutschen Werkbundes," in Kunst und Künstler, year XVIII, no. 2 (1919), p. 90 ff.; P. F. Schmidt, "Werkbund-Krisis," in Cicerone, year XI (1919), p. 704 ff.; O. Bartning, Vom neuen Kirchbau (Berlin, 1919), p. 105.

2. Poelzig remained in charge for only a short time. At the annual meeting of 1922 Richard Riemerschmid was appointed first president of the association. Gropius resigned from the presidential body as early as 1921 as a result of the controversy that arose after the Munich exhibition, but the interest of the opposition in the formal apparatus of the institution had practically evaporated.

3. Cf. Gropius to A. Behne, Sept. 16, 1919, quoted from K. H. Hüter, Das Bauhaus in Weimar (Berlin, 1976), p. 212.

4. Cf., for example, W. Gropius, "Sind beim Bau von Industrie — gebäuden künstlerische Gesichtspunkte mit praktischen und wirtschftlichen vereinbar," in Der Industriebau, year III, no. 1 (1912), p. 5 ff. "All industry today is obliged to face artistic questions seriously so as to be able to give an answer to the demands posed by world competition."

5. W. Gropius to K. E. Osthaus, Aug. 3, 1919 and Aug. 20, 1919; K. E. Osthaus to W. Gropius, Aug. 25, 1919, K. E. Osthaus Archives, Hagen; H. Poelzig to W. Gropius, July 8, 1919 and Aug. 28, 1919, Marlene Poelzig Archives, Hamburg.

6. H. Poelzig, "Werkbundaufgaben," in Mitteilungen des Deutschen Werkbundes, year II, no. 4 (1919), p. 109 ff.

7. P. Bruckmann to the Deutsches Museum für Kunst in Handel und Gewerbe, Sept. 24, 1919, quoted by S. Müller, "Deutsches Museum für Kunst in Handel und Gewerbe," in Karl Ernst Osthaus, Leben und Werk (Recklinghausen, 1971), p. 334. Bosch's statement relates to an idea expressed by Poelzig, who, however, was not speaking of industry in general but of the "industry of art" and of "industrialism."

8. H. Tessenow, "Handwerk und Kleinstadt," in Das hohe Ufer, year I, no. 2 (1919), p. 37 ff.

9. A. Behne, Die Wiederkehr der Kunst (Leipzig, 1919), p. 101 ff.; W. Gropius, "Baukunst im freien Volksstaat," in E. Drahn and E. Friedegg, eds., Deutscher Revolutions-Almanach für das Jahr 1919, p. 134.

10. F. Naumann, Der deutsche Stil, undated [1912], p. 21 ff.

11. K. E. Osthaus, "Die Folkwang-Schule, ein Entwurf von Bruno Taut," in Genius, year II (1920), p. 199.

12. K. Scheffler, Sittliche Diktatur (Stuttgart and Berlin, 1920), p. 14.

13. W. Gropius, " 'Sparsamer Hausrat' und falsche Dürftigkeit," in Das hohe Ufer, year I, no. 7 (1919), p. 180. Gropius's attack on the "shoddy surrogate merchandise" in the simplified furnishings for workers' houses was directed also against certain initiatives of the Werkbund itself, such as the "Einfacher Hausrat" exhibition organized a short time earlier by Bruno Taut and Paul Kurz in the Berlin Kunstgewerbemuseum.

14. Behne, op. cit., p. 102; B. Taut, "Beobachtungen über Farbenwirkung aus meiner Praxis," in Die Bauwelt, year X.

15. Taut, op. cit., p. 12; Gropius, op. cit., p. 180; Behne, op. cit., p. 102.

16. Minutes of the meeting of the presidential council, quoted from Karl Ernst Osthaus, Leben und Werk, op. cit., p. 506.

17. W. Ostwald, in Die neunte Mitgliederversammlung: Mitteilungen des Deutschen Werkbundes, year II, no. 4 (1919), p. 131.

18. Otto Bartning, "Vorschläge zu einem Lehrplan für Handwerker, Architekten und bildende Künstler," in Mitteilungen des Deutschen Werkbundes, year II, no. 2 (1919), p. 42.

19. R. Riemerschmid, "Künstlerische Erziehungsfragen I," Flugschriften des Münchener Bundes 1 (Munich, 1917).

20. Gropius spoke to the regional parliament of Thuringia about Bartning's plan for the reform of the schools of arts and crafts. Bartning, for his part, described the Bauhaus as "a practical experiment to carry out quite a large part of this plan" (op. cit., p. 43).

21. Bartning, "Vorschläge zu einem Lehrplan," pp. 42, 44; Walter Gropius, Programm des Staatlichen Bauhauses in Weimar (Weimar, 1919).

22. H. Poelzig to W. Gropius, July 8, 1919, Marlene Poelzig Archives, Hamburg.

23. R. Riemerschmid in his speech "Von deutscher Kunst," Stuttgart, Sept. 6, 1919, in Mitteilungen des Deutschen Werkbundes, year II, no. 4 (1919).

24. Hans Poelzig to Walter Gropius, July 8, 1919, Marlene Poelzig Archives, Hamburg.

25. Scheffler, op. cit., p. 17.

26. W. Pfleiderer, in Die Form ohne Ornament, Werkbundausstellung 1924 (Stuttgart, 1924), p. 7 ff.

27. Ibid., p. 14.

28. H. Mottek, W. Becker, and A. Schröter, Wirtschaftsgeschichte Deutschlands, vol. 3 (Berlin, 1974), p. 267.

29. W. Gropius to the building contractor Westrum, Nov. 27, 1922, quoted from Hüter, op. cit.

30. H. Poelzig, "Vom Bauen unserer Zeit," in Die Form, no. 1 (1922); W. Riezler, "Über das Verhalten technischer Formen," in Die Form, no. 2 (1922), quoted from Zwischen Kunst und Industrie, Der Deutsche Werkbund, catalog of the exhibition "Die Neue Sammlung" (Munich, 1975), p. 190 ff. and p. 192 ff.

31. R. Riemerschmid, "Zur Frage des Zeitstils," in Die Form, no. 1 (1922), quoted from Zwischen Kunst und Industrie, op. cit., p. 189; L. Moholy-Nagy, "Malerei, Fotografie, Film," Bauhausbücher, 18 (Munich, 1927), quoted from Hüter, op. cit., p. 83.

FINDING THE NORM AND STANDARD, CONSTRUCTING FOR THE EXISTENZMINIMUM — THE WERKBUND AND NEW TASKS IN THE SOCIAL STATE

Hans Eckstein

The founders of the Deutscher Werkbund included some men who were also architects and designers of the Jugendstil (Behrens, Olbrich, Riemerschmid, van de Velde), and it was not without reason that van de Velde wrote in his memoirs that his school of applied arts in Weimar (where artist-craftsmen designed models for industry) was "the root and early bud" of the Werkbund idea. In spite of this, the Werkbund grew into a movement that was the exact opposite of the Jugendstil. And this could not have been otherwise, since the two movements had entirely contradictory objectives. For the Werkbund, apart from purely and simply imbuing the house and objects with aesthetic qualities, as desired by an elite of wealthy patrons with good taste — following a tendency that became characteristic of the entire movement as it attempted to reform the applied arts toward the end of the century — it was desired to imprint a human appearance on everyday reality from which no social class would be excluded. As early as 1903, or four years before the founding of the Werkbund, Muthesius had written: "The salvation and hope for the future is to supersede 'art' in the conceptual connection of art-and-crafts and achieve dignified industrial realizations." And he added, addressing his criticism to the Jugendstil especially: "We do not need sentimental furniture or a luxurious art for the rich, but decent utensils for the common man."

The change of direction toward the social tasks imposed by the times was accomplished by the Werkbund during the twenties. In the great Cologne exhibition of 1914 the industrial art product was the uncontested focus of interest, and the artists of the Jugendstil under the leadership of van de Velde protested with surprising vehemence against Muthesius and his objective of replacing the "extraordinary" by the "ordinary." Indeed, for Muthesius the promotion of the ordinary forms represented the pressing task of the Werkbund, and he saw in the creation of an apparatus of typical forms the necessary condition for every culture of the product of industry and architecture. But artists believed they had to defend and safeguard their right to free artistic expression, a right they feared that Muthesius wished to deny them. In the final analysis this ideological controversy was simply the sign of the situation of conflict existing between an individualistic approach to form and an attitude of concern for social tasks, subservient to the demands of an industry that was mechanized and was therefore reluctant to accept any kind of artistic coercion.

If the Werkbund survived the second decade of its existence, then it owes its survival to the fact that, among the militant forces it numbered in its ranks, those that were victorious had stayed at a distance from both the conservative, retrospective ideals and the attraction of any kind of aggressive modernism, as generally expressed in an extravagant decorative style or, in the architectural sphere, in what Adolf Behne called "the architecture of advertising." In addition, the misery of the postwar situation itself proved more stimulating to architecture and design than any aesthetic ideology. For the Werkbund, the form of the house and the everyday object was, of course, always important — and still is; however, in this case the form was not "invented" but "found," integrated with life and "drawn from the essence of the task, although molded with the means of our times" (Mies van der Rohe, 1923). The most urgent task of the postwar years, that of building homes for people, transformed the Werkbund into a militant movement, a movement struggling for a functional architecture and a form that would be responsive to the industrial product, a "form without ornament." Looking back over the twenties today, we can say that the Werkbund has survived its trial of strength — triumphing over resistance from within as well as without.

A minimal home or no home at all: in the immediate postwar years there was no alternative. At that time to build meant to erect houses that could be let at low rents that the poorest sections of the community could afford. If people did not want to erect slums, with all their notorious deficiencies and their biological and human shortcomings, it was necessary to take a new direction and abandon traditional methods of constructing as well as traditional living habits. The area of habitable space was reduced to 40–50 square meters for family units with 3–4 children, or to even smaller areas for childless couples or single persons. This could be done only by satisfying a number of preliminary conditions: on the one hand, the rationalization of the ground plan and the concentration of the practical basic functions so as to allow for the largest possible family living room and, on the other hand, the design of furniture that was functional in relation to the use to which it would be put and the amount of space available. In addition, it was indispensable that an attempt should be made to reduce building costs by using appropriate new methods (the creation of norms, the standardization of the individual elements, and the rationalization of their assembly).

All countries, including even those that had remained neutral during the First War, found themselves faced with identical problems. The same difficulties existed everywhere; they had to abandon traditional methods and introduce technology into their building methods, so as to reduce the costs of building and to save time. The same resistance had to be overcome everywhere, resistance to the new forms of a type of building that renewed its own systems in order to open up the homes to light and air. Therefore, great courage was needed everywhere, the courage to experiment without departing from the primary object, which was to construct homes that in spite of their limitations of space would be perfect consumer objects capable of satisfying all practical as well as psychic demands.

It was only exceptionally that the Werkbund itself promoted and organized the construction of residential settlements: at Stuttgart in 1927 with the famous Weissenhof Siedlung, in Breslau in 1929 with 103 minimal dwellings and 29 larger dwellings for the Werkbund exhibition "Wohnung und Werkraum" (dwelling and place of work), and in 1932 with the Vienna Siedlung and the larger Siedlung in Neubühl on the outskirts of Zurich. But the Werkbund patronizes many building works and participated directly in their planning and design. However, the design stage was often seized upon by prominent architects, who were leading members of the Werkbund: Martin Wagner and Bruno Taut — Britz Siedlung; Max Taut, Hugo Häring, Mies van der Rohe, Salvisberg and others — other Siedlungen in Berlin; and Gropius — the Törten Siedlung near Dessau constructed mainly by prefabrication.

An adoptive child of the Werkbund was without doubt the big housing project in Frankfurt am Main, the industrial heart of Central Germany. More than in any other German city, in Frankfurt between 1924, the year of monetary reform that determined the strongest upsurge of building in the postwar period, and 1931, the year of the great economic crisis, a team of town planners and architects who followed the ideology of the Werkbund carried out a vast home building program. This was not limited to the planning of residential complexes and individual homes but extended as far as the details of the internal furnishings. The team worked under the direction of Ernst May, who at the time was director of the communal technical studio responsible for house building as well as president of the two largest building concerns of the city; this was one of those rare coincidences that proved historically fertile, since it permitted the necessary systemization of the planning of decentralized residential settlements. The preferred system was that of terrace houses set back from the road; with their green border in front and their garden plot at the rear, these houses conferred on these peripheral Siedlungen the character of garden cities. Buildings of medium height extending over four stories were not excluded; some large blocks were also built, with covered passages. However, the low two-story structure was preferred for reasons explained by May as follows: "The ideal form, just because it is

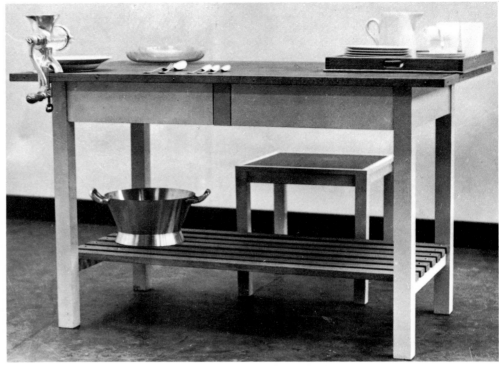

115. Ferdinand Kramer, stove, 1923.

116. Ferdinand Kramer, saucepan, 1924.

117. Ferdinand Kramer, kitchen table, 1925.

118. Ferdinand Kramer, dining room for Oud House, 1927.

119. J. J. P. Oud, terraced houses on the Weissenhofsiedlung, Stuttgart, 1927.

120. L. Mies van der Rohe, block of flats in the Stuttgart Weissenhofsiedlung, 1927.

121. Lilly Reich, one-room flat in the Boarding Haus, Berlin, 1931.

the most natural, is the one-family house arranged on two floors. It assures for the family the peace and domestic privacy that assume particular importance at a time when there is a strong tendency toward collectivism. This is the only form of dwelling that makes it possible for every room to be closely linked with a plot of land, though it might be small, kept as a garden; this means that the living space in the interior of the home is enlarged and integrated with further living space — the living space of the garden. The home that is part of a condominium of several stories will never be able to compensate, for the family and the children especially, for the healthy living conditions that can be offered by the one-family house." Together with the residential homes, collective services were designed and provided: heating plants for central heating (whereas the first homes were still heated by stoves), laundries, shops, communal garages, nurseries, playing fields, schools, old people's homes, community centers, and so on. For these structures, especially in the case of schools, a new style of building was invented in Frankfurt, which remained an example for many years to come.

Seen in this context, the rigorous standardization of the average home, that is, the development of various types of construction adapted to the needs of the home, corresponds to a very obvious and natural process. It always was the case that the needs of daily life, where they were fundamentally the same everywhere, had an influence upon the actual type of dwelling, its furnishings and even its household utensils. At all times the culture of the home, the rooms and household objects, found its natural basis in standardization. Because they condition each other reciprocally, types and norms are necessary both to mass production by craft methods (a process that has always existed) and to industrial production by means of machinery. For this reason one cannot understand how it happened that the word *standardization* could have created such a violent controversy during the Werkbund congress in Cologne and why this caused van de Velde to renege on his profession of faith in socialism, to which he had been converted in 1894. Then he said, "What turns to the advantage of the individual alone is useless in itself; in the society of the future only what will be of general use will be taken into consideration." Now, thirty years later, this maxim of his had become the slogan on which the work of the Werkbund rested, and the good types of housing that were put up in so many places in this same spirit, in spite of much opposition, testify to the force of his idea. In every town, traditional building, which still resorted to artisan methods, put up strong resistance to the technicalization of the productive process. In Frankfurt, however, this resistance was particularly

radical and often bordered on the grotesque.

A well-designed ground plan and the creation of empty homes was something, but not yet enough. It was necessary to offer the residents designs that could facilitate the work of the household in homes that had to be calculated on the maximum saving of space. This need gave rise to the "Frankfurt kitchen," the prototype of built-in kitchens, which later became very widespread. This minimal kitchen measured less than 6 square meters in area, with built-in cupboards, ironing boards folding back into the wall, and an adjustable light running along a rail inserted into the ceiling. The kitchen was designed by Mrs. Schuette-Lihotzky, with the advice of other housewives. Perfectly appropriate in the context of this type of dwelling is the other design that produced the "decent domestic utensil for the common man," envisaged by Muthesius more than twenty years previously, when he had struggled against the artist-cabinetmakers. A system of superimposed containers was designed by Franz Schuster. The other architect who worked at the Frankfurt Hochbauamt, Ferdinand Kramer, designed a whole series of useful and space-saving articles, from the cooking pot and the small iron stove to stools, seats, folding tables, desks and cupboards. The works of Schuster and Kramer for the interiors of small and minimal homes in Frankfurt are among the first examples of a design that was already functional in tendency and was adapted to the conditions of industrial mass production; however, just because it was created at a time when it could not yet be a simple advertising factor for industry, it satisfied aesthetic and practical needs at one and the same time.

A society in which there was communal participation enabled people to buy the entire furnishings on particularly favorable terms of payment. In addition, completely furnished model flats could be visited in every new Siedlung. Therefore, what was achieved at Frankfurt was a complete program of the Werkbund — and in other cities too, although to a less complete extent — although the Werkbund itself was not responsible for financing the scheme in this case.

In 1927 the "house" problem was tackled again by the Werkbund in a personal initiative: the construction of the Siedlung on the Stuttgart Weissenhof. The plan was entrusted to Mies van der Rohe. Unlike other residential complexes that were erected in other cities under the more or less direct patronage of the Werkbund, the Stuttgart Siedlung was markedly experimental in character. It arose indeed as an international exhibition of ground plans and models of the new architecture. Sixteen architects from five European countries showed how it was possible to reduce costs and labor in

running the family and the home by introducing rationalization into the constructive process, using modern materials and technical plants. But they were not concerned exclusively with the material improvement of the home. Behind such materialistic-sounding slogans as rationalization, standardization, objectivity and the formula of the *machine à habiter* used by Le Corbusier was to be found a new sense of life, a desire for humanity and a broader vision, which is too often overlooked by those who follow today's fashion and criticize the functionalism of the twenties. The Weissenhof and the exhibition connected with it, entitled "Living," were intended to show how the modern rational and technical world could be brought into the most intimate area of life, which is and always has been the home, without, on the one hand, its furnishings being denied their technical nature and without, on the other, a rejection of aesthetic values by "form without ornament" (the title of the exhibition organized by the Werkbund in 1924), which was the form most appropriate to industrial production. The official catalog states: "The problem of rationalization and standardization is partial. The problem of the new home is essentially a spiritual problem, and the battle for the new home is only a link in the great struggle for new forms of life." The "machine for living," according to Le Corbusier, "could not be set in motion unless it received spiritual nourishment."

The Weissenhof houses advertised the merits of "liberated living." They wanted to show in what sense the home is not a decorative or a representative object but a human one, and the more it is perfect the more it is human; in other words, it is an object of daily use that satisfies practical needs as well as aesthetic and psychic needs. The furnishing of these homes was not a rejection of art, but a rejection of "L'art décoratif," which led industry to produce furniture and utensils of pleasing appearance. In this connection the Werkbund was in agreement with Auguste Perret, who said in 1925, as Muthesius before him in 1903: "I should like to know who thought of connecting art and decoration to one another. It is a contamination. True art has no need of decoration."

The Weissenhof was a manifesto of functionalism. With this Siedlung and the associated exhibition the Werkbund paved the way to new developments. To introduce these new developments by way of an exhibition with that title was a possibility denied to the Werkbund, because, as Theodor Heuss said in 1958 when he looked back over that period, "the efforts undertaken with imaginative inquiry and critical precision were brought to nought on the day the 'new era' passed through the streets of Germany, beating out the rhythm of an anachronistic military music."

THE DEUTSCHER WERKBUND FROM 1907 TO 1933 AND THE MOVEMENTS FOR THE "REFORM OF LIFE AND CULTURE"
Joachim Petsch

From an examination of the interrelationships that grew up between the Deutscher Werkbund and the numerous movements inspired by the "reform of life and culture," and from a study of the relative journals in which these views were published in the period between 1907 and 1933, there emerges the possibility of analyzing this broad panorama in detail. It represents the most important reformist phenomena that could be observed against the background of economic and social restructuring for which it was partly responsible at the time of the Kaiser's Germany.[1] This is partly because such movements — before 1914, therefore in contrast to the "cultural battle" of the Weimar Republic — present no elements of conflict but can be seen instead as a succession of similar stages in a development that was basically homogeneous. The focus of this present contribution is therefore concentrated on the historical substratum, instead of on a criticism of the programmatic lines of the Werkbund and other reforming groups.

The Kaiser's Germany is characterized by the second phase of the process of industrialization, the stage when monopolies came into being (the end of free competition) inside the largest economic groups — for example, the groups of heavy industry, metallurgy, chemicals and electro-technology — and when there was a tendency toward both mechanized industrial production and an enforced rationalization in vast sectors of these branches; and where, as a result of these tendencies, there was also present a notable increase of industry in relation to artisan production, while the related phenomenon of urbanization grew more and more acute. In comparison with the branches of industry just mentioned, the building sector seems far behind:[2] it is only now that the move toward the manufacturing stage and the mechanization of production is taking place. But the development of the relationships of production and even the objective situation of the productive forces, with its consequent embittering of the class struggle, represent a threat mainly to the pre-capitalist strata, who see their economic position compromised and so, too, their social position — by the progressive disintegration of relationships of production among the lower middle class and the poorer peasant class, and by proletarization. To be included among the category of the middle-class sectors of the population concerned in this process are small businessmen and craftsmen, civil servants in the middle and lower grades, teachers, artists, and peasants, to whom must be added the new category of employees of industry at the lower and middle levels.[3] A middle class composed of these elements is now beginning, moreover, to see its own cultural tradition under threat. This crisis of identity brought about by industrialization led to considerable modifications in the consciousness of these classes and was at the same time the source of the multiple movements directed toward the reform of society, life, education and culture, at the end of the nineteenth and beginning of the twentieth centuries.

The Program of the Deutscher Werkbund
Without underestimating the traditional tendencies present in the Deutscher Werkbund, which will be described fully in the part dealing with the interrelations between the Werkbund and other reforming initiatives, it must be said that among the movements operating in the years before the First War this was the group the majority of whose members most clearly understood the laws already imposed by the system of modern capitalist-industrial production. And the reason these laws were understood was that the association had already realized that artisan means of production would not suffice to meet the needs of the masses; it therefore set itself to solve the contradiction that had opened up between the stage attained by the forces of production and the stylistic mode wherein art was unfolded, to develop a typology of artistic forms that would be appropriate also — and, indeed, especially — to the mass product itself. The majority of the members of the Werkbund (among them F. Naumann) supported the liberal view of public control, where a predominant role was assigned to the development of industry and technology by singling out a basic factor for the advancement of society and its culture. Compared with other reforming forces — where the vocabulary employed and the formal imagery were often identical ("conformity with the material, construction and function," "objective architecture") — the essential difference lies in the acceptance of the productive process, which the Werkbund wanted to see industrialized. By this means, and especially through the adoption of typology and standardization, it hoped to achieve its objective, which was to change the practice of industrialized artistic production ("the ennobling of industrial labor"). In actual fact, the industrialization of the building sector acquired greater significance only after the mid-twenties, although from the very first everyone was absolutely clear about the need to transform the professional methods employed and even the basis of an architectural qualification. Neither the Werkbund's desire to bring about reforms nor the similar intentions of other groups can be detached from nationalistic and imperialistic aims. In fact, in the view of the Werkbund there was only one explanation for the economic and political supremacy of England: it was the product of the cooperation between the artistic and the industrial intelligentsia. Consequently, the "ennobling of industrial labor," within general cultural work, should lead to a national, that is, German, art and produce German quality goods that would be competitive in relation to foreign products. By encouraging and increasing exports, it was hoped to achieve and assure for Germany a supremacy that would be at one and the same time economic, political and cultural.

Movements for the Reform of Life
Even though in the architectural scene the movements for the "reform of life" were less important than those that set themselves to redefine culture, nevertheless, I believe it would be appropriate to devote a few words to the first ones, because, on the one hand, it seems to me that certain fundamental ideological motives and recurrent images conditioned the consciousness of the middle class — especially the cultured bourgeoisie — not only in the years before the First War but also, and especially, during the Weimar Republic, and, on the other hand, they found a welcome, though a partial one, in the Deutscher Werkbund itself. The figures of reformers who appeared on the German scene after the end of the last century with their ideas and their publications — physiocrats, reformers of diet, vegetarians, naturists, and adherents of the movement for the construction of Siedlungen[4] — all had one thing in common: they all rejected the large city, the urban-industrial civilization, in favor of a return to nature, to rural life and crafts, and at the same time they wished to "change the world by means of an individual reform of life." Their reflections did not touch upon state structures, and the family, with its internal authoritarian structure, assumed a central position. Indeed, the family represented the bridge leading to that model of society that thought itself composed of various social groups. Because social Darwinism and anti-Semitism had left a bitter heritage, these were thoughts that were particularly widespread among the reformers. There was no way to stop the process of destroying the landscape by the expanding capitalist industrialization, and the consequent discovery of the *Heimat*, the fatherland or native land with its heritage of traditions and culture, linked these reformers to the Heimatschutzbund. The ecological problem had been understood in its full significance. The reformers followed lines of thought that were already fixed: the hoped-for creation of a new national basis had to come about through a national renewal — and a racial renewal — in the Nordic Aryan man — and this renewal would lead to a bond of unity among all social classes; obviously, no value was assigned to the transformation of the economic order. The essential element inherent in this unity was seen in a new German art, which was to arise as a product of the racial renewal. The concepts employed of "people" and "nation" denied class differences, and, because of the importance soon invested in the German spirit, in the creative force of the Germanic race, no time was lost in imbuing this same race with a "redemptive mission" (pan-Germanism). For identical

122. *A Briebricher, workers' house, ca. 1912, Krefeld-Linn.*

123. *Krupp's Building department, Emscher-Lippe settlement, 1907, Recklinghausen.*

124. *A. Gessner, model of middle-class renting house, ca. 1909, Berlin.*

125. *R. Riemerschmid, Deutsche Werkstätten, 1909, Hellerau near Dresden.*

126. *Paul Bonatz, Henkell Wine Cellars 1907–9 (example of traditional architecture), Wiesbaden.*

127. *O. R. Salvisberg, country house, 1928, Falkenstein, i.V.*

128. *C. Holzmeister, hall for celebrations, 1926 (example of traditional architecture), Salzburg.*

racist motivations, the nationalist groups and circles also rejected Christianity, as being "non-German," and turned to a popular religiosity of Nordic derivation. The rural population was accorded particular importance, since it was considered the "personification of the active Nordic man and the Aryan personality": the peasants represented the backbone of nationalist thought and revival and exemplified the "vital source" of the German people and the Nordic race. For the purpose of diffusing nationalist ideas, schools were given a highly important function, especially the elementary schools: it was expected that a common cultural heritage would "forge" a united nation.

In the twenties the idea of "colonization as a means for the reform of life" had been the basis for the programs of agrarian reform instigated by R. W. Darré and G. Feder. It was meant, too, to lead to the reorganization of the national body ("popular community"): the land would obviously be taken into public ownership and its use shared in common. At the same time, ideas that were antidemocratic (cult of the Führer), antiurban, antiindustrial, anti-Semitic (the difference between passive and active capital) and anticapitalistic (rejection of land speculation and the ideology of profit) were later expounded in the theories of the Kampfbund für die deutsche Kultur (league for German culture).

Movements for the Reform of Culture
The Kunstwart

Compared with the Deutscher Werkbund and for the purposes of the reform of architecture, the first years of the twentieth century saw greater importance devolve to the movements for the reform of culture that came into being as proliferations of the journal *Kunstwart* (a strongly nationalistic and conservative publishing group): the Dürerbund (founded in 1901),[5] the league for the protection of the national heritage (founded in 1904) and — although with some reservations — the German garden-city association (founded in 1902). The *Kunstwart*, founded by Ferdinand Avenarius in 1887,[6] counted among its collaborators men who later became members of the Werkbund: Peter Behrens, German Bestelmeyer, Theodor Fischer, Fritz Schumacher, Heinrich Tessenow and Paul Schultze-Naumburg. The latter acted as an expert in the figurative arts, architecture and applied arts; later, a series of essays published in *Kunstwart* led to the "Kulturarbeiten" of Schultze-Naumburg.[7] But I will confine myself to summing up briefly the aims of the movement linked to the *Kunstwart*, since I would rather go into greater detail when describing the league for the defense of the national heritage, which was its direct continuation.

As was the case with other groups of reformers, the Kunstwart rejected the traditional art of the second half of the nineteenth century, born — as was then said — out of a "desire for enrichment," and turned to the defense of a new national German art. It consequently condemned any kind of flirtation with

England, any kind of attachment to foreign cultures[8] or tolerance of foreign influences. The flat roof, for example, was described as "non-German." A psychological explanation was offered for any art manifestations characterized as "degenerate," because of their decadent features or their rejection of form, or else reasons were sought in the psychic deviations of the term *artist;* this procedure was later returned to in the "cultural battle" of the Weimar Republic and crystallized finally in the exhibition of degenerate art ("Entartete Kunst") of 1937.

When Adolf Bartels joined the journal as literary adviser, greater weight was given to artistic conceptions that were clearly nationalistic rather than national to an extent, with the result that there developed side by side an art associated with race and an art of the tribe. In particular, Bartels identified the peasant class as "the natural source of strength of the people and the state." Therefore, although Schultze-Naumburg collaborated with the Kunstwart at that time and spoke in favor of a "healthy, self-sufficient" architecture, "linked to landscape and place" — which he recognized in the lower middle-class architecture of the first half of the nineteenth century — there were also active inside the movement people who thought very differently: some described "Die Kunst um 1800" (art around 1800) as mostly bourgeois neoclassicism. Unlike Schultze-Naumburg, these men did not go so far as to reject out of hand the use of new materials (iron) and recent methods of production. The desire to create a "German objectivity," to make the industrial product fit into the countryside and the landscape, was met with a positive response in the industrial complex at Dresden-Hellerau.

Any anticapitalist leanings did not indicate that the Kunstwart questioned the bourgeois economic system: the principle of free competition was accepted as a completely natural criterion. On the other hand, the "capitalist spirit" was rejected, because, as it was guided by the profit motive, it placed individual interests before the good of the community. The intellectuals and experts were acknowledged as serving a hegemonic function (which took concrete form in the creation of "cultural" parliaments) and this, together with the efforts made in the fields of education and pedagogy (the stimulation of the individual in relation to his personal natural gifts), was expected to result in social peace, or the peaceful coexistence of all classes, as well as a rise in the level of national culture, which everyone hoped would gain a position of world supremacy. However, pan-Germanism was found unacceptable.

During the war, the Kunstwart became a supporter of *state planning* and a national socialism controlled from above, which was viewed as a dictatorship of the best brains, accepting the existing economic and social order. Since it was a widespread belief that the state's task was to assure the well-being of all its citizens, sociopoliti-

cal initiatives were supported that benefited the workers (an increase in building for the working class, among other things), and, in addition, the large land estates were to be split up in order to favor the rise of a vast peasant society.

The Heimatschutz Movement

During the nineties the movement for popular art and for the preservation of the heritage of regional cultural traditions began to take shape. This movement arose as a reaction to the spread of industrialization and was not confined to Germany but extended into other parts of Europe as well. In Germany, this movement tended — by joining the national and local traditions and the rural or semi-rural way of life ("home" as synonymous with "rural home") of the early 19th century — to form a new local adhesion for the inhabitant of the big cities, and it aspired to a new culmination of the bourgeois culture by the revival of handicraft.

The concept of "Heimatkunst" was thought of by Ernst Rudorff in 1897. The Bund für Heimatschutz, born out of the ashes of the Kunstwart (or a direct proliferation of it), was founded in 1904 by the same Rudorff and by P. Schultze-Naumburg. It contained many local and regional sections, whereas the Heimatbund was an organization to which many associations and societies with different functions and aims belonged. By publicizing its activities very widely — its principal outlets were *Heimatschutz* and *Heimat*[9] — the Heimatschutz movement acquired in a short time a vast sphere of influence over the German middle class and its organizations (such as the Geschichtsverein, the Altertumsverein, and the Wandervogel and Freideutsche Jugend movements). The need to use self-sufficient building systems and local materials had already been felt and supported for a long time by agrarian associations — among others, the Bund der Landwirte (the league of agriculturists) — and had been publicized in the relative professional publications (such as *Das Land*). All these organizations had as their starting point the rejection of the large town, which they described as "non-German," and in leaflets or specialized architectural journals, journals devoted to crafts, to the supervision of monuments and the Dürerbund, they expressed support for the Heimatschutz.[10] The idea behind this movement exercised a great influence on the woodwork departments in the schools of arts and crafts and also on the bureaucracy of the communal technical offices. Indeed, the body of legislation controlling the preservation of the heritage of art and landscape that emerged in those years — for example, the Prussian law of 1902 against the pollution of areas of particular beauty or interest, or the law of 1907 against the deformation of the landscape and village — would be unthinkable if it had not been for the initiatives instituted at that time by men who adhered to the Heimatschutz movement. The rediscovery of national peasant systems and forms

of construction, and, most of all, forms belonging to the local traditions, resulted in two clearly distinguishable stylistic currents: a North German current, specializing in the use of tiles, a wooden structure and a roof with two gables; and a southern structure emphasizing the "sentimental bond with the land," where whitewash and quarried stone were preferred and roofs were overhanging and slate-covered. In the most impressive works there was no lack of quotations from the lexicon of the feudal tradition: the pediment and column. The intention of stressing artisan features, however, cannot be separated from the objective that was then given priority: that of renewing art and architecture in a national and popular sense, giving expression to the historical peculiarities of the locality.

It was not long before national elements in the Heimatschutz embraced anti-Semitic and nationalistic-racist elements. The need for indigenous systems of construction and for local materials in an architecture bound to the soil and landscape found an explanation in the profound sentiment for the nature of the Germanic race and the character of the Nordic tribe. It followed that all non-Aryan elements that were not part of the German race and land were rejected;[11] this rejection covered even the use of foreign materials such as bituminous hardboard for the roof or cement tiles, as well as such nonindigenous forms as the flat roof.[12] Preference was therefore given to the architecture of the period around 1800, "Die Kunst um 1800," which seemed to express the intimate connection between art and race, that irreplaceable bond that seemed likely to become lost in the contemporary "modernism." From the return "to the countryside, to nature," (countryside and nature were synonyms for *Heimat*, local fatherland) the granting of a great hope was expected: that of healing society and creating a "life of social harmony," that harmony that seemed to be put at risk by the large city and the proletarian egalitarianism dominant in it, but also by the logic of profit, which was inherent in capitalism (the Jews). Heimatschutz, the preservation of the rural and peasant fatherland, combined with the preservation of ethnic traditions, was to lead to the equally strong desire to clean and consolidate bourgeois society.

Yet in spite of this, the Bund für Heimatschutz was able to describe with impressive clarity the symptoms and problems of capitalist society — the destruction of the historic images of the town and the original forms of the landscape — and at the same time it rediscovered the peculiarities of the regional styles of architecture. However, the men of the Heimatschutz did not expect that the hoped-for improvement in the practice of architecture and town planning would come from a profound transformation of the existing economic and social system, but, as we have seen, they put their efforts toward a recovery of the "healthy tradition," which

they knew also that they had to continue. For these men, tradition meant provincial and local architecture, as it had existed around 1800 in a precapitalist social structure and in a corporative society.[13] Recourse to tradition would, they hoped, lead to an aesthetic solution of economic and social problems. They therefore firmly rejected the large city, monopolistic capitalism, industrial production and the class struggle between, on the one hand, the proletariat, and, on the other, the academies with their predilection for "classical styles" and "rigid axial schemes."[14]

The great success that came to the movement is explained by the bourgeois origin of the Heimatschutz; it never questioned the traditional way of life of the middle class and posed no threat to its need for tradition and continuity, as did the process of capitalist industrialization.

The Movement for the Reform of the Land and for the Garden City

The so-called movement for the reform of the land and for the garden city undoubtedly formed a part of the mosaic of movements devoted to the "reform of society and life" that grew up after the 1880s. However, this movement was so important that it must be considered separately. The Bund deutscher Bodenreformer (founded in 1898, president A. Damaschke) opposed the practice of urban land development and speculation in metropolitan building zones, since it upheld the principle that such zones should be put to collective use, but it never interfered with private property. Indeed it was the individual ownership of the land that represented the essential condition of freedom and independence and the guarantee for the creative expression of the personality. And these supporters of land reform even came to hope that by extending as much as possible the parceling of landed property the result would be that people who lived in large cities would come to feel they had "roots" in the soil and this would mean that differences of class would be submerged. Like other reforming movements, the Bund deutscher Bodenreformer also rejected large towns and, in particular, the type of apartment house that had developed in the great metropolitan areas, because only home ownership could guarantee the contact with "clods of earth" that was needed. In addition, because this contact could not be achieved when homes were rented, the need was felt to transform the one-family house into a "common good." In the preference for indigenous forms of construction and architecture, in the rejection of the rootless metropolis (the enemy of nature) and in the desire to "return to the land" we see a similarity of views between the Bodenreformer and the Heimatschützer groups. In the former, however, the view of society and art was clearly and more radically nationalistic and racist: the "devastation of the fatherland image" and the destruction of the healthy life of the populace being caused by the destruction of the hereditary patrimony (becoming remote from the Nordic race) and by the "casting out" from Mother Earth, the "original soil of the life of the race." Only by a rehealing of the blood and soil could the race be reinvigorated, and in this sense — following the idea of a corporate society — the employer would have to take care of his own "apprentices."[15] A radical no was said to both capitalism ("seduction of the German soul") and Communism — to Communism because it was reproached for looking for "salvation from the masses" instead of from the *charismatic* leader." The simple architecture of the early years of the nineteenth century represented an exemplary model of popular art to the land reformers as well. The movement for the reform of the land exercised a considerable influence over the movement that grew up during the course of the First War, known as the movement for the home. The "biological" conception of the history of art — where art = history of the race — was initiated and advanced in the twenties by Schultze-Naumburg.

E. Howard, in his conception of a garden city, aimed to provide for an equitable distribution of the goods produced collectively, by means of promoting cooperative associations (in other words, establishing the principle of the social use of the means of production). The Deutsche Gartenstadtgesellschaft, on the other hand, whose principal theoretician was T. Fritsch,[16] in spite of its anticapitalist stance (among other things it rejected land speculation) expounded views that were decidedly racist in character. This group brought no radical change to the existing social structure, as can be seen from their plans for the layout of the garden city: at its center were the villas of the wealthy and the administrative buildings. Since the occupant here lives on his own land (a one-family house occupied by the owner), the garden cities would become the "nursery of German life." Behind this concept of society viewed as a living organism ("popular community"), where it was desired to attain a perfect racial-popular cohesion, there lay the structure of a society of a corporative type. The nostalgic longing for a healthy policy of the land, for an agrarian idyll, and for private communication and precapitalist forms of society (tribe, village, family, corporation) was widespread among the lower middle class and the educated and business sectors of the middle classes. It was only those owning houses or land who put up resistance to the garden cities, because they were afraid they would be unable to let their properties at a good rent in the metropolitan areas as a result of an excessive increase in private residential building.[17]

Conservative Architects

There were quite a large group of architects who remained aloof from the various reforming movements of the early twentieth century in Germany, or at least did not adhere directly to any of them. Yet for their artistic views, which were not dissimilar to those of the organized movements, it is possible to call this group conservative. It consisted mainly of architects who were members of professional associations (journal: *Die Deutsche Bauzeitung*), and the vast majority of them were teachers at the Academies of Fine Arts.[18]

As they saw it, architecture was not a product of the general prevailing conditions nor a sociopolitical, technical and aesthetic process; they placed the work of architecture in a single context — that of the artist, whereby to build equals a purely artistic matter — and therefore interpreted architecture as a stylistic task, pure and simple.[19] Starting from the concept of a creative spirit — architect = spiritual producer — these architects thought they occupied an area situated beyond the conditions posed by a merchandise-producing society and tried to find an individual mode of production that would be valid within the ambit of architecture. The surface area and, with this, the facade were at the center of their individual efforts, but, by individualizing the form of their architecture, they hoped at the time to succeed in tackling new problems of society. Their architectural style had historical associations; it was objective, was rich in highly differentiated elements, met with favor among a broad sector of the bureaucracy of the building industry, especially among the upper class, and imposed an unmistakable appearance on the official architecture of the Kaiser's Germany. Some of these artists were also members of the Werkbund (Bestelmeyer, Wilhelm Kreis), and in 1914 they asserted their own artistic individuality in support of the "aesthetic opposition" (Henry van de Velde); in other words, they denied that economic conditions could have any bearing on the quality of the work[20] and took up a position against industrialized artistic work, which created types and therefore schematized and standardized the forms of construction. While acknowledging that machinery represented a way of making manual work lighter, they radically repudiated modern methods of production and held the conviction that only craft work could assure the hoped-for architectural individuality (artistic facade = technical nucleus). Even in the journal *Die Deutsche Bauzeitung* just mentioned, nationalist ideas were very quickly allied to racist tendencies. The modern type of construction was rejected — with its basic characteristic, "sterile uniformity" of the "leveling standard" — because it did not "beautify the fatherland,"[21] but the main accusation against architecture was that it deliberately followed foreign models. In place of that, what was wanted was an art of "authentically Germanic derivation," which would be established on "German territory" and personify the "Germanic essence." Alongside the monumental and imperial architecture of the Kaiser's Germany, local art too was defended — with the single exception of Bestelmeyer. At a sociopolitical level the ideal now

generally held was that of a "strong state" that would regularize social inequalities. Class antagonisms in society were explained on biological grounds: the differences in class were due to an incontestable natural law. Regret was expressed for the progressive exclusion of the individual and his loss of function as a free creative being, and with this came a new type of slavery (great industries with their own planning departments: architect = "salaried employee"), so that "artistic freedom" became more and more eroded. At first, the *Deutsche Bauzeitung* came out against the setting up of corporations, but after 1917 it gave its support to the drawing up of professional registers, which would assure the existence of the artist-architect as a free professional.

Reforming Movements and the Werkbund

From a study of the positions adopted and the accounts (which appeared in various publications of the groups of reformers of life and culture) of the nature, aims and activities of the Deutscher Werkbund, one may say as a generalization that its foundation was welcomed as a positive step,[22] so that the Werkbund was joined by groups of societies or associations — for example, the Bund für Heimatschutz and the Gartenstadtgesellschaft — as well as individual architects of different orientations and adherence — P. Bonatz, G. Bestelmeyer, T. Fischer, K. Frick, W. Kreis, to quote but a few.[23] What bound them together was, on the one hand, their rejection of the art of the second half of the nineteenth century and of extreme individualism, and, on the other, their desire to renew art itself by creating a new national style. In the Werkbund, nationalist ideas acquired a more decidedly racist character only during the course of the First War (e.g., Bestelmeyer and H. Muthesius). The Werkbund included crafts in its reforming efforts — in the initial phase craft was actually given first priority — and hoped for a renewal of art to come from the "cooperation of art, industry and crafts," while (with the exception of a very few buildings such as the Fagus offices) remaining within the framework of architectural tradition. At the same time it did not question the existing economic and social order in any way. For these reasons there could coexist within the Werkbund artistic tendencies that were contradictory and opinions that were extremely diversified or in direct contrast to each other; very soon, however, this diversity led to conflict within the association. During the twenties these internal differences brought various groups of reformers of life and society into open conflict with the Werkbund.

In the 1912 Werkbund yearbook Muthesius wrote in favor of the Heimatschutz but at the same time advised a certain "caution" toward the movement and the groups that supported popular art, and he attacked the presumed "beneficent serum of 1830." He had, in fact, realized what a grave risk was concealed in the indiscriminate support of the art of the local "fatherland": it could be converted into an impediment to constructive progress and therefore to the stylistic evolution of a whole epoch.[24] The distinguishing feature between the Werkbund and other reforming groups is apparent here especially, in the position adopted by Muthesius in favor of the modern type of production and, with it, of industrialized mass production. This explains, among other things, why the Deutscher Werkbund was supported by the most advanced sections (the ones most in favor of the policy of exporting) of industry and commerce and their relative associations — AEG, BASF, Deutsche Linoleumwerk, Farbenfabriken Bayer, Hapag, Mannesmann, Baustoff- und Textilveredelungs-industrie, associations of various industries, Deutscher Handelstag — as well as the state bureaucracy (e.g., the Prussian Ministry for Industry); indeed, there were many industries that even became members of the Werkbund. But the historical scene was not at all homogeneous; at the same time other groups that also supported the reform of culture, and with them the conservative wing of architects, denied industry the role of "civilizing agent of the present" and criticized the "industrial neoclassical sentiment" of the Werkbund. The discussion reached its climax in the controversy that erupted in 1914 in the interior of the Werkbund itself between Muthesius and van de Velde, which almost led to the group breaking up. The points in dispute could be reduced to two questions: Industrialized work or creative individual work (that is, craft work)? Aesthetics of the machine or artisan art?[25] This was then a repetition, in new terms, of the dispute that occurred in 1907 concerning the reform of the applied arts, which led to the birth of the Werkbund.

The artistic opposition supported first and foremost the precapitalist systems and models of society (because it was from the authoritarian and corporative state that some of them expected economic security; most of them, however, shared the liberal concept of free initiative). This line of thought found a wide following, especially among the craftsmen, who feared that the triumph of industrialized mass production might reduce the importance of their professional role (for example, painters, masons, carpenters). The same fear, which was the fear of losing the basis for their own existence, was shared by small farmers and tradesmen. The Fachverband für die wirtschaftlichen Interessen des Kunstgewerbes, or association for the defense of the economic interest of applied arts, repudiated the Werkbund as the "enemy of German art."[26] But the potential adversaries of the Werkbund were the workers belonging to associations of the building industry or agriculture, who were more afraid of the possibility that their work category might become proletarianized, so that their traditional role would be

reduced to that of the figure of a "day laborer." For the novelty of its ideas — modern production and promotion of provisions for social reform, especially in the improvement of living and working conditions — the Werkbund was far in advance of any of the other groups of reformers.[27] But in the first phase of its activity the Werkbund never stopped to ask itself whether and to what extent a vast renewal of culture was possible inside the capitalist economic and social system, and even less so did it concentrate on this theme;[28] for this reason a criticism of the movement on the basis of such criteria would be antihistorical. On the other hand, it is an undeniable fact that even in the initial phase, some of its members hoped that the new way in which industry was organized would result in weakening and then bringing to an end the traditional power structure.

The Weimar Republic
Now that I have fully described the various groups that were active in the Kaiser's Germany and acknowledged the weight their influence had on the formation of the views of the nationalistic and conservative forces of the Weimar Republic, I feel authorized to abbreviate the account of the second phase, which ended in 1933. The economic and political development under the Weimar Republic, though it undoubtedly brought about a certain democratization of the political relationship with the ruling class, did not produce any substantial change; in fact, it left the economic and social structures of the Kaiser's age fundamentally unaltered.[29] Instead, there occurred a progressive reactionary movement among the lower middle and middle class (the middle sector of society), for whom the proletariat with its organizations (trade union parties) as well as capitalism (the Jews) were to be accounted responsible for the economic, social and cultural crisis, which represented a direct threat.[30] These sections of the population were unwilling to renounce any of their social prestige, and through the medium of their organs and professional associations (Reichsverband des deutschen Handwerks, Reichsverband des deutschen Dachdeckerhandwerks, Reichsverband der deutschen Mauerstein-, Ziegel- und Tonindustrie, and Deutscher Wirtschaftsverband für das Baugewerbe, as spokesmen of the small and medium industries) they started an intense campaign against industrialization and technology, against unemployment and the consequent increase of their own proletarianization. At the end of the twenties the opposition parties of nationalistic orientation were finally absorbed by the NSDAP. The trend toward the "Neues Bauen," the new way of building — the Deutscher Werkbund itself was considered the initiator and main supporter of this trend — was impeded for economic reasons (the rejection of large-scale production and mass residential building), technical reasons (bad

quality of the building and poor materials) and ideological reasons ("cultural Bolshevism"), and its forms were considered the most clear indication of the threat to culture. But the most significant difference as compared with the previous climate under the Kaiser's Germany can be seen in the new attitude of the parties: in the Weimar Republic the parties made themselves the spokesmen for the various professional groupings, while at the same time racist, nationalistic and pan-Germanic tendencies nurtured the programs of the Right. It goes without saying that the so-called cultural battle conditioned the political debate to a far greater extent than was the case in the initial phase.

The Werkbund in the 1920s
When the Werkbund took up its activity again during the twenties, the results of which could be seen in a series of exhibitions (Berlin, Breslau, Cologne, Mannheim, to quote but a few), this did not reflect a greater political influence on the part of the association, but the opposite. Its sphere of activity was in fact now confined within the fields of technical and aesthetic experimentation. This can be explained by two new factors: on the one hand, some members (e.g., Bruno Taut) tried to influence the theoretical discussions on architecture by associating themselves with the Arbeitsrat für Kunst, which emerged from the Novembergruppe; on the other, a great mistrust in the parties had grown up and had produced what was an inevitable consequence in any party system: the loss of important spheres of influence. This "attitude of noninvolvement" was defended in various contributions that appeared in the publications of the Werkbund, but it was also criticized. The defenders explained: It is not the task of the Werkbund to discover what is the source of the "crisis" and how it can be eliminated, in the same way as it is not the artist's function to change the social structure.[31] This attitude was criticized in particular by such men as A. Behne and A. Schwab and the left wing of the "Neues Bauen" (H. Schmidt, H. Meyer).[32] They attacked the "polish of the surface" and the adoption in architecture and town planning of aesthetic principles alone; at the same time they refuted the belief that technical rationalism by itself could annul and overcome economic interests.[33] For these men the rationalization and standardization of the building industry and forms of construction were still far from being the realization of social ideas: to arrive at this point it was necessary to go beyond the capitalist policy of house and residential building and also to have a new land policy.[34] But Schwab knew who was to be the inquiring mind in this process and wrote an article that appeared in the Werkbund's journal *Die Form*, mentioning the absence of the building trade union at a congress of the Reich research institute, the Reichsforschungsgesellschaft.[35] In spite of

129. *Lechner and Norkauer, middle-class home, 1927–28, Weilheim.*

130. *H. Bökels, exhibition "Creative Nation," 1937, Düsseldorf.*

131. *K. Dübbers, roadman's house, ca. 1935, Eisenach.*

this, just because it cooperated with industry, the Werkbund was viewed with mistrust by the SDP and the unions. In reality, however, so far as the vast majority of its members were concerned, the Werkbund did not consider itself either a professional organization or a specialist association, which would have to uphold individual interests, but defined itself as a "defender of form"[36] and thus clarified its role, to ask questions relating to form — in other words to seek for a new style, in the center of its own architectural interest.[37]

In the ambit of this contribution, it does not seem appropriate at this point to devote further space to consideration of the various positions coexisting within the Werkbund or to describe the development of the movement under the Weimar Republic. However, it now becomes necessary to recall the various reactions to the current of the "Neues Bauen."

The conservative and nationalistic elements, with the exception of Schultze-Naumburg, never made a complete break with the Werkbund and remained within the organization[38] — among others were included O. Biber, E. Fahrenkamp, K. Frick, H. Giesler, E. Haiger, P. L. Troost — but for its adversaries the Werkbund always remained synonymous with "Neues Bauen," because the architects who followed this general trend transferred their field of activity to a wider sphere, in parties, associations and organizations, so contributing in a substantial measure to the cultural politicization of vast groupings of opinion.

Movements for the Reform of Life and Culture and Nationalistic Movements

During the last two years of the war, nationalistic ideas took possession, to an ever-growing extent, of the thought of the middle class and parties of the Right, who were in any case already disposed to welcome them. For example, in 1917 the journal *Deutschlands Erneuerung* called for a radical renewal of the German people. Only one method could achieve this: the construction of "healthy rural colonies" and the "elimination of dead branches." The program also anticipated that a peasant art, equally healthy, would replace the "deformed" manifestations of the avant-garde (Expressionism). Finally, the large towns, considered the strongholds of Judaism, were put on trial. Racist nationalism became widely followed, especially in the circle or group of Saaleck around Schultze-Naumburg; in this connection I believe there is no need to speak of other theoreticians and other associations (Stahlheim, Werwolf) or journals. After the revolution, Schultze-Naumburg left the Ring and the Arbeitsrat für Kunst and with other like-minded companions, Bonatz, Bestelmeyer, E. Högg and P. Schmitthenner, formed the self-styled "nationaler Block," or national block. In 1927 this group — with the exception of Högg — issued a manifesto of its own, which was essentially a violent attack upon the "Neues Bauen." Later, when a new tax on buildings was imposed — and violently

contested by the middle class (owners of houses and lands) — and 50 percent of that tax was assigned to social building, the planning of large residential complexes was undertaken in a modern style. The process of a complete radicalization of racist tendencies became irreversible and, under the influence of H. F. K. Günther and R. W. Darré, Schultze-Naumburg, the Bund für Heimatschutz, and other similar reforming groups for life and culture, it was welcomed by vast sectors of the middle class. Art was thought to be connected with race, and consequently the "blood" was thought indispensable to its form;[39] and history, too, was thought to be determined by the law of race. Meanwhile, a campaign was set in motion against modern art and architecture, judged to be "non-German" and "not bound to the soil of the Fatherland," or, in other words, "racially degenerate." On the basis of the distinction between art that was "in conformity with the race" and art that was "extraneous to the race," the art of the first half of the nineteenth century was reevaluated, since in this art the people still expressed their bond with "Mother Earth." In the second half of the century, however, the mixture of races had determined an irreversible process, whereby individuals were uprooted and art became degenerate. Peasants were then considered to represent the true substance of the German people, so that in the "colonization of the countryside," on the one hand, and in the "purification of the race," on the other, were seen the only two possible ways to rediscover the active Nordic man and the Aryan personality. After 1930 this principle became the slogan for the "national revolution."

The organization that propounded these reactionary, racist and nationalistic ideas was the Kampfbund für deutsche Kultur, which incorporated them into an organic program. But the beginning of an organized cultural work that was already clearly national-socialist[40] coincided with the formation — by A. Rosenberg — of the Nationalsozialistische Gesellschaft für deutsche Kultur in August 1927. As it specifically stated in its statutes, the task of this society was to summon up "all defenses against the forces now dominant in disintegration" and to "enlighten" the German people on the "connections between race, art, science, and ethical and military values."[41] The league gathered around itself various groups and circles with racist, nationalistic and pan-Germanic views, and set itself the task of "founding a new culture based on a German affinity, which would oppose Marxism, the parliamentary system and modern art and architecture."[42] In 1931 the Kampfbund was transformed into a mass organization with many professional sections: architects and engineers had their own Kampfbund deutscher Architekten und Ingenieure. Beside Rosenberg and Schultze-Naumburg, the principal theoretician, orator and publicist of the league was A. von Senger. According to Senger, it was the "Bolshevist spirit" ("torch of Moscow") that in-

spired the "Neues Bauen," which he described as a reaction of "underdeveloped" and "racially enfeebled" men.[43] Therefore, the "Neues Bauen" was seen as an attack upon the middle class, since this current threatened the existence of craft work and even the industries of the middle class (brick making and stone masonry). The "love of Mammon," or large-scale industry and international capitalism, known for scorning human life, was the acknowledged protector of the modern trend in architecture. Behind such slogans was a clear allusion to precise German realities: whereas administrative offices and the sales establishments of the commercial capital and the new commercial pilot sectors, such as the electrotechnical and chemical industries, preferred avant-garde forms, that is, the forms of the "Neues Bauen," in contrast, German heavy industry — in order to create an image of its own industrial might — returned to the monumental architectural forms of tradition. Behind the constructions of popular mass building von Senger saw — mistakenly — the imprint of American capital.

The founding of the Bauhaus was obviously not due directly to the efforts of the Werkbund. But many of the basic objectives of the Werkbund were, in fact, realized in the Bauhaus: a three-year artisan and spiritual apprenticeship before studying the trade, crafts workshop as a teaching model. The controversy that erupted in 1924 around the Weimar Bauhaus shows clearly that the nationalist and bourgeois parties represented in the regional parliament of Thuringia, and, behind the parties, the Thuringian crafts circles (builders' associations), the representatives of the Bund für Heimatschutz and the relative press outlets (*Anhalter-Anzeiger*) were not so concerned about the type of professional training given by the Bauhaus as they were about the aesthetic viewpoint expressed in its works — the new forms of industrialized building production. The argument led to the fall of the government of the Left (SDP) and the transfer of the Bauhaus itself from Weimar to Dessau, where from the very first it met with violent opposition from the parties of the Right. The controversy surrounding the Bauhaus in 1924 marked the beginning of the "local cultural battle," in which there participated, apart from the social strata, groups and associations mentioned, also the universities and some of the communal bureaucracy. From Thuringia the campaign soon spread to other cities, for example, to Stuttgart (Weissenhof Siedlung), Karlsruhe-Dammerstock and Dessau (Törten Siedlung). At that time the Werkbund was synonymous with "Neues Bauen"; the wave of denigration submerged even its own members, who were called "agents of Bolshevism." The Dessau Bauhaus was even stigmatized as a "Communist cell" and the Dessau buildings described as "too cerebral."[44] People often quoted the comparison made by Bonatz between the Weissenhof Siedlung and an outlying district of Jerusalem. The principal objections were that there were no national and historic bond and no consideration of the site into which the buildings were inserted.[45] The opposition to the Siedlungen was based, on the one hand, on economic reasons (the ruling social and building policy with the protection of tenant's contracts was castigated) and, on the other hand, on ideological reasons (the "Marxist Siedlungen" lacked "the bond between the occupant and the soil," and their architecture destroyed love for the fatherland, for the nation and for the family). The national socialist critics justly recognized the two aspects of modern architecture, as defined by Schwab; the "upper bourgeois" aspect and the "proletarian" aspect; this is because the architecture was constructed and occupied mainly by these two social classes.

In December 1929 Thuringia elected as Minister of the Interior and of "popular education" a national socialist (W. Frick, who remained in this office until 1931); the Weimar college for engineers was restructured and placed under the directorship of Schultze-Naumburg. The struggle that ensued against the "Marxist depauperization" represented a foretaste of what became the norm after 1933: the frescoes by Oscar Schlemmer were removed from the college, which remained under the control of Schultze-Naumburg until 1940.

Therefore, the conviction held by the lower middle and middle classes that they could serve as an intermediary between capital and labor and so eliminate mass production, at the same time overcoming class divisions through the collective consciousness, was shown to be illusory, and this is confirmed by the history of the Third Reich. The same failure awaited the other hypothesis, that is, the hope that it might be possible to improve living conditions, or even to eliminate the power structure of society, simply by renewing the technique of construction, stylizing form and creating new forms. With regard to the Werkbund of the twenties, one may say, speaking generally, that it lacked depth of thought as applied to politics. At all events, the Werkbund associated itself with other groups of middle-class origin who had an excessive belief in culture, education and teaching, and because of their narrow outlook it underestimated the strength of the economic and social components of society. Its history during the twenties shows that the Werkbund was not as it was termed the *drudge* of capitalism and it was even more untrue that the new forms could be ascribed to the simple desire to assure greater profitability to industrial production. It is by looking at its history that we can judge what is the only legitimate interpretation to be accorded this group: it was the artistic movement that contributed to developing the new style and to bringing it into architecture.[46] The economic crisis brought complete paralysis to the building sector. The building industry and rental accommodations shared the hope of the various nationalist movements that only a "strong state" could accelerate the economic revival. But the "national revolution" brought to the lower middle and middle classes the exact opposite of what was anticipated from fascism: their economic situation worsened but was compensated for in ideology. All the movements for the "reform of life and culture" were dissolved after 1933.

1. Parts of the essay are based on: J. Petsch, *Baukunst und Stadtplanung im Dritten Reich, Herleitung, Bestandsaufnahme, Entwicklung, Nachfolge* (Munich, 1976). Documentary sources: specialized architectural journals.

2. The principal causes must be ascribed to two factors: on the one hand, there was an enormous army of unskilled labor: on the other, a market saturation, especially in the sector of residential building, had created unfavorable conditions for the investment of capital. As a result, small and medium firms made up most of the building industry.

3. Cf. H. -U. Wehler, *Das Deutsche Kaiserreich, 1871–1918* (Göttingen, 1975).

4. A disparaging description of the movements for the reform of life can be found in: J. Frecot, J. F. Geist, and D. Kerbs, *Fidus 1868–1948: Zur Ästhetik bürgerlicher Fluchtbewegungen* (Munich, 1972).

5. The Dürerbund was the organization of the readers of *Kunstwart*. The Kunstwart was the organization for the diffusion of the Dürerbund's ideology.

6. Cf. G. Kratzsch, *Kunstwart und Dürerbund* (Gottingen, 1969).

7. P. Schultze-Naumburg, *Kulturarbeiten 1–9* (Munich, 1901–10).

8. Cf. many articles published in *Deutsche Bauzeitung* between 1909 and 1912.

9. The *Heimatschutz* was edited and published by the council of the presidency of the Bund für Heimatschutz; the *Heimat*, by the Deutscher Verein für ländliche Wohlfahrts und Heimatpflege.

10. The journals included *Architektonische Rundschau, Deutsche Bauzeitung, Zeitschrift des Rheinischen Vereins für Denkmalpflege und Heimatschutz, Die Denkmalpflege, Flugschriften des Dürerbundes*.

11. Cf. *Walhalla, Bücherei für vaterländische Geschichte, Kunst und Kulturgeschichte* (Munich, 1905 ff.).

12. Cf. the essay "Heimatschutz" in *Architektonische Rundschau*, year XXVII, no. 2 (1911), p. 15 f.

13. Cf. P. Mebes, *Um 1800. Architektur und Handwerk im letzten Jahrhundert ihrer traditionellen Entwicklung*, 2 vols. (Munich, 1908).

14. Cf. E. Hartig, *Erziehung zur bürgerlichen Baukunst* (Aachen, 1906).

15. O. F. Weinlig, *Haus und Heim im Kleinen* (Düsseldorf, 1911), p. 7.

16. Cf. T. Fritsch, *Die Stadt der Zukunft* (Leipzig, 1896); id., *Antisemitischer Katechismus* (Leipzig, 1887).

17. Cf. the statements of the secretary-general of the Zentralverband der Haus- und Grudbesitzervereine in: Gartenstadt, year VIII, no. 3 (1914), p. 57.

18. The traditional distinction between Baukünstler (artist-architect) and Bauingenieur (engineer-architect) is here preserved. The sphere of technological building is accepted, as is confirmed by the many articles on "technical masterpieces" that appeared in the *Deutsche Bauzeitung*.

19. Cf. J. Petsch, op. cit. (n. 1), p. 41.

20. Cf. principle 9 of Henry van de Velde, which declares: "Quality is not created by the spirit of exports." Published in U. Conrads, ed., *Programme und Manifeste zur Architektur des 20. Jahrhunderts* (Berlin, Frankfurt, Vienna, 1964), p. 27.

21. Cf. *Deutsche Bauzeitung* (n. 8).

22. Positive statements were made, for example, by the following journals: *Architektonische Rundschau, Dekorative Kunst, Deutsche Bauzeitung, Deutsche Kunst und Dekoration, Kunstgewerbeblatt, and Kunstwart*.

23. See the list of members of the Werkbund for 1908.

24. The exhibition of the Werkbund in Cologne in 1914, in which the village of the Lower Rhineland (under the direction of J. Metzendorf) had central importance, shows in what sense and to what extent the Heimatschutz influenced the work of the Werkbund.

25. On the program laid down by the Werkbund see S. Müller, *Industrialisierung und angewandte Kunst: Deutscher Werkbund zwischen 1907 und 1914* (university thesis, Bochum, 1969).

26. *Kunstgewerbeblatt*, the organ of the applied arts associations, came out in favor of the Werkbund.

27. In actual fact, A. Loos had even before this arrived at solutions that were stylistically new, although they must be defined as "artisan purism." Cf. Müller, op. cit. (n. 25), p. 21 f.

28. Exceptions are H. Waentig and H. P. Berlage. Cf. H. Waentig. *Wirtschaft und Kunst* (Jena, 1909); H. P. Berlage, "Baukunst und Kleinkunst," in *Kunstgewerbeblatt*, no. 18 (1907), p. 183 f. Waentig was doubtful whether a new culture was possible in the capitalist economic system, whereas Berlage postulated a change in the existing relationships of production.

29. Cf. W. Ruge, *Weimar: Republik auf Zeit* (Berlin, 1969); H. A. Winkler, *Der Mittelstand, Demokratie und Nationalsozialismus: Die politische Entwicklung von Handwerk und Kleinhandel in der Weimarer Republik* (Cologne, 1972).

30. The policy of financing the war by loans during the First War led to inflation, which hit the middle class hardest. However, inflation was blamed not on the sectors of society who had wanted war but on the Republic, and the SDP in particular.

31. Cf. W. Riezler, "Front 1932," published in *Die Form; Stimme des Deutschen Werkbundes 1925–1934*, ed. F. Schwarz and F. Gloor (Gütersloh, 1969), p. 75.

32. Cf. the articles published A. Behne and A. Schwab in Werkbundarchiv 1, ed. J. Frecot and D. Kerbs (Berlin, 1972).

33. Cf. the essays by A. Schwab, "Menschenwirtschaft und Raumwirtschaft in Deutschland" and "Typen der Theorie des Städtebaus)," published in *Die Form*, op cit. (n. 31), p. 180 f. and p. 184 f.

34. Many of the left-wing architects of the "Neues Bauen" emigrated to the Soviet Union at the end of the twenties.

35. A. Schwab, "Zur Tagung der Reichsforschungsgesellschaft," in *Die Form*, op. cit. (n. 31), p. 137.

36. Riezler, "Front 1932" (n. 31).

37. The author agrees with Julius Posener in believing that in the final analysis the "Neues Bauen" was a "new style."

38. Cf. list of the members of the Werkbund for 1928.

39. Cf. P. Schultze-Naumburg, *Kunst und Rasse* (Munich, 1925); H. F. K. Günther, *Rasse und Stil* (Munich, 1926).

40. H. Brenner, *Die Kunstpolitik des Nationalsozialismus* (Reinbek/Hamburg, 1963), p. 8 f. The various nationalist circles are fully described in this volume.

41. Ibid., p. 8.

42. Two principal stylistic currents may be distinguished: for the first, the point of departure remained the architecture of the first years of the nineteenth century, whereas, for the second, it was felt necessary to concentrate efforts toward studying and developing regional traditions.

43. Cf. A. von Senger, *Krisis der Architektur* (Zurich, 1928). id. *Die Brandfackel Moskaus* (Zurzach, 1931).

44. E. Blunck, "Das Bauhaus in Dessau," in *Deutsche Bauzeitung*, no. 17, 61, year 1927, p. 153 f.

45. Cf. J. Joedicke and C. Plath, *Die Weissenhofsiedlung* (Stuttgart, 1968).

46. Cf. C. Friemert, "Der 'Deutsche Werkbund' als Agentur der Warenästhetik in der Anfangsphase des deutschen Imperialismus." in W. F. Haug, ed., *Warenästhetik: Beiträge zur Diskussion, Weiterentwicklung und Vermittlung ihrer Kritik* (Frankfurt, 1975). p. 177 f.

THE THIRTIES AND THE SEVENTIES: TODAY WE SEE THINGS DIFFERENTLY
Lucius Burckhardt

Most of the technical inventions now in daily use were already in existence in the thirties. There is something surprising about this statement, because we always think we have made a great step forward. But the advance that has been made from 1930 until today pertains mainly to technology rather than to the technique itself. I remember that television existed in my childhood, but there were no public transmitter stations; however, it was already possible to see television in research laboratories or exhibitions. With the possible exception of the transistor technique, although here again the progress is technological, all the discoveries had been substantially made already. The innovation brought about in the period after the Second War was in effect to combine these discoveries and put them to use not only in the products themselves but in the actual processes of production. And this is the step forward that, in my view, has had the effect of modifying human consciousness. In the form in which inventions were presented in 1930 they were adaptable to luxury goods: cameras were available for those who could afford the high cost of buying them; radios could be heard, it is true, but sets were incredibly expensive; cars existed, but who could afford one? The enjoyment of these goods was not available to everyone and was voluntary. Those who were poor had no access to such things, and, if, in fact, they came into contact with modern technology and new inventions, the only relationship the poor had with them was to be found in their function as producers, never as consumers and users. However, production techniques remained conventional. The very fact that so perfect an optical instrument as a Leica existed caused a sensation, but the technique used in its manufacture was completely conventional. The photographic lenses were ground by hand, the camera was made of welded brass, by hand also, then lacquered, and so on. The process of participation in the technique then in the stage of evolving was carried out by the consumer, and for this reason it has been an inconstant phenomenon. Those who were poor were obviously excluded, while those who were rich could participate if they liked but could remain apart from the whole process if they preferred. There were many rich people who did not take photographs, did not listen to the radio or drive a car — in other words, did not participate. For those who were poor,

Ills. 132–149 photographed by Theo Gröne.

132, 133. Siedlungen of the "Neues Frankfurt": Hellerhof includes rental apartments and presents a valid example of the architecture of welfare. Praunheim is a condominial property.

134, 135. The exterior of the Hellerhof has remained unchanged.

136. The cramped dimensions in the interior permit few alterations.

94

however, the fact that they were deprived of the benefits of technology was an imposition.

Today the situation has reversed. Technization is now an inherent part of technology. It is therefore not apparent in the consumer sector but is confined to the ambit of production. And, here, participation is enforced and obligatory. The civilizing effect is for this reason very different: whereas in the past — when participation in the product was a spontaneous and voluntary choice — a given product might have had an influence upon someone who by personal choice exposed himself to its influence, today, in contrast, the influence of the place of work is obligatory and no one can remain apart from it. The street that has to be passed through in order to reach one's place of work is obligatory; the overcoming of distance is obligatory, as is the changing of jobs as part of the background of rationalization and automation of the work itself. The majority of places of work are adapted to automation or semiautomation, which depends on work done in laboratories and on electronic data processing.

This influence of technical products, which no longer applies only to the consumer sector but equally to that of production, causes effects upon our view of aesthetics. Such effects are far-reaching, extending from profound modifications of consciousness to the most banal consequences. To give an example — the place of work determines effects that have repercussions even on private space: technology conditions the image of the kitchen and the whole technique of living, where there are products of the new technologies testifying to the means of production. Against such a background, our aesthetic viewpoint, or our way of seeing the world, changes. The effect produced by the obligatory nature of this participation on the productive sector leads to the technization of life. Even the care of health has abrogated to itself new techniques: people are no longer nursed at home but trust themselves to technology, as it has been learned by professional practice. Even the home is mechanized, although here a contradictory tendency has appeared — that is, the pioneers of the thirties had developed minimal and functional homes, because in the intention of the avant-garde the home had to become more and more of an instrument; in other words, it had to lose some of its own importance to the advantage of collective life. The Bauhaus was by now convinced that life had to become collectivized and as a result the individual house would lose in value. To this conviction was associated the hope that capitalism would be superseded and replaced by a new, cooperative

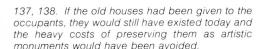

137, 138. If the old houses had been given to the occupants, they would still have existed today and the heavy costs of preserving them as artistic monuments would have been avoided.

economic system. But capitalism has remained, and not only has the home not become inessential, but it has acquired even greater importance. The home is our last refuge. I can very well imagine a culture where the home is not important, and, in fact, I find such a concept ideal. Among Eastern nations, for example, the importance of the home is irrelevant, and great cultures are possible without the home being granted a prime role. For us, however, a suggestion of this kind is at present unreal, since in our society the house creates and constitutes a refuge, which clearly represents something more than an instrument for living. Today we attribute ever greater importance to the home, and indeed more and more "free spaces" are constantly being brought into it to a degree that would have astonished the pioneers of the mechanization of the home. The home has thus become a place where one can remove oneself from the world and attempt to put up resistance to the coercive participation required of us by the technical process.

It was hoped in the past that technology would create a civilizing influence on a unified society, that it would manifest itself clearly, become transparent and lead to well-defined forms. It was hoped, too, that ugly things would be ugly only because they were transitory but would become clear and appropriate once they were conceived in their definitive form. A convincing example of the time was the bicycle. In its conception, the bicycle is perfect, ready for use; therefore it is clear and appropriate in its parts and could not be better. But technology has not followed this path. So far as form is concerned, it did not adopt this approach. In our day electrotechnology is the predominant technique, and it is far from clear. It is not accessible to design. In the final analysis, the designer has nothing left to do other than to furnish designs for the gray containers that contain a tangle of wires. When the lid is lifted, we do not know whether the instrument we are looking at is a record player, a measuring instrument or a telephone apparatus. Only from the switchboard, which is the work of the designer, is it possible to define the object. In this sense, therefore, one cannot say that technology has become "transparent," and design continues to limit itself — now more than ever — to hiding the technique. Technology has not given us the pleasure of revealing itself and making itself accessible to design in the sense that the inventor could find revealing and clarifying forms. We must therefore record the fact that one of the expectations of 1930 has not been fulfilled.

139, 140. In Praunheim the entrances themselves denote the proud status of the owners.

But it seems to me that yet another expectation was disappointed: technology did not have the result of collectivizing life. The hope was that technology would have relieved us of some of our labor and that this would become collective or else performed by specialists, so that we could achieve a higher level in our lives. The first technical products were colossal plants. The new kitchens were collective kitchens. Recently, I saw the central vacuum-cleaning plant installed by the Danish architect Arne Jacobsen at the Hamburg electricity-generating station. But the great vacuum-cleaning plant is now at a standstill. Indeed, this is now the destiny typical of technology on a relatively large scale, which was meant to have taken away some of the burdens of domestic labor and allowed us to have a new and different form of life. The invention of small engines has annulled the liberating and progressive value of large mechanical plants intended for collective use; small items of household equipment have kept women in their usual position of slavery, and in fact have even made things worse, because these objects are not exactly cheap and in order to obtain them a great amount of money is needed. Today every home possesses these small items, whereas, if they had been bigger and used collectively, they could have effectively made life easier for everyone.

Building, too, has not followed the path that the avant-garde foresaw and imagined. It is true, of course, that in the period after the end of the Second War, and also at the Hochschule für Gestaltung in Ulm, the climate was such that people could hope for a new way of building. Their dream of a house that could be assembled like a ship or airplane did not come to pass, however. Engineers of undoubted talent, like Jean Prouvé, who worked on light prefabrication, or Frei Otto, who partially realized supporting structures that appeared light and open, had to admit in the end that building did not follow this path. Sail-shaped roofs — when they assume the dimensions of the roofs of Olympic stadiums — no longer had the desired lightness and, moreover, proved extremely costly. Therefore, the light prefabrication that could be applied by anybody and could make it possible to transport walls and build houses without difficulty did not come about. Today prefabrication is very heavy and essentially the exact opposite of what was hoped for; although it is really primitive, only building contractors are able to put it to use. The explanation for the fact that all these hopes proved false is to be sought in problems of a technical order, for example, the problem of insulation. It is necessary that buildings must incorporate a minimum weight so as to allow for acoustic and heat insulation. On the other hand, the failure I have pointed out is also undoubtedly due to the actual structure of the building system, the building industry. In the building sector the bigger the societies and their capitals are, the sooner the innovation came to a halt.

The start of the international style in the twenties, the start, that is, of the formal renewal promoted by the avant-garde and later to become dominant, was an aesthetic experience that affected only a small minority. A tiny group of people applauded the proposed innovations, while a large group reacted indignantly to a message they could not understand; the great mass of the people obviously remained excluded. There is no doubt that it was a great shock to the modern movement when it became known that the competition for the construction of the Palace of the Soviet had not been won by a design of the architectural avant-garde. The people who had taken power in Russia wished to construct a building that could express this dominion, and for this they turned to traditional styles of architecture, where they could recognize their power. But this was the precise moment when architects removed all distinguishing marks that could be understood by the people, and proposed rational and functional buildings. This is a situation that undoubtedly became more radicalized in Russia, but even in our society things were probably not very different in substance. The architectural scene was dominated by traditional buildings. Modern architecture represented too great an advance, and, in contrast to what was the case during earlier revolutions in style, the public was not capable of learning how to harmonize its own aesthetic expectations with the new message. Today we find ourselves in a very different situation. The ratio between old buildings and new houses has been reversed. Before, among the great mass of old buildings, we had at the most one modern building. And at that time there were many who believed this new construction to be the tangible sign of the future hope that the world might assume a more rational appearance, where houses with larger windows would let in more light and transparency, so that it would be possible to penetrate both into the interior of the structure itself and into its social relationships. The conviction that a world like this, of which these few new buildings were the herald, could come into being or that there could be an experiment similar to the one that a small group of intellectuals then carried out would no longer be possible today. Equally unlikely is the probability that the vast ranks of the conservative middle class could be scandalized by suggestions for modern buildings, because the percentage of new buildings is too high. The change in ratio has produced a considerable effect: the contingent of old buildings, which have in the meantime become the minority, is seen in a new light, a way of looking at them that we might term *nostalgia*. This redefinition proceeds along two directions: on the one hand, the old buildings are seen in a depressing light, whereas, on the other, they are revalued. The fact that in most cases homes are situated in new buildings fixes the norm for constructions appropriate to private residences. Those whose social status is perhaps not very secure may find themselves in a rather embarrassing situation if they live in an old building and their guests express surprise at the height of the rooms. In the past, high rooms were a sign of nobility, whereas today, under the impression of the four-fifths or nine-tenths of new residential dwellings with a ceiling height of 2.50 meters, it is by no means certain that very high rooms do not in fact signify the decline of a neighborhood. Within the existing heritage of old buildings a discrimination is arrived at on the basis of the availability of new houses.

But at the same time a semantic transformation also occurs, in other words, a reinterpretation of the connotations imparted by old buildings, and in particular the marks of "nobility," which today we no longer view in the traditional way. In particular, those groups of people who reject the marks of authority choose to move into the old buildings that emanated prestige in the past. Houses that at one time were the traditional homes of bankers, officials and the bourgeoisie are now occupied by student communes, which interpret their connotations differently from the original. The reinterpretation of these connotations, or the fact that such buildings can assume a new function, represents a liberating experience for the new occupants.

In modern architecture (if one accepts the premise that *architecture* can be compared with language) we have to do with previously established semantic elements, which can be employed at discretion or used by anyone in the way he prefers. Even the acquisitions of the avant-garde have become current language. The very fact that modern architecture may have destroyed the system of earlier architecture has as its immediate consequence the erection of a series of new buildings that were initially stimulating and that nevertheless still represent an irreplaceable experience for us also. Today, however, any speculator at all can adopt again the language that was new at that time and have houses designed by his employees. These houses will have all the elements of the language of that time, but these elements will not be able to contain that message — they will simply be envelopes.

141. *On the garden side the solarium is built as an outbuilding.*
142, 143. *The new technical equipment enormously reduces the living space of the kitchen.*

The other determining cause in the change of our viewpoint, or our way of seeing things, is connected with the difference in the relationship of the general public to the intellectual élite, the group that decides on new aesthetic orientations. Here, the radical transformation that has occurred was brought about by the vast movement under the name of pop art. It is a movement directed from above, and at the same time, from below. The innovatory wave overturned our traditional views of harmony and design to such a point that it determined a remarkable change in our very way of looking at things. In this connection we need only consider the way of furnishing homes, or simply the general way of dressing, to understand how far this process of transformation of customs has attacked their foundations and how deep it has gone, subverting the classical idea of harmony with which we were brought up; today we no longer dare combine colors in the way that was done in 1930. The pop movement equally represented the acknowledgment of the obsolescence of beauty — the admission that the model of beauty is always historically conditioned, that beauty must irreversibly become obsolete, and that it has the character of a given historical moment; moreover, the evolution of beauty can be put to the test. In architecture the pop wave educated our eye to appreciate the constructions of the general public: orchards grown outside the city in people's free time are beautiful, slums are beautiful, the complexity in the architecture of tall houses is beautiful, and restorations of buildings are beautiful. In short, and speaking very generally, everything is beautiful where the distinguishing features of various epochs are legible and where it can be seen how time has been dominated by man.

These developments appear particularly contrary to the spirit of the Werkbund. Has not the Werkbund always supported clarity of design, perfection of its realization and "good form?" And if the sensibility and sense of beauty of the public have changed, should the Werkbund for this reason deny its own principles? If we think back to its origins, we see that the guiding principles of the Werkbund have their roots far deeper than in good design pure and simple. Its original struggle against industrial kitsch and the extravagances of the Jugendstil must without any doubt be understood as a reform of the decisional hierarchy in the planning phase: a reform whose purpose it is to create values for daily use that the user can appropriate to himself in order to arrive at the surmounting of the relationship between producer and consumer, which was so desired.

144, 145. *The old drawers and ironing board attached to the wall still function.*
146. *Here the old kitchen equipment was thrown out.*
147, 148. *The bathroom was changed more than the kitchen.*
149. *The furnishings of the bedroom no longer respect the views of the pioneers.*

SANATORIUM PURKERSDORF

THE OSTERREICHISCHER WERKBUND AND ITS RELATIONS WITH THE DEUTSCHER WERKBUND

Friedrich Achleitner

Historical Context

Even the name is problematical: the Oster-reichischer Werkbund should really be called the Wiener Werkbund. For if it is true that the ideas of the Werkbund were accepted (or even followed) in some regions of Austria also, it is just as true to say that the discussion — if it may be so defined — took place almost exclusively in Vienna. The task of the Deutscher Werkbund, which was originally national, created an impact in Austria only among circles that were linked by traditional affinity with Germany, but it was only very rarely that the wind that blew from the Reich reached as far as the capital of the monarchy on the Danube — to be precise, twice only, in 1912 and 1930, when two congresses of the Deutscher Werkbund were held in Vienna.

In addition, the activity of the Austrian Werkbund was concentrated mainly in two fairly short seasons: between the year of its foundation in 1913 and the Cologne exhibition of 1914, and from 1929 to 1932, that is, until the inauguration of the Viennese Siedlung of the Werkbund. But Vienna was not the soil on which the ideas that informed the Werkbund could flourish. The capital of the Hapsburg Empire felt it necessary to preserve its image of refinement and nobility, and therefore preferred to keep the world of industry out of its consciousness. To this attitude was added that hostility — a hostility that had been lovingly cultivated — toward every kind of theorizing. This feeling was typical of the artists and architects of Vienna and culminated in their strong tendency for the original, and in their traditionally skeptical view of progess and the spirit of the time. This was reflected in an ironical detachment from their own work and scorn for the work of others. Last but not least, in all sectors of life their love for the arts-and-crafts objects, the charming and unreal creation, was paramount. But one must not overlook another precise historical reality: by about 1912 Vienna had already passed through all the principal stages of the modern movement in architecture — the architectonic doctrine of Otto Wagner, the concept of "Western" culture of such men as Adolf Loos, the half-century of activity of the Thonets, and even the world success of the Wiener Werkstätte.

When the Werkbund was founded, the Viennese Secession had lost its initial impetus in a natural process of decline and especially in the idleness of the dispute, while the Werkstätte had passed their zenith with the Brussels Palais Stoclet. Moreover, the Austrian monarchy could not be halted in its advance toward war, while its society revealed manifest symptoms of disintegration. Unlike Adolf Loos, Josef Hoffmann did not see (or through his

150. *Adolf Loos, Steiner house, 1910, Vienna.*

151. *Josef Hoffmann, design for the Purkersdorf Sanatorium, 1903.*

152. *Josef Hoffmann, table cutlery, 1904.*

153. *Josef Hoffmann, porcelain coffee set, 1935.*

154. *Otto Wagner, seat for the Postsparkasse, Vienna.*

155. *Otto Wagner, stool for the Postparkasse, Vienna.*

own gifts and ambitions did not wish to see) the historical logic of this development and gave the final answer to the demand for ostentation advanced by the dying Austrian bourgeoisie. Whereas Loos recognized the problems and tasks of an architecture that was intended to be socially directed and looked for an appropriate form in which the challenge could be met, Hoffmann's late works, on the other hand, returned to the distinguished style of a nobility who lost its fortunes.

Otto Wagner, Thonet and the Wiener Werkstätte and Adolf Loos Again

The "functionalist doctrine" of Otto Wagner is comprehensible only if seen in the context of the system of historical references found in the famous Vienna Ring, and only if it is understood as a final proliferation of the optimistic faith in progress. However, the following hypothesis is justifiable: if his school, the much quoted Wagnerschule, had understood the master, if the course embarked on in the counter hall of the Postsparkasse had been continued — if only by a few students — and also, if the architects of the Vienna Secession had not bound the furniture designed by the Thonets to a formal dictate of fashion, then it is certain that the founding of the Werkbund would have occurred under different signs and auspices. But Vienna was not prepared to draw these conclusions. And this was why Otto Wagner's school transformed itself into a fortress of reaction, as if it were called upon to produce the shroud in which to enfold the "beautiful corpse" of the Danube monarchy, instead of showing the way to meeting new problems. It goes without saying that some of Wagner's students were involved in residential building in Vienna in the twenties and used their experience in the planning of great blocks, which were perfectly fitting to the historical idea of a great city, a metropolis. They dominated the architectural scene but remained embroiled in the concept of the artist-architect that they had developed under the Jugendstil.

With regard to the situation of industrial production in Austria, we may recall just one example (although it would obviously need greater study in a wider context): the Thonet phenomenon. During the second half of the nineteenth century a model of industrial planning and production developed that was unique because, from its starting point of a new method for treating wood, it succeeded in creating a complex of norms; deriving from this technique, however, in the course of its evolution this model, too, was interfered with or its development was hindered by the intervention of architects and artists. Here, what was to become the essential idea of the Werkbund was realized at a practical level even before it was formulated as a theory, but the problems relating to "form" were already apparent in all their complex network of decision. Seen from this angle, the foundation of the Wiener

156. *Thonet chair.*

Werkstätte (in 1903, by Josef Hoffmann, Kolo Moser and Fritz Waerndorfer) was in itself a "reactionary event," if for no other reason than that it followed the model of Asbhee in London. We must remember that paramount importance was accorded to the individual article produced by craft methods, the luxury article intended for the exclusive level of taste found in the small class of society at the head of the social hierarchy; this tendency obviously culminated in a radical rejection of any kind of social aspect of production. Proceeding by paradox, the artistic collective individuality belonging to the Wiener Werkstätte developed an elegant and refined aesthetic system (partly influenced by English and Scottish artists). The much vaunted geometrical simplicity represented a marked antithesis to traditionalism and the Jugendstil, but in detail it was even more artistic, pretentious and exclusive. It would certainly be a gross error to see in a seat designed by Josef Hoffmann in 1902 a functional form; it is the pure expressive form of a typical artistic attitude in an equally typical historical situation. In the same light one must interpret the reason why there was not within the Wiener Serkstätte a development taking a progressive direction, instead of a using up and wearing out of forms. The ascetic period, and probably also the one that was most significant viewed in a historical perspective, was quickly exhausted, and, with the change in the commercial situation and in the figure of the patron himself, there was a move toward a more ostentatious style in which — around 1914 — Josef Hoffmann could already exhibit his characteristic and individual historicism (or neoclassicism).

Hoffmann's tireless research into form concealed a profound aversion for any kind of repetition. For this reason he took no part in the discussion on standardization (the controversy between Muthesius and van de Velde).

It is said of him that no sooner did a purchaser show an interest in a certain article than Hoffmann offered him another, finer and more beautiful. This may be no more that an invented anecdote, but this story is perfectly symptomatic of Hoffmann and the spirit of the Wiener Werkstätte. But at the same time, this attitude reveals another marked characteristic of this institution: in the Wiener Werkstätte economic criteria held no sway.

Adolf Loos became the critic and conscience of his time, thanks to his experience of English culture and, also, through lack of commissions; not only did he understand the specific situation of Vienna during those years, but at the same time grasped the motivations behind the move of the Secessionists to the Werkbund and gave his own interpretation of them. In his preface to *Trotzdem* in 1930, he wrote, in the following self-congratulatory terms: "I have emerged victorious from the thirty-year struggle: I have set humanity free from superfluous ornamentation. 'Ornament' was once the epithet of 'beautiful.' Today, thanks to me, it is the epithet of 'mediocre.' Of course, the echo that rebounds believes it is the voice itself. The perfidious book *Form without Ornament*, published in Stuttgart in 1924, says nothing about my battle and at the same time falsifies it."

On the occasion of the founding of the Werkbund in 1908, in outspoken terms and with all his polemical vigor, Loos took a stand not against the idea of the Werkbund but against its leaders. In an essay with the not very complimentary title "I Superflui," (The Superfluous) he wrote:

> They have now met at a congress in Munich. Once again they are telling our industry and our artisans how important they are. In order to justify their existence, at the beginning, ten years ago, they told people they had to introduce the art of craft work. The artisan himself could not do so. He was too modern. . . . All the factories that until that moment had managed to keep this superfluous phenomenon away from their premises reached the summit of their capacities. It is only the products of these industries that are representative of the style of our time. They are so in tune with the style of our time that we — and this is the only criterion — do not feel at all as if they would have a style: they conform to our thought and our sensibility. Our car, our drinking glasses, our optical instruments, our umbrellas and walking sticks, our suitcases and our harnesses . . . our jewels and clothes are modern. They are so because nobody who is unskilled in these fields has presumed to interpret the role of tutor in these workshops.

In the same year Loos again expressed himself on the subject of the Werkbund, but this was the last time and he said no more on the subject. Time worked on his behalf. "The objectives are good. But they will never be attained by the German Werkbund. The members of this association are men who are trying to substitute a new culture for our present culture. Why they do so, I do not know, but I know this will never succeed. . . ."

The Vienna Exhibition in the Spring of 1912

On the occasion of the fifth congress of the Deutscher Werkbund, which was held in Vienna, the Imperial Museum of Art and Industry organized an imposing exhibition, which did not fail to make a great impression upon the German visitors. Viennese applied arts, moreover, appeared far in advance of the German industrial product. Austria had spared no efforts in order to show itself worthy of possessing a Werkbund of its own.

The speech delivered by Adolf Vetter — "The Significance of the Idea of the Werkbund for Austria" — documents a situation that has been romantically glorified, confused at a theoretical level, and particularly subject to German wishes, so testifying to an attitude that twenty years later was to prove fatal to the newborn Austrian Werkbund.

> He who correctly understands the Werkbund movement [Vetter raved] knows that in harmony with its own nature it must as the first priority bind itself to the soil on which it is born and be national;

a culture rooted in collectivity is the only possible culture, yet it can develop and receive guarantees only where the people conscientiously cultivate their own ethnic peculiarity, even though at first this may be less elegant or refined than that of foreigners. . . . . According to our conviction, nationalism can expect, from many points of view, to be deepened and truly ennobled by the triumph of the ideas of the Werkbund: indeed, these ideas are in essence nothing but a purified nationalism.... The thoughts of the Werkbund could strengthen the national efforts and fill them with new contents. They could appease the national struggle by setting it nobler aims and giving it purer forms.

On the other hand, the hope formulated by Vetter must have sounded typically Viennese to the ears of the Germans: "May the Werkbund contribute to the result that large consumers — every time they consume — consume quality and content themselves with ordinary simplicity if they should lack the means to acquire pure luxury. . . ."

The Cologne Exhibition of 1914

There is no doubt that sooner or later the Werkbund exhibition held in Cologne in 1914 will be critically reexamined and consequently reevaluated. Until today, people have modestly confined themselves to making reference to only a few works: the theater of van de Velde, the factory and offices by Gropius, the pavilion for the glass industries by Bruno Taut. This is so, partly because all the other buildings were not very usable in the lines of development of modern architecture; even the classicism of the Austrian pavilion is more in line with the architecture of the pre-Fascist era or forms part of the last signal of bourgeois traditionalism. Anyone who examines the Cologne exhibition with an open mind cannot fail to be surprised at the great amount of nationalistic romanticism "barely emerged from the German heathlands" that was here poured out. And anyone looking still more attentively, and especially at the product of German applied arts exhibited at Cologne, will no longer be surprised at the great success won by the Austrian exhibitors.

Yet this success did not help Vienna. The outbreak of war dissipated any further illusion concerning new outlets for trade, just at the time when the arts-and-crafts ideology of the Vienna artists was definitely fixed. In 1916 Max Eisler wrote in Österreichische Werkkultur, the volume published by the Austrian Werkbund:

And finally we come to the essential: recently at the Cologne exhibition Austrian applied arts showed that their specific sphere was crafts, whereas industry was a secondary field; one might say therefore that this relationship is the reverse of the one that exists in German production. This may be harmful from an economic viewpoint, but from the artistic angle it is certainly an advantage. For this reason we always keep closer and closer to the source of all industrial art, and consequently we constantly provide an incentive for those movements that pursue the most radical practical

157. Josef Hoffmann, reception room, Werkbund exhibition, Cologne, 1914.

Pages 106–7

158. Oswald Haerdtl, Österreichischer Werkbund, 1930, entrance.
159. Josef Frank, tearoom.
160. Ernst Lichtblau, pavilion for foreign visitors.

and social objectives that are remote from us, and protect them from the risk that they might possibly move too far away from their origins. The special quality of the Austrian pavilion at Cologne, unlike other parts of the exhibition, is, in the final analysis, to be seen in connection with the fact that . . . ,we have almost exclusively produced artisan art that is close to its genuine source. By this not only have we consolidated our own prestige, but also — in the heart of the grandiose industrial zone of the German Reich — we have clarified, for ourselves and others, our specific role in the framework of collaboration with Germany: this was the most important thing.

Austrian Exhibition of the Werkbund, 1930
A Change of Scene

The Austrian Werkbund's yearbook issued in 1929 contained the following statement: "As a result of the prolonged stagnation that has occurred inside the Austrian Werkbund, many of its adherents have grown less interested in the aims of the organization. In the year following the unification of the Werkbünde, which was a step taken in order to obtain good results from such unification, several satisfactory events have occurred already, although we must not forget we are now passing through a phase of slow reconstruction. . . . Only nine months separate us from the congress of the Deutscher Werkbund in Vienna. This period requires the contribution of all vital forces. . . ." The president at that time was Dr. Hermann Neubacher, director of the Gemeinnützige Bau- und Siedlungsgenossenschaft "Gesiba"; the vice-presidents were Josef Hoffmann and Josef Frank. Together with Frank, the young members who formed part of the presidential council were Oswald Haerdtl and Walter Sobotka. In the committee there were such names as Max Fellerer and Oskar Strnad.

The participation of Josef Frank (the only Austrian architect) was of particular importance to the planning of the Stuttgart Werkbundsiedlung: he was asked to design a house. In circumstances which have remained obscure, Loos was dismissed. On that occasion Frank was therefore enabled to observe from close at hand the new situation that had arisen within the Deutscher Werkbund. His "Speech about the Werkbund" — the principal contribution in the 1929 yearbook — is an introduction that is theoretically sound, lively and appropriate to the new programmatic line of the Werkbund that had just been reformulated. Without any doubt, Frank's essay was far and away the best contribution written on the subject by an Austrian. Starting from that moment, the activity of the Austrian Werkbund grew at an incredible rate: it reached its climax, and at the same time its conclusion, in the Vienna Siedlung.

The main reason for this is that the Siedlung was erected just before the congress of the Deutscher Werkbund, which required a worthy framework in

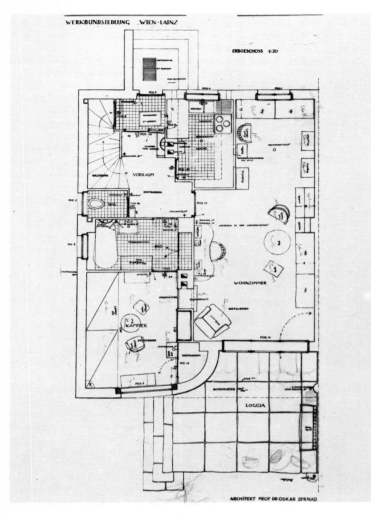

WERKBUNDSIEDLUNG „WIEN-LAINZ

ERDGESCHOSS 4:20

VORRAUM

WC

BAD

KAMMER

WOHNZIMMER

LOGGIA

ARCHITEKT PROF DR OSKAR STRNAD

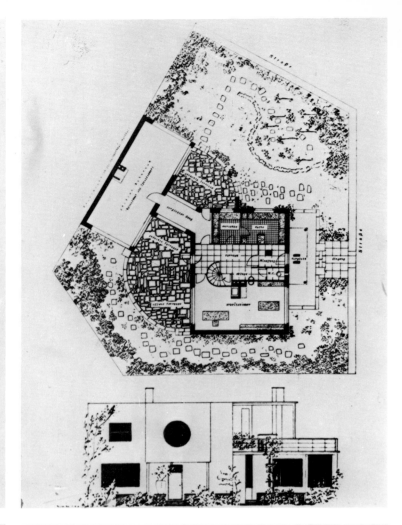

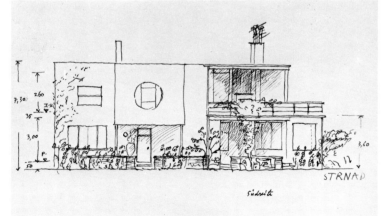

Südseite

STRNAD

which to display itself in a great exhibition organized by the Austrian Werkbund. But the conclusion of work on the Werkbundsiedlung, which had been anticipated for the same year, had to be postponed because of a series of events outside anyone's control. The artistic control of the exhibition was assumed by Josef Hoffmann, who reached his sixtieth birthday in that year. This subject was chosen: "How a culturally modern large city can be helpful to strangers." The catalog states more clearly: "This time the Österreichischer Werkbund has set itself the task of presenting alongside products of Austrian industry, crafts and fashion [note the order! F.A.] a great number of public places, which now represent the daily experience of the modern civilized man, and, at the same time, to enliven the exhibition by showing the visitor . . . some of these services in full operation." The Werkbund used its best people. Mention may be made here of the main ones with their relative tasks: Josef Frank (tearoom), Hugo Gorge (confectionary pavilion), Oswald Haerdtl (porch, administrative hall of the Austrian tobacco monopoly and sales kiosk, fountain, pavilion of industry), Josef Hoffmann (large central hall, cafe with terrace), Karl Hoffmann and Felix Augenfeld (cafe), Clemens Holzmeister (inn), Ernst Lichtblau (pavilion with tourist office, musical instruments shop), Walter Sobotka (hotel lobby), Oskar Strnad (bar, shop for Lobmeyr), E. J. Wimmer (beauty salon), Carl Witzmann (wine bar).

Vienna wished at all times to present itself as a happy, joyful city "with a cheerful spirit and a refined sense of existence." There was pride in "the great number of slightly aroused talents, highly developed," and for the occasion the industrial product went so far as to make a pact with the applied arts. "And the two tolerate each other well," wrote Max Eisler; "in fact crafts have agreed to place themselves under the discipline of the machine and its exactness. As always, the center of interest is quality. But now even among us this no longer means a smug self-satisfaction, but what is decent and good." However, the peace was of short duration. Other conflicts came to the fore. Opposite the elegant, filigreed, luxurious tourist pavilion by Ernst Lichtblau stood the inn by Clemens Holzmeister, built with a rough-hewn technique. Josef Frank was already engaged on his book *Architektur als Symbol*: it was a desperate attempt to render accounts concerning everyone, or so it appeared. Now, however — as we view it from a distance — it is judged the work that questions the validity of the so-called international architecture; it is an emotive, sometimes disconcerting, work, but at various moments it explores connections with lucid intelligence. It is the moment of truth about Vienna, the "new German architecture," the Werkbund, the Bauhaus.

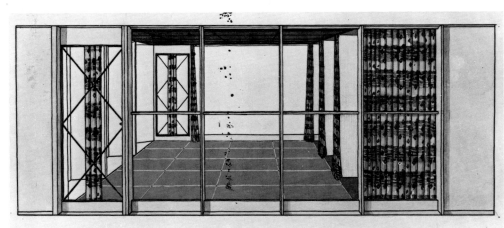

161. Oskar Strnad, house on the Werkbundsiedlung, Vienna, 1931–32, ground plan.
162. Oskar Strnad, house 13 and 14, Werkbundsiedlung, Vienna, garden side.
163, 164. Oskar Strnad, design for his own house, ground plan and sketch.

165. Carl Witzmann, exhibition room for applied arts.
166. Eduard Josef Wisgrill, sketch for a beauty parlor.

167. Werkbundsiedlung, Vienna, general view, 1932.

168. Josef Frank, house on the Werkbundsied-lung, Vienna, 1932.

The Vienna Siedlung, 1932

Before these conflicts broke out within the Werkbund, a final effort was made, resulting in the Vienna Siedlung. The person who was responsible for directing the work, as well as for choosing the architects, was Josef Frank. His presence explains why at this last attempt at "self-representation of Viennese architecture" Loos was also present and of the German architects only Hugo Häring was included, of the French André Lurçat and G. Guevrekian, and of the Dutch Gerrit T. Rietveld.

The idea of the Vienna Siedlung differed fundamentally from that of the Stuttgart Siedlung: rationalization and standardization were excluded, as was experimentation in new building methods. Even apart from the by now obligatory skepticism with which this type of progress was viewed, the industrial area of Austria was quite unsuited to such developments. The essential reason for the Vienna Siedlung was to make the maximum use of space and create the greatest living comfort that could be compatible with the principle of minimum expenditure of space. The Siedlung is a single coherent attempt to show how it was possible to offer a great variety of types of homes with this condition in mind. From the same point of view, town planning, too, was limited to the alignment of houses inside the network of the residential complex, to be used during the visit to the exhibition. The garden city theme had already been widely considered in the first attempts of Loos, Frank and Schuster, and here it was applied to local conditions. Although today the constructions seem to be interconnected by a formal compatibility (as well as by the grown up vegetation), yet at their basis one can still discern the wish that they should exemplify individuality and should attest to the fact that each architect can create his own individual treatment of space even though he has to work in extremely circumscribed conditions. From this viewpoint the Viennese Siedlung of the Werkbund can be seen as a clear antithesis of the Stuttgart Siedlung, in its general tendency. The same may be said, too, if not to an even greater extent, concerning the interior decor. Frank fought against the dictates of any kind of aesthetic system, and for him each object always had its own individuality.

The Siedlung houses were intended for the middle class, whose financial position necessitated modesty. But the ideal model remained bourgeois. Throughout his life Adolf Loos had tried to reconcile the comfort of the bourgeois house with a restricted space: the Vienna Siedlung was the public recognition — to be understood from this angle — of his efforts in this direction, although he himself (with his collaborator Kulka) was put in charge of the planning of the houses with the best display of the rooms.

Once the Siedlung was established (for the

Viennese there was once again something to talk about), the process of the Werkbund's disintegration began. President Neubacher (at that time illegally a national socialist and future burgomaster of Vienna under Nazism) withdrew his collaboration with the Werkbund "because of pressure of professional work." Josef Hoffmann resigned as well. This happened because the Right disliked the "Semitization" of the Werkbund. In spite of this, at the extraordinary plenary assembly held in July 1933 (under the chairmanship of Oskar Strnad) — with 173 votes in favor and 101 against — faith in the old presidential committee was confirmed. But nothing could now heal the breech within the Werkbund. The Jewish social democrat Josef Frank then tried to get the Werkbund to admit new members, and Oskar Kokoschka and Ernst Krenek were enrolled. In September 1933 the journal *Die Form* stopped publishing accounts of the Werkbund's activities: the connection between what was happening in Germany and in Vienna was now obvious.

On February 24, 1934, the Neuer Werkbund Österreichs was founded. Clemens Holzmeister was its president, and Josef Hoffmann and Peter Behrens vice-presidents. The preponderant presence of the Right in the new Werkbund was certainly not concealed: all Jews and Left-wing militants or sympathizers were dismissed. But it would be an error to identify the Right, which was divided within itself in any case, with national socialism. It must be said that in Austria the conservative forces were concentrated in the nationalist and Austro-fascist field, and here political Catholicism played a dominant part. But these were the same forces that later joined open conflict with German Nazism.

Under Dollfuss, Clemens Holzmeister was appointed "Staatsrat" für Kunst, or adviser on artistic matters. Vienna was practically in the hands of the conservative forces of the province, and the change that occurred in the administration of the city had repercussions on the cultural field, where the liberal component and the intelligentsia of the Left were substantially deprived of power. Out of the "old Werkbund" what remained was a movement of opinion, a circle of impotent people (information transmitted orally). By 1934 Josef Frank emigrated to Sweden, and this date marked the end of the first phase of the history of the Werkbund.

In spite of the split in the political front, the factions of the old and the new Werkbund were not really enemies. For example, Oswald Haerdtl and Max Fellerer, more for their personal relations with Hoffmann and Holzmeister than for other reasons, joined the Neuer Werkbund. Haerdtl, who was an assistant and later a collaborator of Hoffmann, shared the latter's ambitions in the sphere of industrial design, although in architecture he

169. *Hugo Häring, house on the Werkbundsiedlung, Vienna, 1932.*

170. *André Lurçat, residential block on the Werkbundsiedlung, Vienna, 1932.*

favored the more progressive wing.

The organ of the architects' association, the journal *Profil*, published the communications of the Neuer Werkbund. But not much was being written and even theoretical work seemed to have stopped. At last people could once again design in peace and organize feasts. Art (of course, only art that was acceptable to the regime) again received public social commissions; architecture became monumental once more. Josef Hoffmann organized a new exhibition of applied arts, significantly entitled "Liberated Crafts." It seemed that the Viennese world was again "in order." In London, Austria was considered an Alpine, Baroque province, with tourist ambitions; in short, the region advertised by the products of its crafts, by its fashion in village dress and by its hunting trophies.

The various ideologies may clearly be discerned from the buildings put up by the old and the new Werkbund. In the house on the Wenzgasse in Vienna, and in the essay based on this house ("Das Haus als Weg und Platz"), Josef Frank has left us his impressive spiritual testament: "A well-organized house must be 'founded,' implanted like a city: with streets and paths that necessarily lead to squares free of traffic, where people can find rest. . . . It resembles those beautiful old towns in which even the stranger can immediately orientate himself without having to ask where the town hall or the market place is situated."

After Loos and Frank, Ernst A. Plischke was the only person who succeeded in formulating a convincing theory of building — from the household utensil to the country house, from the city dwelling to administrative offices. Unlike Frank, Plischke did not adapt applied arts to a style that was peculiar to Vienna (Frank simply relates it), and he attained a purity of architectural language that rehabilitated Viennese architecture of the 1930s and assured its place in history.

There were of course many architects in Vienna who continued to follow the ideals of the "old Werkbund": Walter Loos, Walter Sobotka, Hans A. Vetter and others.

Vienna and Germany, and Loos and Frank Again

"The object of daily use lives as long as its material lasts, and its modern value resides in its solidity. Wherever I interpret the object of daily use by decorating it, I shorten its life, because, since it then is subject to fashion, it dies sooner. Guilty of this murder performed on the material is, it must be said, feminine whim and ambition — and ornamen-

tation at the service of woman will surely live forever. A useful object, a textile or upholstery, whose duration is limited in time, remains at the service of fashion and is therefore ornamental." Ornament is a question of the consumer, wrote Loos in the same article ("Ornament und Erziehung," 1924), and in the footnote he expressed his resentment against the Germans, who by their purism failed to understand the battle he had fought. The note reads:

I hold the Germans responsible for the misunderstanding between consumer and producer. A German knows nothing about the common value of humanity that forces the producer to produce forms required by the community. He believes that it is the producer who is imposing these forms, and this is why he speaks of the tyranny of fashion. Owing to his slavish nature, he feels subjugated and so tries to make the world pay for what he has suffered. He sets up associations in order to create a German fashion — the Wiener Werkstätte and the Deutscher Werkbund are his already — to impose on humanity in this way his own will in questions of form. The German essence must cure the world from this sickness. It must, but will not. It wishes to create by itself the form to be imposed on life and does not want to find it imposed upon itself, confectioned by some association of businessmen. The same hegemonic caste of producers has made social democracy forget that the worker must be taken into consideration in his quality of consumer also. For more important than the amount of his weekly salary is what he can afford to buy with his salary.

Frank's critical gaze turned also to the West. He devoted a whole book to this question, polishing off Vienna in a few short sentences: "Dominant here is a marked uniformity among all those who build without making distinctions of degree, so that the university professor and the foreman occupy the same terrain everywhere; perfectly secure in their ignorance, they carry on, neglecting all problems, of whatever type they may be, and this produces a calming effect on the eye, the complete futility 'not infected by the pallor of thought.' . . . Frank had abandoned this particular Vienna. What remained, however, was the discussion concerning "the new architecture," and this was a challenge that he, whether as a Viennese or an Oriental, could not fail to meet. And it was this challenge that led him to a surprising form of resignation, since Frank had to attack the men he most esteemed and since the colleagues who remained to him in 1930 were all members of the Deutscher Werkbund and wrote in *Die Form*. This is probably the viewpoint by which one can understand Walter Riezler's mild, comprehensive, yet honest review of *Architektur als Symbol*, since Riezler was obviously very familiar with the situation in Vienna.

Frank, who was influenced by Loos and close to Hugo Häring, saw in functionalism nothing more than a motivation for a new ornamentation, but this time it was a more intolerant and exclusive ornamentation than the one based on tradition could have been. The "new truths" expressed so intolerantly seemed to him new lies and instruments of power:

Steel is not a material but an ideology. Seats were really invented in order to serve as a seat for the commission for war damage compensation, and show the seriousness of German efforts. This is ideology for propaganda: It will enlighten every visitor, in the same way as the "authenticity of the material," expressly used, which cries out to whoever looks at it, "I am honest," and at the same time preaches to him in moral terms, "I do not wish to appear more than I am and therefore I am better than you. Go away and be like me." But how likable were the men who used imitations — of the material, of course, not of the spirit — men of an authentic modesty, of an arrogance that at the most was material but never *ideal* and lacking any ethics. . . . But the new German feels he is under a moral obligation to be seated uncomfortably and does not want to know anything else exists. "The god who made iron grow did not want to have wooden furniture . . ."

I cannot quote the whole book but could perhaps include one other passage, the one on "organized taste," which was the central problem of the Werkbund:

Organized good taste is the real enemy of any vital progress. The whole German organization that has been created for the single purpose of affirming it and giving it value, so that by displaying art and science it can give Germany complete supremacy, has shown that it is not even good taste. Indeed nothing can be more in bad taste and mortifying than absurdly to impose a pretentious system. . . . Today anyone who wants to create something that is really alive cannot, on the basis of one principle or another, neglect or set aside certain things just because he considers them tasteless or even immoral. Humanity is not composed of puritans. Yet the German arbiter of taste, wishing to scale the heights of his own viewpoint, from where he can judge everything, sits with his red pencil in hand and gives marks for ethical merit. Anyone who wants to create something that is alive must accept everything that is alive today. The spirit of the time, including its sentimentality and its exaggerations, including its bad taste, which though bad is at least alive . . .

Resignation or prophecy? Both are present in the East. To round off our examination, we may recall that many attempts were made in Austria after 1945 to reactivate the Werkbund, especially in Vienna and Upper Austria. Exhibitions were held during the fifties. Now, however, the Austrian Werkbund is in a deep coma.

171. Gerrit Rietveld, houses 53–56, Werkbundsiedlung, Vienna, 1932.

172. Ernst A. Plischke, table and chair for the Werkbund exhibition in Vienna, 1931–1932.

173. Applied arts room in the exhibition of the school of applied arts of the Österreichisches Museum, Vienna.

THE FOUNDATION OF THE SCHWEIZER WERKBUND AND L'OEUVRE

Othmar Birkner

Swiss Art

Is there such a thing as Swiss art? This question was often asked in the years around 1913 when the Swiss Werkbund and L'Oeuvre were founded. But — as Raoul Nicolas remarked in 1922 — in no other country were there so many artists in proportion to the population as in Switzerland. There were altogether about a thousand painters and sculptors.[1] But did these artists not look toward France, Germany and Italy, according to the region of Switzerland in which they lived? Albert Brüschweiler spoke of the "native provincial sobriety" of the Swiss writers who started to look for "national material" after 1914.[2] In confirmation of this rebirth of patriotism, Brüschweiler quoted the description by Johannes Jegerlehner *Grenzwacht der Schweizer* (Swiss frontier guard): "Their white heads shone in the misty landscape . . . the arms of four thousand soldiers pointed to the sky, from four thousand mouths sounded the oath of allegiance 'We swear' . . ." It was a Hodler picture! And Hodler, who had never studied abroad, was considered the most significant exponent of native Swiss art. Hodler really created a Swiss school, which he believed should be distinguished by "simplicity, clarity, unity of composition, and, most importantly, repeatability of color." But these concepts were not applied to painting exclusively. The German architectural journal *Moderne Bauformen* in 1911 claimed to have discovered "the hidden originality of Switzerland." "In its natural freshness, almost rugged at times, Swiss art is never without interest. . . . In summer and winter Switzerland is full of bright color: white, blue, and green, in the most diverse tones, but always robust, energetic and limpid."[3] Among the most important expressions of Swiss architecture, this journal cataloged the works of Nikolaus Hartmann (St. Moritz), Otto Ingold (Berne), Karl Moser (Karlsruhe and St. Gallen), Heinrich Müller (Thalwil), Martin Risch (Chur), Robert Rittmeyer (Winterthur) and

174. *Cupola of the art pavilion by Otto Schäfer and Martin Risch in the Exhibition of Applied Arts, Chur, 1913.*

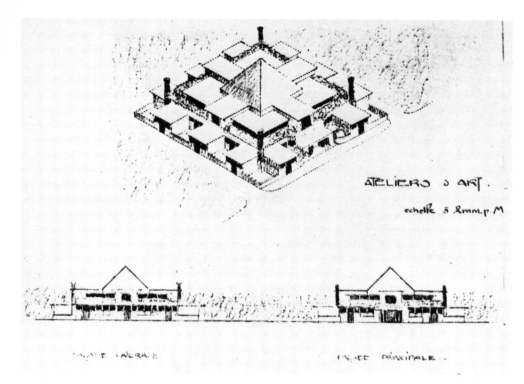

ATELIERS D ART.

echelle 5 2mm.p.M

FAÇADE LATRALE

FAÇADE PRINCIPALE

Rudolf Streiff (Zurich). All these architects were among the founders of the Swiss Werkbund in 1913. Their works were considered "Swiss architecture," that is to say, an art that always took particular account of the cultural individuality of each canton. "An autonomous quality" had developed out of a "long hypogenic evolution."[4] For example, Nikolaus Hartmann and Martin Risch reinterpreted in a highly original way some of the traditional forms that were typical of the Grisons Canton, as confirmed by the exhibition of Grisons industry held in Chur in 1913. Priority was given to local materials in use before the construction of the railway. Not the style, but the quality of the natural stone, for example, had to be the determining factor for the form of the detail. The sculptor Wilhelm Schwerzmann used rough-textured tufa in his architectural decorations and colored the grain of the stone preferably red, blue, and green. For roofs Otto Ingold used the convenient forms found in peasant homes in the Bernese Oberland. He liked to work in wood on interiors, and in his churches and the houses for the painters Cuno Amiet and Emile Cardinaux he transformed the wooden parts into a "feast of prime colors."[5]

It seems likely that in these developments a certain part was played by the movement for the protection of the national heritage, which was then being widely followed more or less everywhere. The Swiss association for the defense of the national heritage was founded in 1905 and was very active at that time in matters concerning modern architecture. Already in 1906 the first numbers of the journal of that name published plans and reproductions of the works of Karl Indermühle (of the Swiss Werkbund), Max Häfeli (founder member of the Swiss Werkbund) and Otto Pfleghard; the intention was clear — to propose models for imitation.

Die Schweizerische Baukunst was the title of another journal first published in 1909; this was the organ of the Bund Schweizer Architekten, or Fédération des Architectes Suisses, an association founded the year before. In the introductory article published in the first number it was stated explicitly that "Swiss architecture" had to be transformed into a "popular question" — popular, that is, in the

175. *Charles Edouard Jeanneret (Le Corbusier), design for a studio for the Ateliers d'Art, La Chaux-de-Fonds, 1910.*

176. *J. Perrenoud & Cie., Cernier, bedroom with wall decoration by Charles L'Eplatteneier, 1922.*

sense that the architects just mentioned who worked during those years had to adapt their ideas to the native architecture, which remained anonymous, for the purpose of promoting at the same time a "new tradition," which would be both modern and national.[6] However, anyone who is regarding the years of the First War as the period of the founding of the Swiss Werkbund and L'Oeuvre, will have seen the development of "Swiss art" in a much less favorable light. Hodler died in 1918, and the great exhibition held in the Kunsthaus, Zurich, in 1917, devoted entirely to his work, was viewed as a "sublime funeral ceremony," "the final evidence of the Helvetic spirit in Switzerland."[7] And in 1918 Paul Baudry lost no time in stating that in western Switzerland not only did people speak French, but they painted and sculpted in the French way as well. The Helvetic spirit in art therefore "had been an adventure, luckily without too serious consequences."[8]

Contemporaneity of the Swiss Werkbund and L'Oeuvre

As may be imagined from the situation just described, the founding of the Swiss Werkbund and L'Oeuvre occurred at the point of intersection of two epochs. On the one hand, their birth is a milestone within a period that was particularly dynamic and rich in initiatives, although it would very soon have been exhausted even had it not been for the First War. On the other hand, ideas already anticipating a development that was to extend even beyond the twenties were apparent within it.[9] First, people in Switzerland were by no means certain that the Werkbund and L'Oeuvre were capable of safeguarding the achievements made around the turn of the century. To many people, for example, the Swiss Werkbund seemed nothing more than an imitation of the German Werkbund, and therefore not a very appropriate instrument for nurturing a quality or mode of expression of a typically Swiss nature.[10] It might have been possible to draw up an unmistakably clear picture if the various geographical areas had really cooperated actively. But then, as now, this was impossible. As an example: as soon as the

177. Otto Ingold, entrance pavilion to the exhibition of decor at the third Swiss National Exhibition, Berne, 1914; wall paintings by Hermann Huber.

178. Alfred Altherr, inner courtyard in the exhibition of the Swiss Werkbund, Zurich, 1918, with small theater and fountain.

116

Schweizerische Baukunst supported works mainly belonging to German Switzerland, the need was felt to juxtapose to the Swiss Werkbund and its journal *Werk*, which began publication in 1914, an association like L'Oeuvre, also with its own journal. The two associations were formed in two cultural centers that were already active: Zurich and La Chaux-de-Fonds. In La Chaux-de-Fonds, Charles L'Eplattenier was in charge of the École d'Art, founded in 1870, with the clear aim of training good engravers for the clock industry. When he was appointed director in 1903, L'Eplattenier immediately decided to restructure the school, extending its field of interest to cover all the arts: "from architecture to decor, from monumental architectural decoration to knickknacks."[11] L'Eplattenier was an exceptional teacher, who, "according to many of his students, not only emanated an incredible charm, but at the level of art education created a system that was very new indeed at that time."[12] Among the students of his "Cours Supérieur" were Charles Edouard Jeanneret (Le Corbusier), the sculptor Léon Perrin and the architect-decorator Georges Aubert. These students were among the founders of the Ateliers d'Art Réunis, which worked in many spheres: furnishings, trinkets, furniture, tombstones, and so forth. Jeanneret was later sent to Germany to gather critical documentation on the teaching of the applied arts. He published the results of his research in 1912 under the title *Étude sur le mouvement d'Art décoratif en Allemagne*. All these experiences — whether they were personal to him or known through the medium of his students — made L'Eplattenier one of the promoters of L'Oeuvre. The founders' meeting took place in 1913 at Yverdon under the chairmanship of the architect Alphonse Laverrière, who had also been president of the committee that founded the Swiss Werkbund. Jeanneret was also one of the founding members of L'Oeuvre. Lausanne was chosen as headquarters of the association.[13] Committees were set up to take responsibility for different aspects of the work. The propaganda committee was to concern itself with publications, lectures and exhibitions, as well as to make contact with

other associations; it also had responsibility for establishing a "Musée du Beau et du Laid." It is interesting in this connection to note that it was not only the Swiss movement for the defense of the national heritage that took up Paul Schultze-Naumburg's idea of example compared with example. The committee for the promotion and development of the applied arts organized competitions and conferred prizes on those industries that had particularly distinguished themselves in this sector. Other committees were active in the field of teaching, trying to improve the teaching of the applied arts and bring the teaching to a uniform standard; another of their functions was that of promoting authors' rights.

The Gewerbemuseum of Zurich was inaugurated in 1875, and in 1877 — following the example of the Austrian Imperial Museum of Art and Industry in Vienna, which had an arts and crafts school of its own — it established the school known as the Artisan School of Design and Modeling. Especially in the period when its director was Jules de Praetere, the museum was a very lively center and a reliable point of reference in the field of professional education. In 1907 alone it organized 12 exhibitions, in which there were shown works by Henry van de Velde, William Morris, Richard Riemerschmid, and the like. From 1912 to 1938 the institute was under the direction of Alfred Altherr (Basle).[14] Altherr was a pragmatic architect and artist-craftsman, who began his career as a cabinetmaker and ship designer, but was able to show his natural organizing talent and his surprising versatility when he founded the Swiss Werkbund. The broad spectrum of the Schweizer Werkbund under his direction can be appreciated, if for no other cause, from a study of the first leaflets published by the movement itself, which dealt with the most diverse topics, such as advertising design, toys, garden planning and religious art. In the first three years of its existence the Swiss Werkbund initiated design competitions for advertising posters, book covers, lamps and postage stamps. Among the many itinerant exhibitions, the most important initiative, again under the direction of Altherr, was the great exhibition of the Swiss

Werkbund held in Zurich in 1918. This exhibition considered every aspect of the bourgeois "culture of the home" and offered ideas for workers' Siedlungen and dwellings for the working class. It was a shining beacon against the background of the war, a great step in the movement to promote the economy and encourage craftsmen and artists. This exhibition created a far greater interest, in neighboring countries as well, than did the third national Swiss exhibition held in Berne in 1914.[15] The Schweizer Werkbund now felt itself strong enough to look to the future with new ideas and new programs.

1. R. Nicolas, "Malerei und Plastik," in J. Ruchti, *Geschichte der Schweiz während des Weltkrieges 1914–1919*, vol. 2 (1929), p. 359.

2. A. Brüschweiler, op. cit. vol. 2, p. 529

3. C. H. Baer, "Neuere Schweizerische Architektur," in *Moderne Bauformen*, year X (1911), p. 57.

4. H. Bloesch, "Schweizerische und Eidgenössische Baukunst," in *Die Schweizerische Baukunst* (1913), p. 177.

5. A. Baur, "Das Landhaus eines Malers," in *Schweizerisches Jahrbuch für Kunst und Handwerk* (1912), p. XIII.

6. Baur, "Zur Einführung," in *Die Schweizerische Baukunst* (1909), p. 1 ff.

7. Cf. n. 1, p. 368.

8. Cf. n. 1, p. 360.

9. Cf. here, "The New Life-Style," p. 49.

10. Bloesch, "Ein Schweizerischer Werkbund," op. cit., quot. 4, p. 162.

11. St. von Moos, *Le Corbusier — Elemente einer Synthese* (1968), p. 15.

12. A Monteil, "La Chaux-de-Fonds feiert Charles L'Eplattenier," in *National Zeitung*, no. 141 (1974), p. 31.

13. J. Gubler, *Nationalisme et Internationalisme dans l'architecture moderne suisse* (1975), p. 42 ff. Further information and facts have been kindly provided by Jacques Gubler, since accounts of the foundation and other important documents have been lost.

14. O. Birkner, "Gründung und Entwicklung des Kunstgewerbemuseums," in *1875–1975, 100 Jahre Kunstgewerbemuseum der Stadt Zürich* (1975), pp. 7–12.

15. Cf. n. 9.